African Culture and the Christian Church

By the same author

MISSIONARIES TO YOURSELVES
(ed. with Eugene Kataza)

African Culture
and the
Christian Church

An Introduction to Social and Pastoral
Anthropology

AYLWARD SHORTER WF

 GEOFFREY CHAPMAN
London   Dublin   1973

Geoffrey Chapman Publishers
35 Red Lion Square, London WC1R 4SG

© 1973, Aylward Shorter

ISBN 0 225 66028 8

First published 1973

Printed in Great Britain by A. Wheaton & Co., Exeter

Contents

To

CHARLES IMOKHAI
MATIA SSEKAMANYA
ALEXANDER CHIMA

and Graduates
of
The Pastoral Institute of Eastern Africa, Gaba

Introduction

THE idea behind this book was to supply the widely-felt need for a textbook in social anthropology for use in African seminaries of theology and philosophy; in pastoral institutes, catechetical centres, missionary language schools, university departments of theology and religious studies; and in courses and seminars for priests and religious. There are many excellent introductions to sociology and social anthropology, but few of these have a specifically African orientation, and none of them make the pastoral applications which interest the priest, religious or religion teacher. The sociology course given in many African seminaries has, up till now, consisted very largely of a study of the industrial sociology of the Western world and the social documents of the Church, most of which deal with Western structures and problems. More recently, several popular books on African traditional religion have come onto the market, and some are being used as textbooks. They tend to follow the life-cycle of the individual and, although they are not usually the work of professional social scientists, they profess an academic, rather than a practical or pastoral, interest. Time and again I have been asked by priests, sisters and seminarians to recommend a book in the field of pastoral anthropology and I have been obliged to confess that nothing exists in print. At the Pastoral Institute of Eastern Africa, to which I am attached, there has been a steady demand from outsiders for the lecture notes that accompany my course in pastoral anthropology, and this has convinced me of the need to turn these lecture notes into a published book.

The term 'pastoral anthropology' may be a source of confusion in some quarters, especially to professional anthropologists familiar with the problems of African pastoralism! However, the term aptly symbolizes the marriage of two disciplines: social anthropology and pastoral theology. This is not, of course, a book about African pastoralists, but a book for Christian pastors and potential pastors in Africa! In many ways it resembles an ordinary introduction to social anthropology by attempting to present, in a coherent and popular form, the findings of contemporary anthropologists and sociologists. The difference lies in the African and Christian emphasis. This emphasis governs the selection of topics and examples presented. As far as the African character of the course is concerned, the attempt is made to give an overall view, and examples have been taken from all over the continent south of the Sahara. The Christian emphasis takes the form of practical pastoral applications, and it is in this that the originality of the course consists. This is an entirely new and original field, and is the product of discussions and exchanges that have taken place over the past five years with students from every part of sub-Saharan Africa.

The lecture course was originally made for students of the international Pastoral Institute of Eastern Africa in 1968 and was repeated in the following two years. In 1971 it was completely revised and re-written, and was repeated in that form in 1972. Some of the lectures were given at major seminaries to students from Uganda, the Sudan, Tanzania, Malawi and Zambia. Some were also given to national seminars for clergy, religious and laity in Kenya and Rhodesia. Still other lectures were given at missionary language centres in Uganda and Tanzania, to groups of religious sisters and brothers, and to sixth forms in a number of schools. The present book represents yet another revision in an attempt to present the lecture course in an expanded and more readable form.

A few sections of the book have appeared as articles in the *African Ecclesiastical Review*, but they have been revised here and integrated into a much broader context. Several ideas contained in this book have also been used by the Pastoral Institute's secondary school religion series *Developing in Christ*, which is a work of collaboration by the Institute's staff-members. In that series the ideas in question appear in the context of a religion course for first- and second-formers, and not in that of a systematic introduction to African anthropology for pastoral purposes. However, this book should also prove useful as source material for teachers of the *Developing in Christ* series. Some sections of the book have also appeared in Pastoral Papers put out by Gaba Publications.

I would like to record my gratitude to all those who have contributed to this book through discussion and advice, my fellow staff-members at the Pastoral Institute, the students of the Pastoral Institute and visitors to the Institute, as well as the seminary and other audiences before whom many of the ideas contained in this book were first aired. Finally I wish to thank Mr Evarist K Kimalempaka who typed the manuscript.

Aylward Shorter WF
The Pastoral Institute of Eastern Africa,
Gaba, Kampala.

I Nature, Purpose and Methods of Pastoral Anthropology

ANTHROPOLOGY is the study of man—not man as an isolated individual, but man in his own community, man as the product of his society. African anthropology is the study of man in Africa.

Pastoral anthropology is the application of anthropology to pastoral needs and programmes. In Africa it is the essential tool for developing an African Christianity, and this, as Pope Paul VI told Africa, 'is an immense and original undertaking' (discourse at the closing of the first meeting of SECAM, Kampala 1969[1]). It is an entirely new field, in which the main burden of responsibility rests with Africans themselves.

Two consequences follow: Firstly, the study of man in Africa for pastoral purposes must be systematic. Anthropology is a branch of modern social science, and pastoral anthropology is therefore scientific. This textbook is not just an orientation course about African social customs for newly-arrived missionaries. It is assumed that the student already has knowledge and experience of 'man in Africa', either as an African pastor or teacher—born and educated in an African society, and possessing a common knowledge of that society—or as an expatriate missionary with a more recently acquired, and a necessarily more marginal, knowledge. The purpose is to give both Africans and 'marginal Africans' the equipment for a systematic (and not a common, or impressionistic) understanding of their own experience of human situations in Africa, in order to help them fulfil their pastoral obligations effectively. This brings us to the second consequence.

The study of man in Africa from a pastoral point of view, no less than the development of an African Christianity, must be a work of collaboration. Many of the facts dealt with in this

1

book will be not unfamiliar to you, but we shall attempt to put them in a new light, and to obtain a new understanding of them. The aim of the book is to form general hypotheses and make general interpretations. These will be illustrated by examples taken from the author's own field experience (limited to a rural area of southern Tanzania), and by examples taken from published and unpublished accounts of other African countries, peoples and areas. It is up to the reader to make his own modifications and applications to his own pastoral field. This book can give you the tools for solving your pastoral problems but it cannot, obviously, do the work for you.

We shall not deal with dying customs and moribund social practices, but with ideas and behaviour current in contemporary Africa. Because of the cultural fragmentation of Africa and the uneven process of development, some problems may appear less important to one reader than to another; but it is not the intention of the author to give prominence to any one cultural area more than to others. Illustrations will not be given for their own sake but for the sake of the general propositions they support. It is hoped that readers will not only make their own pastoral applications but will contribute from their own experience to a deeper understanding of the facts, remembering all the time that nobody has a monopoly of *Homo Africanus* and that there are many differing, but authentic, traditions which deserve to be called African.

One of the purposes of the book is catechetical : to discover those values and life-situations in contemporary African societies which can form a basis and a framework for preaching and for developing an African Christianity, a Christianity relevant to Africans today. Another purpose is moral : to acquire a correct understanding of contemporary African beliefs and practices, and to apply to them the relevant principles of a developing moral theology. Hitherto, these beliefs and practices have often been imperfectly understood by moral theologians. Yet another purpose is concerned with liturgy and with the social apostolate : to consider ways of handling African cultural material and African social institutions, in order to install a living Church in Africa. Interest will centre chiefly on liturgical adaptation, on preparation for marriage and parenthood, and on the problems of conversion.

In a few short chapters it is impossible to give a complete anthropology of *Homo Africanus*. In any case, comparative material is still so deficient that it is not worth trying. It is possible, however, to give readers the elements of sociological theory and structural analysis, and to apply Christian principles systematically to the generalized concepts which emerge from a study of African material when scientific methods are used. The Church in Africa needs anthropologists, and the attempt must be made to turn the reader into a mini-anthropologist who can observe and judge systematically and correctly for himself. The aim is also to give a number of examples of anthropological themes, and of their use in Christian catechesis; examples of areas of conflict and concordance between African social institutions and Christian ideals; and practical methods of encounter (adaptation).

Anthropology means 'the science of man', and since the Second Vatican Council the word has become increasingly popular in the sense of 'the efforts by which man achieves an understanding of himself'. In so far as he employs transcendental and *a priori* arguments, he is in the realm of pure speculation and philosophy, especially if he is considering man's ideal and destiny. In so far as his arguments rest on the truths of divine revelation known by faith, he is in the realm of theology.

Pastoral anthropology is not philosophy or theology. It is a natural science subject based on *a posteriori* arguments. It is concerned with behaviour as well as with ideas. It studies what men actually think and believe. In doing this, it can and should provide material for philosophical and theological anthropology. An African theology, should, in any case, be based on natural science anthropology. In this book we are, however, not primarily concerned with African theology, but with the less speculative and more practical problems which arise from the preaching of Christianity in Africa.

Physical anthropology is the study of man as a physical organism. It includes human physiology or biology (study of man as a living being), human morphology or somatology (study of human body forms, pigmentation, etc.), genetics (study of heredity and inherited variations), and human evolution (study of fossil remains of early man to determine how human beings have evolved). Human physical facts can take on social dimension and become social facts. For example, the visible impact of differences in body form and pigmentation can lead to racial discrimination; or the high incidence of twin births in Africa can lead to the elaboration of twin rituals. Social facts can occasionally have repercussions on human physical development : for example, prescriptions and preferences in choosing marriage partners can have genetic consequences. In general, though, pastoral anthropology and physical anthropology have little in common. Pastoral anthropology is social and not physical. We can agree with the following quotation from G K Chesterton:

'It is a pity that the word Anthropology has been degraded to the study of anthropoids. It is now incurably associated with squabbles between prehistoric professors (in more senses than one) about whether a chip or stone is the tooth of a man or an ape; sometimes settled, as in that famous case, when it was found to be the tooth of a pig. It is very right that there should be a purely physical science of such things, but the name commonly used might well, by analogy, have been dedicated to things not only wider and deeper, but rather more relevant' (*St Thomas Aquinas*, New York 1956 ed, p. 160.)

Colonial governments in Africa used to employ anthropologists to advise them on 'native affairs'. They were especially in demand in British colonies, where an attempt was made to rule the people indirectly through their own traditional, political institutions. The government anthropologists delineated tribal boundaries, and helped the administration decide who were the legitimate local rulers. Colonial anthropology has been defined as 'how to take away the natives' land according to native custom'!

Although much good work was done by colonial anthropologists, it was often spoiled by a sense of racial superiority. They were very fond of the word 'primitive', an ambiguous term which meant 'simple', 'pre-technical', 'exotic', or 'strange in European eyes' (implying a judgement of African societies as being somehow morally inferior). However, the term could also mean 'primitive in time' or 'at the origins of human development'. Early anthropologists believed, without a shred of evidence, that the simplest societies were examples of stages in

European development. As a result of all this, anthropology received a bad name after political independence.

African pastoral anthropology is not concerned exclusively, or even mainly, with 'backward' rural areas. It is equally interested in the development of towns. It does not aim at perpetuating tribal divisions in modern African states and keeping people in 'human zoos'. It is interested in socio-economic improvement and social change. It is not concerned with the past, but with the present and the future. Some educated young Africans affect to despise anthropology. Okot p'Bitek, the Ugandan poet, has satirized their shallow sophistication as not being in the real interests of Africa.

He puts these words into the mouth of Ocol, the victim of his satire, who represents the opposite extreme from the colonial anthropologist.

> 'We will arrest
> All the village poets
> Musicians and tribal dancers,
> Put in detention
> Folk-story tellers
> And myth makers,
> The sustainers of
> Village morality;
>
> We'll disband
> The nest of court historians
> Glorifiers of the past,
> We will ban
> The stupid village anthem of
> "Backwards ever
> Forwards never".
>
> To the gallows
> With all the Professors
> Of Anthropology
> And teachers of African History,
> A bonfire
> We'll make of their works,
> We'll destroy all the anthologies

Of African literature
And close down
All the schools
Of African Studies.'
(*Song of Ocol*, Nairobi 1970, pp. 29–30.)

Psychology studies the nature and functioning of the individual human mind, and not man's social context. Social psychology studies the reaction of the individual to social pressures and stimuli. Group psychology studies the art of interpersonal communication from the point of view of the individual. As we shall see, pastoral anthropology studies the social facts which psychology either takes for granted, or only studies indirectly.

Pastoral anthropology must also be distinguished from ethnology and cultural anthropology. What do we mean by culture? Sir Edwin Tylor, a famous ethnologist, defined it thus: 'that complex whole which includes knowledge, belief, art, morals, law, custom and any other capabilities and habits acquired by man as a member of society'.[2] The important phrase is 'acquired by man as a member of society'. In other words, culture refers to the whole range of human activities which are learned, and which are transmitted from one generation to another through the processes of learning. We shall see that culture from this point of view is concerned with social facts, and is the proper object of anthropology. However, culture can be divided into intellectual culture and material culture. Ethnology is concerned with the study of material culture, and seeks to compare and classify different human societies on the basis of the characteristics of their material culture, artefacts, techniques, economies, and so forth.

Cultural anthropology (as it has developed—chiefly in America) has attempted to deal with the whole range of culture: all the non-biological aspects of human life. In practice, it has subdivided itself into a variety of studies of both material and intellectual culture: particular aspects of culture, learning theory, and so on. Pastoral anthropology, unlike ethnology and cultural anthropology, studies culture and items of culture as social facts relating to a social structure, or a systematic whole.

Human beings are naturally gregarious. As soon as individuals start living together they generate society, and their actions and interactions, both at the level of behaviour and at the level of ideas, become social facts. Society is the relationship of individuals to each other, within a network of relationships, or in relationship to a group. Social facts are human relationships which take on enduring shapes or patterns in people's minds. They are the components of society. When we speak of society or of social facts, we are not speaking of visible, concrete things. These things are of the logical, relational order. They are a way of looking at, a way of talking about, the concrete actions of individuals. Society and social facts exist only in the minds of people, but they are none the less real for that! According to Emile Durkheim, the great French anthropologist, the social fact has three basic characteristics :[3]

(i) *it is general*
—that is to say, it is an experience shared by a number of individuals at the same time. For example, in African societies many young men pay livestock or money to the families of their brides (bridewealth). This fact is seen as general.
(ii) *it is transmissible*
—that is to say, it is capable of being transmitted from one group of people to another, and from one generation to another. In other words, it outlives individual human beings themselves. For example, the custom of bridewealth continues over many generations; and some peoples who never practised it have learnt about it from those who did.
(iii) *it is compulsory*
—that is to say, each member of society is more or less obliged to reckon with it. Most individuals accept it without question, a few rebels reject it, but even they are influenced by the fact they reject. It determines the course of their rebellion. Social facts just happen. Nobody in Africa knows who invented bridewealth. Individuals contribute to the continued existence and development of the custom, but they are not entirely free in front of it.

Social science is the discipline which studies society and social facts. In social science it is customary to speak of sociology and social anthropology, but these terms refer to differences in emphasis and method rather than to any really significant differences between the two. The difference is partly one of scale : sociology tends to deal with social problems on a wide scale and with numerically larger groups of individuals; social anthropology tends to deal with small-scale problems in groups of relatively few individuals. As a result, sociology tends to be more impersonal and statistical, dealing with behaviour, while social anthropology tends to concentrate on inter-personal, or face-to-face, relationships, and to be more interested in ideas. Concentrating on the small group, social anthropology can go more deeply into the subject, placing the social fact in its structure or whole context. As we shall see, anthropology places emphasis on structures or 'wholes' for a full understanding of social facts. Because of its interest in inter-personal relationships, anthropology is very much concerned with communication between persons, and between the person and the group. The most fundamental form of personal communication is symbolism. Anthropology is concerned with basic loyalties, beliefs and values which help to realize personality. It is easy, therefore, to see why anthropology should be of service to a movement of renewal in the Church which has adopted the personalist approach and which stresses community values. Pastoral anthropology is a form of social anthropology.

The fact that the anthropologist tends to study small groups and communities does not mean that he confines his interests to African tribes or to purely rural areas. Parkin studied two housing estates in Kampala; Marris studied a location in the city of Lagos; Arensberg studied a community in the west of Ireland; and Frankenburg studied English villages, small towns and urban communities. Man always tends to set up communities and to live in communities : anthropology is therefore as relevant to Europe or America as it is to Africa or Asia.

Societies are more or less strongly influenced by their physical environments. The physical environment offers those who live in it a number of choices for solving the problem of living. A society is determined by its environment in so far as the choices are limited; but it is free in so far as it can accept or reject the different alternatives and can modify its environment through the diffusion of ideas, materials and techniques. The Masai people of East Africa, for example, live in a land which is equally suited to farming, hunting or stock-raising. Why did they choose to specialize in stock-raising? The choice was their own.

The West African Yoruba cultivate yams in a forest zone. They could have been specialized hunter-gatherers, but they chose agriculture.

The adaptation which a society makes to its environment, choosing and arranging material things according to the society's own expanding desires and in relation to the scarcity of these things, is called its economy.

Society, however, has to adapt its social institutions, its patterns of residence and movement—even its systems of beliefs and values—to the economy it has chosen. This external adaptation is called social ecology, and the social ecology provides the society with many of its most characteristic symbols, forms of expression and ways of acting. Human groups are nomadic or semi-nomadic (transhumant) hunter-gatherers and pastoralists; shifting or settled cultivators; or town dwellers engaged in industry, commerce, social services, or the professions.

A society also has its own cultural tradition, and its social institutions must make an internal adaptation to this as well as to each other. Obviously, the physical environment exerts less influence on town communities and the economy is less rigid. However, town communities may still be strongly influenced by a cultural tradition, deriving their symbols from the physical environment and economy of their former mother-land, as in the case of Jewish communities in Western cities and tribal communities in African towns.

Anthropology studies social facts, but simply making an inventory of social facts serves no useful purpose, even though that is what a great many amateur anthropologists do. Social facts are not meaningful by themselves; they explain one another. The anthropologist must therefore see how they possess a pattern or structure. In this way he will understand them and their importance.

Social facts have one or more functions which relate them to one or more other social facts in space and time. The anthropologists who belonged to the so-called 'functionalist' school believed that one could discover the structure of social facts simply by enumerating the functions which connected them. Bronislaw Malinowski, who was one of the founders of functionalism, is a typical example of this.

In his fieldwork among the Trobriand Islanders of Melanesia,[4]

Malinowski discovered that the people carried out a form of ritual exchange, known as *kula*, in which red shell necklaces were passed in one direction and bartered for white shell bracelets, passing in the opposite direction. To go on a *kula* expedition it is necessary to build canoes, and canoe building is a major social activity in the Trobriand Islands. In order to build a canoe successfully the islanders utter magic spells, and these magic spells have stories or myth charters to explain their origin. The myths, however, are inherited matrilineally (from the mother's brother) and this necessitates an understanding of Trobriand kinship and marriage systems. The organization of a *kula* expedition is in the hands of chiefs, and chiefs owe their authority and prestige to their productive yam gardens. However, productive yam gardens, in their turn, depend on a chief being a polygamist and having many wives to cultivate for him.

This brings us back once more to kinship and marriage. The social facts when they are related to each other by their functions, accordingly form a vicious circle :

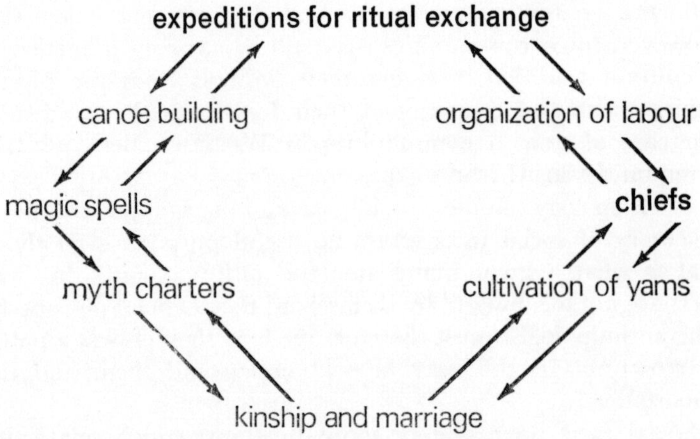

Fig 1.

In his first book, Malinowski entered the circle through the *kula* expeditions, but in other books he entered it at different points : magic spells or yam gardens, for example. He could have written a hundred books about the Trobriand Islands, all of which would have been fundamentally the same book! The picture he gives of Trobriand society is the picture of an anthill : a ceaseless round of activity which has no overall explanation.

A structure can be said to integrate many parts, but one does not discover it by functional analysis (studying the relation of the individual parts to each other) alone. A structure is a 'whole' which has a logical priority over its parts. The anthropologist should be studying the teleological (final purpose) functions of social facts towards the structure—the relation of parts to the whole. Malinowski and the functionalists made the mistake of thinking that a structure was the sum total of its parts, the social facts. They had too concrete a notion of structure. Social facts do not *form* a structure, they *have* a structure. Structure belongs to the logical order. It exists in the minds of men. The functionalists made the mistake of concentrating on the behaviour of people, and neglected the ideas of the people. Consequently, they missed the structure.

A structure is an idea, theory or model which integrates many different social facts. Empirical reality consists of a network of interrelated parts (like the vicious circle quoted above), but this reality only makes sense to the observer when it is referred to an abstraction in his own mind. This abstraction is the structure, model or pattern. The structure is simply a way of looking at, or thinking about, a number of social facts in such a way that they make sense and have a unity.

The structure is primarily what Claude Lévi-Strauss has called a mechanical model : that is to say, an integrating theory which is already inherent in a people's culture. It is mechanical because people accept it, without having to think about it or test it. It is taught to them by society. They may be only partially or intermittently conscious of it, but it underlies their actions and decisions. In so far as the structure is delineated by an observer, measuring the facts closely, or engaging in probabilistic dialogue with the members of the society, it is what Lévi-Strauss calls a *statistical model*—statistical because it is established by the counting of observed or probable instances. In an anthropological study, the mechanical and statistical models overlap. The anthropologist has to discover the mechanical model and test it statistically.

Evans-Pritchard, one of the pioneers of structural anthropology, or structuralism, has given a classical example of the method in his study of Zande witchcraft beliefs.[5] Among the Azande of the Sudan, witchcraft, oracles and magic form a complex of beliefs and rites which only make sense when they are seen as a system. According to this system witchcraft causes death, oracles reveal the identity of witches, and magic can either protect the witches' victims or punish the witches. This is a mechanical model. Evans-Pritchard himself observed that death was treated as evidence for witchcraft, that the oracles tended to confirm this, and that magic was made to avenge death and protect from death. This is a statistical model.

Society does not merely have a single structure; it has many structures, and these structures are interrelated. Thus Evans-Pritchard, in the study cited, shows how the structure of witch-craft belief has implications for the political structure, the kinship structure, the neighbourhood structure and the structure of morality in Zande society.

Lévi-Strauss has shown that structure is the 'language' of social activity. On the analogy of linguistic analysis, he has built up methods of structural analysis. Just as people speak their own languages without necessarily being conscious of their structures (grammar, syntax, phonetic structures, etc), so people take part in social activity without necessarily being aware of the structures that underlie it. To lay bare the structure of a language, or of social activity, helps people to understand both of them better.

Structure is not static. It can be thought of as a process, a configuration of developing elements, which human minds are seeking to organize and render intelligible to themselves. Human beings have an innate structuring capacity, and are propelled by an innate structuring force, which assists them to perceive and understand reality. Lévi-Strauss has set himself the high task of searching out this innate capacity—'the constraining structure of the mind'.[7] Many anthropologists are sceptical and remark that it steps out of social science and into the realms of philosophy. Lévi-Strauss has stimulated a school of philosophical structuralism of doubtful achievements. For the majority of anthropologists, structuralism and structural analysis are simply methods to be used to understand society and social facts better.

We have now examined the nature and purpose of pastoral

anthropology and its methods of studying human societies. These societies, however, are not static, but are subject to change— often rapid change. We must therefore study the important question of social change in the next chapter.

Notes

[1] Pope Paul VI's closing address to the Bishops of the Symposium of Episcopal Conferences of Africa and Madagascar, July 1969, *Gaba Pastoral Paper* no 7, p. 48.

[2] Tylor, Sir E B, *Primitive Culture*, London 1891.

[3] Durkheim, E, *Règles de la Méthode Sociologique*, Paris 1895.

[4] Malinowski, B, *The Argonauts of the Western Pacific*, London 1916.

[5] Evans-Pritchard, E E Y, *Witchcraft, Oracles and Magic among the Azande*, Oxford 1937.

[6] Lévi-Strauss, C, *Structural Anthropology*, London 1968, (pp. 31–34, 55–66, and 67–80.

[7] Lévi-Strauss, C, *The Raw and the Cooked*, London 1970.

Suggested further reading

Beattie, J H M, *Other Cultures*, London 1964.

Benedict, R, *Patterns of Culture*, London 1935.

Evans-Pritchard, E E Y, *Social Anthropology*, London 1951.

Forde, D, *Habitat, Economy and Society*, London 1963.

Goldthorpe, J E, *An Introduction to Sociology*, Cambridge 1968.

Lane, M, *Structuralism*, London 1970.

Mair, L, *An Introduction to Social Anthropology*, Oxford 1957.

Wilkins, E, *An Introduction to Sociology*, London 1970.

2 Social Change, Political Ideology and Urbanization

THE classic picture of traditional Africa is of a medley of homogeneous, self-sufficient and static social units or 'tribes'. Africans were often presented as robots who unquestioningly accepted the dead weight of immemorial custom. This picture was false, and it is partly due to the 'microscopic' methods of the anthropologist. These methods have certainly made possible the study of whole structures and the deep penetration of coherent systems of ideas, as we saw in the last chapter. But they created an illusion of stability, and made social change—when it came to be recognized and studied—appear unnecessarily dramatic and difficult to understand. Of course, societies are changing all the time, and in African societies, as in all societies, there was an area of free, individual choice, and an opportunity for relative non-conformism. Non-conformists are always potential agents of social change.[1]

The tribe has been defined as a whole society, having a high degree of self-sufficiency at near-subsistence level, based on a relatively simple technology, without writing or literature (other than oral tradition), politically autonomous with its own distinctive language, culture, sense of identity and religion.[2] Such a definition no longer holds good and it is arguable if it really held good even in pre-colonial times. The tribe, in fact, was not so highly self-sufficient. Even if in the past it was more integrated, it was never a fully integrated system.

There were many tribes because populations were small, and different ecological adaptations were made by relatively isolated peoples living in the same, or similar, environments. However, this isolation must not be overstressed. The tribe was, and still is, a category of interaction. It explains certain divisions, oppositions, alliances and modes of behaviour that exist between and towards different human groups. Today, in the changed modern situation, the tribe operates within a wider system and possesses new goals and new areas of application. For example, it can be a means of working out conflicts and of casting blame in urban, or political, situations. Tribal loyalty today is sometimes more important than family loyalty.

Tribal (or ethnic) loyalty is an ideology of unity, rather than an identity of political or economic interests. The cultural symbol of unity, be it language or custom, is more important than economic solutions or political structures. This explains why ethnic loyalty can be fiercer today than in former times, even though the tribes have lost their political autonomy.

The limits of tribes were not clear in pre-colonial times. There were different points of reference for tribal loyalty, relative to geographical position or to custom. For example, in Tanzania the words *Nyamwezi*, *Sukuma* and *Dakama* are geographical terms, meaning Westerners, Northerners and Southerners respectively. The particular group with which a speaker identified himself would depend upon his own geographical location in relation to other people. In Uganda, practically the only feature which distinguishes the Gisu from many of their neighbours is their custom of circumcision. The people in Nigeria who go by the name of *Nupe* are socially divided in many ways, and not all of them belong to the Nupe kingdom. Allegiance to primary groups and other sub-groups was often much stronger among African peoples than allegiance to the more nebulous tribe.

This brings us to an explanation of the distinction we make between primary and secondary groups. Briefly, a primary group is an intimate, social, interpersonal group which tends to absorb 'the whole man'—for example, the family-community or the rural village community. A secondary group is a more distant, impersonal group which affects only a segment of the individual's life—for example, the dispersed category of people who form a clan or a mask society, or (to take modern examples) a parent-teacher association, or a trade union. The distinction between primary and secondary groups is, of course, artificial.

There are many gradations of group, and any number of over-lapping or concentric sub-groups may make up a tribe.

Change can come from inside or outside a society, but it is usually external contact with people belonging to other groups and cultures which gives the potential agents of change within a society their opportunity. To give the impression, however, that Africa had to wait for the coming of Europeans for any social change to take place would be wrong. African societies enjoyed regular internal change as a result of the conflicts and changes already provided for within their structures. A good example of this is provided by the conflicts that raged over Anuak kingship in Sudan and the possession of the Anuak emblems, symbolic of the shifts in inter-village relations.

African societies also experienced structural change by which the structures, or patterns, of social relationships and social facts were transformed as a result of interaction between different groups and influences external to the tribe. Migrations, like that of the Lwoo peoples in East Africa; conquests, like that of Usuman dan Fodio and the Fulani in Nigeria; and long-distance trade, like that of the Nyamwezi across Tanzania, or the medieval trans-Saharan caravans, were all instances or agents of structural change.

Change in modern Africa is both structural and organiza-tional. By organizational change we mean a change in the scale of social relationships. Secondary groups become more important and numerous, and there is a greater intensity of co-operation and communication between the different ethnic groups or social units over a wider geographical area. Examples are systems of communication, postal and telephone services, radio networks, transport, labour migration, the holding of meetings at regional, national and international levels. New social systems or struc-tures come into existence : for example, the mass media are systems linking audience, market researchers, distributors, spon-sors, advertising agencies and legislative bodies. All of this does not mean that the face-to-face experience of the primary group necessarily disappears, but it may mean that its importance is reduced.

An important feature of organizational change is the growth of pluralism. Social groupings, structures, and even whole cul-tures, are multiplying. This is a growing phenomenon throughout the world and Africa is influenced by this through her contacts with outside countries, and through her acceptance of a technology which has been developed outside Africa to serve different value systems. Moreover, Africa has her own complexity with which to encounter world complexity! The most important fact about puralism is that it is not simply a plurality of social groups, but a plurality of value-systems and cultures.

Another feature of organizational change is what is known as functional interdependence. This means that social units go in for specialization and come to serve, and depend on, each other. For example, a particular community may specialize in the production of a certain cash or food crop, or in a particular industry sited in their region.

These processes of change have important consequences in modern Africa. One of these consequences is known as congruence of values. This simply means that there is a growth of a common identity. An obvious example of this is what is known in independent African countries as 'nation building'. However, there are many other forms of common identity that are larger than the tribe but smaller than the nation; and there are other identities which overlap national frontiers or even transcend the nation altogether. Such are religious loyalties; adherence to cultural values or political ideologies bequeathed by former colonial powers, such as the French or British 'way of life' or Marxist Socialism; regional and pan-African ideals and organizations, such as support of anti-colonial liberation movements, the East African Community, or the Organization of African Unity. The actual area of congruence may be small; and although organizational change brings more with it than the merely passive co-existence of different cultures and value-systems, it seldom goes so far as to achieve a wide measure of congruence. Pluralism of culture has to be accepted in modern Africa. This means that so-called 'national cultures' imply a developing mutual knowledge of and by the different ethnic groups, and an increased appreciation and sharing of each other's heritage.

Organs of mass media play an uncertain role in bringing about congruence.[4] Their audience is divided and interrelated in many different patterns already, and on top of this there is a variety of patterns of attention, interpretation and response.

Very often distributors are more interested in the attention of their audience without worrying whether this attention implies approval or disapproval. Radio and television are limited in their effect, since they are a continual 'flow' which can be disregarded or switched off. Films make a greater impact, and going to the cinema is a social occasion. Yet, here again, people go to the cinema with many different intentions : for example, seeing a 'good film', having a rest, getting a distraction, doing some necking and petting, keeping oneself 'up to date', learning, enjoying an art-form, indulging a private fantasy, having a love affair with a film-star, getting a thrill, and so on. Films, moreover, are a highly conventional language which is difficult to understand, especially when they are produced by a different culture. Too often a film is an occasion without a message. Newspapers have a limited scope in countries with a traditional, oral style. In Africa they are nearly always organs of government propaganda, and people automatically tend to develop a deaf ear for propaganda. In spite of these limitations, it is clear that mass media can be a force for congruence if they are effectively used.

Another consequence of these processes of change is incorporation. This term refers to the degree of interaction and mutual influence of various social units and systems on each other. It is not an even process. There are continual shifts, variations, migrations and stratifications. Each unit is continually adjusting to other units and to the whole. This is a further aspect of the plural society. The degree of cohesion varies from day to day, and social units take on different degrees of importance with respect to each other. Even in countries where incorporation is the ideal, complete incorporation can never take place. Complete absence of incorporation does not exist either—there is always interaction in a plural situation.

Today the tempo of change is extremely fast, and periods of stablility between movements of change are short. Not only are new cultures and sub-cultures coming into being; they are coming into being with great rapidity, within a single lifetime. Generational cultures, or cultures which are exclusive to particular generations, are appearing, and we speak of the new 'youth culture'.

There are frequent misconceptions about social change.

People often speak about 'culture contact' or 'culture clash' or the 'diffusion of culture traits'. It is important to remember that it is people, not things, who contact one another and who influence, and react to, each other. Writers frequently stress the negative side of social change in Africa and this is a theme of some modern African writers. The picture commonly painted is one of traditional cultures being destroyed or replaced by a Western, urban culture. In fact, people often manage to re-adjust their cultures to changed social situations. The process of change in Africa is often referred to as 'detribalization'. This is a highly misleading term, since it suggests that tribes no longer have any existence or relevance in the modern situation. The term refers to the process by which the individual learns how to apply his ethnic loyalties to new social situations. It could equally well be called 'retribalization'. There is much in African tradition which is relevant today, and much which, whether relevant or not, is tenacious or resilient. It must always be remembered that there is both continuity and development in social change, and that one system is never completely replaced by another. Rather, a third *new* entity comes into existence as the term of change.

Cultures can also co-exist because they relate to different situations. For example, rules of conduct in the village differ from rules of conduct in the town, because these are different situations. The man who goes from village to town, or back from town to village, will necessarily change his rules of conduct, but he does not reject them forever. He will revive them when he returns to the other situation. When a man goes to a new situation—say from village to town—he does not have to abandon his village culture completely. Some elements of this culture are unsuited to town life, but others survive. In fact, village standards are often maintained in African towns because town populations are so mobile and the people are returning regularly to the villages.

Both the people who bring the changes and those who accept them can be selective in what they bring and what they accept. Africans are not just passive victims of Westernization. For reasons of self-interest, Westerners may deny certain aspects of their culture to Africans, while African societies have their own censors who decide how much of the external influence is good for them. An African government might decide, for example, that mini-skirts, wigs and soul-music are bad for its own nationals; another might be discriminating about the foreign programmes shown on its television network.

More important still, change may be only superficial. Observers may believe that Africa is changing radically because Africans are adopting a machine technology imported from Europe, European fashions, and European modes of transport. In fact, the deepest cultural levels may remain impervious to outside influences. Technology is a part of culture, but it is not the most important part. It is a coin of exchange. Because Africans, Indians and Japanese all make use of a technology that originates in Europe, it does not mean that they have all adopted a European culture, or that their culture *is* European. Western technology is simply absorbed by them and made to serve many other cultural ideals.

Obviously, the adoption of a new technology brings other cultural changes in its wake, especially in the scale of social relationships, but it does not, and cannot, take the place of all facets of traditional culture. To talk of a 'world culture' originating in the West is misleading.

There are, of course, many cultural levels. Here we shall take note of four main levels in the cultural make-up of a person.[5]

The industrial technical level concerns techniques, fashions, and modes of behaviour which are imposed on a man from outside, and to which he gives allegiance easily, either because they do not affect him directly, or because they are ephemeral. Such are, for example, means of transport, fashions in clothes, techniques in industry. These things are easily changed.

The domestic technical is a deeper level because it concerns a man's own home life, and at home he is more himself. Examples are his diet and his conventions for cooking, eating, sleeping, and spending his leisure time. Such things are slightly more resistant to change than the industrial technical.

The value level goes even deeper. A value is the priority or worth which a man gives to persons, things, actions. Values are interrelated and form a hierarchy in people's minds. This hierarchy explains their choice of courses of action. For example, generosity may be a value, or honour or success may equally well be values. In one society bearing children may be a greater value than conjugal love for its own sake; or distributing wealth may be a greater value than conserving wealth. Values derive from the final and deepest level.

This final level is the ultimate cultural coding of the person. It is the view which society teaches him about man and man's relationship to the world, to other men and to facts of ultimate concern. The view of man is the product of the interaction of environment, history and human traditions, and it is the hardest level to change. It is what ultimately makes a man Muganda, and not Kikuyu, Chagga and not Chewa, Ibo and not Yoruba. It is a view on what man is and what his destiny is. This area of ultimate concern may be more or less explicitly religious, but implicitly it is a religious phenomenon. Thus religion is the core of culture. Men need a religion to provide a framework of thought and symbolism which will help to integrate them into society.

It would be idle to pretend that there are no casualties in an era of organizational change. There are many. Chief among the negative consequences are tribalism and particularism. Tribalism is the imbalance of posts, privileges, opportunities, profits, advantages, assets and so on, between tribes. It is the situation in which the whole is made to serve the part, the nation serve the tribe, rather than vice versa. Even in modern Africa there is still a need to do one's 'tribal arithmetic'. Particularism is the conservative commitment to an old style of life which is so highly specialized or so isolated as to make people reluctant to change. An example would be an ethnic group within its own environment and with its own economy which was opposed to modernization. Several cattle-raising peoples in East Africa are guilty of, or have been accused of, such particularism : for example, the Karimojong of Uganda and the Masai of Kenya and Tanzania. Another example would be any social structure or hierarchy of values, the supporters of which see modernization as a threat to their highly integrated (although irrelevant) system. A church or a religion could fall into this category.

Organizational change takes certain notable forms. One of these is the creation of political ideologies which are clearly aligned with change and with the widening of scale, but which also stress their continuity with an ideal past through symbols of African authenticity. This is their strength, and we shall examine these ideologies more closely later in this chapter. However, since they are aiming at incorporation and a certain level of congruence of values at national level, they tend not to strike very deeply into the cultural personality. They may also be handicapped by the tools of government bequeathed by a former colonial administration, education system, penal system, civil service and so forth, which are ill-adapted to the new political ideals. Political leaders often derive their power from a strong tribal base and may seek to imbue their tribe with a 'national vocation'. Depending on the history of the nationalist movement, other leaders may have succeeded in building their power upon multi-tribal, or even non-tribal, centres.

Urbanization is a very obvious form of organizational change and one which will be dealt with in detail below. However, it is often remarked today that the real revolution in contemporary Africa is not the urban revolution, but the rural revolution. People sometimes speak of the urban mentality spreading to the rural areas, or of the people in the countryside anticipating urbanization. Such ways of speaking may suggest that there is a stricter bond between town and country than is in fact the case. Nevertheless, it is true that a modern mentality is affecting the countryside and bringing about a social revolution there. New structures have been created—government structures, administrative, educational, medical and many other structures. People are now striving for positions in these structures, and formal education, as a qualification for these positions, has taken on considerable importance. There is also increased social mobility resulting from the training and posting of people within these wide structures. Economic changes are also taking place; market trading, cash-crop farming and industries have begun. There are considerable material incentives for taking part in the new activities and a considerable spirit of competition. With the new opportunities come new statuses and new roles. Women are freer than before, emphasis is placed on individual responsibility, and there is a demand for a more personal approach to be shown by authorities and office-holders.

In this situation of social change traditional religion is ill-adapted to help the African find meaning in his life, and to integrate him with his society. Even though traditional religious ideas had a wider-than-tribal currency, they were taught on a tribal or community basis through the ancient, expressive, community rituals. These rituals are disappearing or becoming family affairs. Instead, the instrumental rituals of power and competition, divination, witchcraft accusation and sorcery, are being strengthened. Many popular spirit-possession and millennarian movements are coming into being. These movements look forward to the rebuilding and transformation of the traditional society, the millennium or golden age; and their preoccupation with bodily ills symbolizes the ailing traditional, social body which they hope to cure. People are hoping in vain to rebuild a strong, homogeneous society again.

The established religions stand a much greater chance of being able to adapt the ancient religious symbols of Africa and articulate them in logical forms related to technological development and social change. Islam is very often handicapped by the fact that it has merged so successfully with the traditional structure that it suffers the same disabilities and is exposed to the same threats. Its chief asset is that it offers the African the sentiment of belonging to a world-wide religious communion. Nevertheless, in many cases knowledge of the Koran has become synonymous with the wielding of magical power, and the role of women within Islam appears to conflict with the new tendency for them to acquire independent status.

Christianity has come to Africa in many forms and the various Churches tend to operate within sub-cultures of their own. The Churches seem to be very reluctant to change, operating as they do through outmoded authoritarian structures and impersonal law systems. Although they have been slow to seek explicit continuity with African tradition, the Christian Churches do, in fact, find support from the more stable elements in African society, rural and ethnic structures. Christian tenets, although they are often in conflict with traditional values, also tend to buttress selected values in traditional society. Christian leaders frequently express the hope that a stable and homogeneous church structure can be restored. The Churches, therefore, run a serious risk of particularism and irrelevance in so far as they are unable or unwilling to recognize modern pluralism and the rapidity of change.

The independent Churches, which we shall study in a later

chapter, are able to compensate for some of the deficiencies of the established Churches. They offer a more thorough-going African adaptation; they cater for the casualties of Church marriage legislation; and they take an interest in the sick, the depressed and the deviant. They exhibit many of the characteristics of the spirit-possession and millennarian movements in their attempts to compensate for the breakdown of the traditional social order. In general, their lack of sophistication does not augur well for their survival in their present form. The chances are that their development will be towards more orthodox forms of Christianity.

The best hope for religious development in Africa lies with the established forms of Christianity which possess powers of expansion, penetration, and creativity. However, the Churches must be prepared for a greater degree of flexibility and adaptation and abandon their dream of a homogeneous Christian culture. They have to steer a middle course between particularism on the one hand, and, on the other, disorientation caused either by an intoxication with change for change's sake or by bewilderment at the rapidity of change. They have to form Christians who can act as bridges between the different units and systems of a plural society, discovering elements of continuity and interaction and promoting a greater incorporation and congruence of values. In doing this they can learn a great deal from the two examples of development and continuity in social change that we are going to demonstrate: political ideologies (African Socialism) and urbanization.

The political ideologies of independent Black Africa usually go by the name of 'socialism'. As we shall show, they differ widely from European 'scientific socialism' or Marxism. Moreover, the policies of so-called socialist régimes in Africa may differ very little from those which are not called socialist or which explicitly reject the title. Senghor, Nyerere, Sékou Touré, Nkrumah, Dia, Kaunda, Mboya have all called themselves socialist; Haile Selassie, Tubman, Houphouet Boigny, Mba have not.

Early writing about African Socialism was vague. It presented the African way of life as a kind of vague collectivism, opposed to the individualism of the Western world, and this collectivism was praised or blamed according to the point of view of the author. For example, Dudley Kidd wrote a book in 1908 called *Kaffir Socialism* as an argument in favour of *apartheid*!

Early African politicians tended to be Marxists. This was all right as long as they were fighting the battle against colonialism. On gaining independence, two things happened: firstly, Marxism was found to be inapplicable to the African situation in practice; and secondly, Africans realized the need for an authentically African ideology which would enable them to play an original role in world affairs. Africa needed to make her own specific contribution to human development. Even as convinced a Marxist as Nkrumah was forced to repudiate the Marxist basis of Ghanaian socialism in 1964 in favour of a more authentic African communalism, while Sékou Touré (who remains a Marxist) also makes verbal appeals to African tradition.

African Socialism has been called 'a series of unanalyzed abstractions',[7] and while it is true to say that it is poor in its theorizing, and diverse in its approaches, it has a common theme: co-operative living, man-in-community. African Socialism claims to be rooted in African traditional society and this element of continuity is the measure of its opposition to Marxism. On the other hand, it has to transfer the ideals of traditional society to a much larger social scale. This is the element of development and change.

The poet Okot p'Bitek is sceptical about the African basis of this socialism, but he has to admit that there is some truth in the appeal to tradition:

'Can you explain
The African philosophy
On which we are reconstructing
Our new societies?

I hear a faint flute
Playing in the moonlight,
It is Leopold Senghor's tune
Of African Socialism,
Do you hear
That distant drum?
Is that not Mwalimu
Nyerere's Ujamaa?

The Osagyefo
Is silent,
The anthem of
United Africa
Is drowned by
The sound of guns!

Tell me
You student of communism
And you Professor of History
Did Senegalese blood
Flow in the veins
Of Karl Marx?
And Lenin,
Was he born
At Arusha?'

(*Song of Ocol,* Nairobi 1970, pp. 83–4.)

The appeal by African Socialists to tradition is explicit. In the words of Nyerere, 'our first step, therefore, must be to re-educate ourselves; to regain our former attitude of mind. In our traditional African society we were individuals within a community' (*Ujamaa,* Nairobi, pp. 5–7).

African Socialists emphasize the interaction between individual and community in African tradition. In contrast to Marxism, which is prepared to subordinate the individual to the collectivity by constraint, Senghor insists that the individual must be drawn to co-operate freely, otherwise he will be depersonalized, and Mboya states categorically that man is not a means to an end but an 'end and an entity in himself'. African Socialists lay stress on the 'co-operative' character of their socialism.

The Marxist revolution is a revolution against capitalism, but African Socialists point out that there was no capitalism in traditional Africa. 'We neither needed nor wished to exploit our fellow men' (Nyerere, *Ujamaa,* p. 7). Some go further and claim that there was no private property in traditional Africa, but true common ownership. This is partly true. As far as land was concerned, it was more of a common 'non-ownership' than a common ownership. Land could not be bought and sold, nor alienated. Kings and chiefs gave people licence to clear and cultivate land, and the continued use of the land by an individual depended on his diligence. Individuals were responsible for the use to which the land was put, though they often called in friends and neighbours to work on it in co-operation. Consumption was in common, depending on mandatory gift-giving and mutual assistance in the family lineage village, chiefdom and tribe. Distribution, however, was not necessarily equal. There was thus a progression, from individual responsibility, through co-operative production, to common consumption.

African governments are not excluding private investment by foreign capitalists in their countries, but they are attempting to stifle incipient capitalism among their own people, so that private property does not become a significant factor in their countries' economy. African governments are seeking an effective monopoly of material wealth.

Marxists speak of a class-struggle, but African Socialists point out that there were no classes in the traditional Africa. This claim is true, if we take a class to be 'a group whose prestige and influence depends on its economic superiority or inferiority'. There were no such classes in Africa, even in areas where there was considerable durable wealth, although there were castes of closed-status groups manipulating wealth. These were not based on a monopoly of wealth alone, since entry into these groups was by birth, and the groups were supported by cultural and religious sanctions. A good example is provided by the cattle-owning aristocracies of some Lake kingdoms in Eastern Africa. There were also age-sets in the highly stratified pastoral societies of Eastern Africa, but these strata were essentially mobile and open. Similarly, among societies like that of the Ibo of Eastern Nigeria, there was a system of ranks and titles which successful individuals could take at certain moments in their lives.

On the other hand, classes in the strict sense are in the process of formation in modern Africa, since high wages have to be paid for skilled workers and members of the professions and there is a growing disparity between the wage-earners and the rest of the population. Governments are legislating to try to prevent the gap widening. Marxists speak of the wage-earning industrial workers as the 'proletariat', the poorest and lowest class in society, but in Africa the poorest class is the non-wage-earning subsistence farmer. It is also the peasant farmer, and not the capitalist, who is the parasite. African leaders are continually exhorting farmers to work and to collaborate in the development of the country. The obligation to work was certainly traditional but it was not so urgent, nor was it so strictly a communal responsibility.

African traditional societies often had a multiplicity of social institutions, but they were focal-institutional—that is to say, they were penetrated and dominated by a single institution such as centralized chiefship, a unitary system of stratification, or a single kinship complex. This institution was multi-functional. Today African countries have a single party organization to which all other institutions are subordinated and this party operates through multi-functional institutions such as the local school. Thus a school may organize political meetings and even polling on election day. Marxist régimes are usually totalitarian, governing by force rather than by consultation. Although there is always a strong temptation on the part of single, focal, institutional societies to be totalitarian, there is a genuine attempt on the part of some African countries to be democratic and to set up mechanisms for consultation. There is no doubt that discussion and consultation were important features of traditional African policies. One of the most successful experiments in combining democracy with the single focal institution has been Tanzania, and there is more than a grain of truth in President Nyerere's comparison of the Tanzanian Parliament to a group of elders meeting under a tree!

Marxists teach that religion is an alienation and that the socialist must be an atheist. African Socialists say that they are non-atheists. Some even go so far as to say that they are, and must be, believers. Senghor maintains that, for men to co-operate as persons, they must be attracted by the love of a super-person (God). The only alternative is for men to use force on each other. Senghor believes that it is love, and not hate, which must be given the greater role in socialization. Mboya has even described the African code of conduct as the law of 'universal charity'. It is love, and not hate, that makes us persons and integrates us in a community. African Socialists always stress the fact that man is only fully man if he is part of a community. According to Senghor, love is the 'essential energy' and 'heart' of Negritude. Hate is the essence of tribalism and the perversion of tribal culture and loyalty. A godless society is a loveless society, and Africans have traditionally believed in God.

Both Senghor and Kaunda are strongly influenced by the work of Teilhard de Chardin. For both men, Teilhard's idea of a positive evolution of universal civilization towards a culmination expressed in theistic belief provides a means of integrating the African contribution into the scheme of world progress. As Kaunda puts it, the African Socialist should be a believer, because it is the believer who is forced to ask big questions, however crude his answers. The believer's mind is open to the possibility of continual development because he believes in a human development that is infinite. African Socialism desires to contribute to human development at a much deeper level than Marxism. It claims that Africa has an essential lesson to teach humanity, a lesson forgotten by the countries which colonized her. African Socialists give the lie to Marxists when the latter call their socialism a science. A political philosophy must always be an ethic and not a science. Africans are not socialists for the sake of socialism, but for the sake of man, and their socialism is the art by which man lives. True religion is man-centred. It does not alienate man from himself, but fulfils him and directs him towards his right end. True religion promotes brotherhood and co-operation; therefore it is directed towards man-in-community and harmonizes with the aims of African Socialism.

So far we have been dealing with the aspect of continuity : let us now consider the aspect of development or change. The essence of African Socialism is co-operative living and working for the good of all. This is founded in the mutual respect for, and involvement with, one another that characterized traditional society with its network of mutual rights and obligations.

The basic problem for African Socialism is how to transpose the characteristics of a small-scale, traditional society to the level of a modern nation-state. What level of community does one take as a starting point, and how far does one go with the process? Kaunda and Mboya often speak of the village as the ideal, Senghor and Nyerere of the extended family. The difficulty is that, in order to understand the level of the small community, one must refer to other levels. The family cannot be understood without reference to the lineage, the lineage without reference to the village, the village without reference to the

29

chiefdom, and so on. The more the loyalties are extended, the weaker the sense of community becomes. The task of African Socialism, therefore, is to extend the fullest experience of co-operative living to the widest possible community. Some African leaders, like Sékou Touré, speak as if the community were the entire nation, and Marxism generally tends to stress the total community at the expense of its component communities. Nyerere stresses another Communist experience, local collectivism, and is trying to build up a nation composed of village communities (*Ujamaa* villages) which are much more cohesive and productive than the old type of villages. He bases his programme on the doctrine of *Ujamaa*, or making the extended family into an 'ever-extending family'. He wants people in Tanzania to extend the practices of equality, mutual respect and assistance beyond the limits of the extended family and apply them to fellow-villagers in the first instance, and thereafter to fellow-Tanzanians, fellow-Africans, fellow-human beings.

With the creation of a modern state, it is necessary to have labour organizations. In capitalist countries such organizations are consumptionist, existing to secure better pay and better working conditions from the employers. As long as the colonial powers were the employers, consumptionist unions made sense. Their role was seen as part of the struggle against colonialism. But with the coming of independence it was asked 'Whom are the unions fighting? There are no capitalists for them to fight. They can only be fighting against the government itself, and impeding the country's development.' The labour unions are therefore enlisted in the crusade for more work and higher production. They exist, not to get a larger slice of the cake, but to produce more and contribute more. This is an exact parallel with the evolution of labour unions in Russia and other Communist countries.

African Socialism shares the concept of alienation with Marxism, but it applies it differently. It is not capitalism which causes the alienation of the African so much as colonialism, and African Socialists see their task as a continual fight against colonialism and neo-colonialism, which is forever trying to rob the African of his dignity and his rights, his culture and historical heritage, and to stifle his voice in world affairs.

Although African Socialism rightly claims to be carrying over into the modern situation certain values and principles derived from traditional African society, it has had to bypass, and in some cases depose, the traditional rulers. The colonialist régime, following its policy of indirect rule, built these rulers up into paramounts, transforming them into servants of an alien administration. In countries like Uganda, where there was a strong authoritarian tradition, and a group of highly centralized kingdoms, the onslaught on traditional rulers has been more bitter —so much so that it has almost prejudiced the very appeal to African tradition itself. Obote's *Common Man's Charter* is a tirade against feudalism. The following is a characteristic passage :

'We do not consider that all aspects of the African traditional life are acceptable as socialistic now. We do not, for instance, accept that belonging to a tribe should make a citizen a tool to be exploited and used for the benefit of tribal leaders. Similarly we do not accept that feudalism, though not inherently something peculiar to Africa or Uganda, is a way of life which must not be disturbed because it has been in practice for centuries' (no 21).

Bede Onuoha of Nigeria gives three basic trends in African Socialism. They are fraternity, leadership and dialogue. He also adds that planned development is a characteristic of African Socialism borrowed from world socialism, but that it has received a corrective from African tradition in that it must be carried out in harmony and not in conflict. African foreign policy, based on the positive approach of African tradition, includes the following postulates : autonomy, positive neutrality, pan-humanism.

The following are some of the ideologies known collectively as African Socialism :
i)   (Senghor) *Negritude*
Based on the African's intuitive method of understanding reality through symbolism. The African lives in 'symbiosis' with reality (he shares in the life of what he observes). He participates in apprehended reality to such an extent that he is assimilated by it, rather than assimilating it himself. He prefers the symbol to the narrow Marxist abstraction. African symbolic expression is the key to his philosophy of positive integration.
ii)   (Nkrumah) *Consciencism*
Based on deductions from the existence of the human conscience,

and on traditional African humanism and communalism. There is no need for a class-struggle in a largely pre-technical, already communalist, society. Consciencism seeks a connection with the egalitarian, humanist past; it seeks new methods and techniques from colonialism; it has to crush incipient capitalism and erase the colonialist mentality; it has to defend the independence and security of the people. Nkrumah hoped to introduce his ideology all over the continent of Africa through a single political party working in every country. No other African country has accepted this idea of one party for the whole of Africa.

iii) (Sékou Touré) *Communaucracy*

The aim is to develop Africa as a third force between the Communist and capitalist camps, but the thinking is basically Marxist. The country (French Guinea) needs a dominant party organization operating in the general, and not in a class, interest. Sékou Touré focuses on the humanism of the early Marx because it fits in better with African traditional values. He is more of a sociologist than an economist.

iv) (Nyerere) *Ujamaa*

This form of socialism is 'an attitude of mind' by which people will tend to treat their fellow-citizens as kinsmen, will co-operate with them, and feel responsible for them in a common effort, not to share wealth which does not yet exist, but to create wealth which can later be shared. Nyerere sees the human community as a value in itself; it does not exist merely as a means to an end. The concrete expression of the *Ujamaa* theory is the Arusha Declaration which deliberately exploits the assets already in hand : the work and intelligence of the people and the productiveness of the land.

v) (Mboya) *African Personality*

African Socialism accords with the African personality. It is a code of conduct which confers dignity and security on people. Man is an entity and end—not a means to an end. Such mental attitudes provide a positive framework for economic expansion and modernization.

vi) (Kaunda) *Humanism*

The African revolution must be centred on man and man's possibilities. It must make the African more aware of his responsibility in relation to the evolution of the universe. People are valued for themselves and human need is the criterion of progress. Humanism means a mutual, inclusive kind of society, like the traditional society of Africa.

vii)   (Obote) *Common Man's Charter*

This is the strategy of the 'move to the Left'—a moderate form of socialism. The heart of the Common Man's Charter consists in putting political power in the hands of the majority, and of raising the standard of living and *per capita* income of ordinary people. It hopes to bridge the gap between the common man and the privileged class, but makes no direct economic onslaught against the privileged class. It attacks very strongly all sectionalism and factionalism, both tribal, political and religious. This is because of the historic conflicts and rivalries of Ugandan history.

Our second example of continuity and development in social change is that of urbanization.[8] If urbanization means crudely 'the numerical increase in the populations of towns and cities', then it is certainly true to say that it is an important phenomenon in the African continent today. For every one person living in towns of more than 100,000 people fifty years ago, there are now sixty-two persons. This is a more rapid increase than in Asia, where the increase over the same period for towns of the same size is only 44. However, numerically speaking, Africa is the least urbanized of the continents. The degree of urbanization reached by Africa in the 1960s resembled the degree of urbanization of the rest of the world in 1900. Little more than 7% of the population of Tropical Africa lives in towns of more than 5000 inhabitants, whereas 30% of the rest of the world does. Only 5% of the population of Africa lives in cities of more than 100,000 persons and 4% in towns of between 20,000 and 100,000. In the whole continent of Africa there are only a dozen cities with a population of more than half a million. The largest city is Cairo with three million.

Urban growth in Africa is an uneven process. Some towns are growing fast, while others are hardly growing at all or are remaining stationary. To demonstrate this, over the ten years from 1957–67 the annual overall population increase for the whole continent was 3%. In the city of Nairobi it was 6%; in the city of Accra it was 12%. Between 1957 and 1967 the city of Dar-es-Salaam grew by 109%, although Tanzania as a whole grew by 34%. Tabora town (Tanzania) grew by 36%, only 2% above the national average during the same period. Between 1948 and 1959, Kampala City grew by 71%. Sociologists call this uneven growth the phenomenon of the 'super-city'.

The super cities have grown fast in the past ten years. What were the causes? Will this rate of growth be maintained? An analysis of the figures shows that political causes are more important than economic ones and that it is unlikely that the sudden increase precipitated by independence will be maintained. Urbanization is a prerequisite of industrialization, but the reverse is not true. Although the city wage-earners represent a majority of the wage-earners in the country as a whole (for example Nairobi 21%, Dar-es-Salaam 30%), those employed in industry and even commerce are in the minority. The public services account for a greater percentage. For example, in Nairobi 28% are employed in public services, only 19% in commerce, and only 18% in industry. More important still, there is a yearly increase in the unemployed and the under-employed. In Kampala between 1958 and 1961 although the total population of the city rose, the number of wage-earners dropped and the labour force decreased from 36,635 in 1958 to 27,878 in 1961. Leslie found in Dar-es-Salaam that 19% of men between the ages of 16 and 45 had no work.

There are not many industrial towns in Africa, and those that are industrial go in for mining rather than manufacturing. More often the majority of wage-earners in the town is engaged in administrative, social or agricultural services to the surrounding country.

The growth of the super-city is often uneconomic. Although the population continues to grow, there is a failure to provide more jobs in the cities, or to specialize labour. In South Africa, in Rhodesia, and formerly in Zambia, industry relies on maintaining an unskilled urban population which it is able to control and employ. In most African super-cities, a large proportion of the people have no jobs, no skills and no means of acquiring them. Sociologists used to believe that the growth of cities was an indication of sound economic growth. They now know that cities can become a parasite on the economy, retarding economic growth and failing to stimulate productivity. The cities are swollen with refugees from rural distress who strip the countryside of its manpower, inhibit agricultural development, earn nothing in town, and return without skills to compensate for the loss. The growth of the super-city is therefore ambiguous. This is the phenomenon known as 'over-urbanization'. African governments are doing their best to counteract it by curbing the growth of cities by law, encouraging people to stay on the land, and siting industrial projects more evenly. If this policy is successful, we shall see a decrease in the rate of growth of the super-city.

We have seen that the biggest group of wage-earners in the city is employed by the public services. This is because the African super-city is essentially a power phenomenon, a centre of dominance in the country as a whole. This is not such a new thing in Africa. It was true of the ancient pre-industrial towns and centres of population, such as the metropolitan kingdom cultures of West Africa and the temple cities of the Yoruba of Nigeria, the latter being centres of politico-religious dominance, deriving their existence from the sacred power of the Oni of Ife.

The modern African super-city has a key function in the surrounding country. The populations of African countries are small. Only eight out of some fifty African countries have populations of more than ten million (less than the population of Greater London). Cities and leaders are few. This scarcity of leadership and cities, coupled with small national populations, make possible the domination of a whole country by a small élite operating from the super-city and planning the economy on a nationwide scale. The city makes educational and economic growth in the country possible. From it emanate the organs of mass media which have a greater political than cultural significance.

Historically, the city can be observed as a growing concentration of control. In Kampala, for example, the city began as the political centre of the kingdom of Buganda, with the king's court numbering some 13,000 people in the mid-nineteenth century. This political centre attracted other power centres—political, religious, educational, medical, economic. Kampala being a city of hills, these power centres were established on the different hills: Mengo hill, Kampala hill, Namirembe hill, Rubaga hill, Kibuli hill, Makerere hill, Mulago hill, Nsambya hill, and Nakasero hill. In the valleys and swamps between the hills there grew up commercial and industrial areas and African housing locations. High-income residential areas were situated on other hills—Kololo hill, Mbuya hill, and Tank (Muyenga) hill.

One cannot, however, discuss urbanization in Africa simply in terms of absolute numerical growth, or assume that it will follow the same historical pattern as urbanization in Europe and America. Town populations in Europe are comparatively stable; in Africa they are not.

Although a majority of town-dwellers would like to stay in town, scarcity of jobs and poverty of conditions make it impossible. Parkin found only one householder in Nakawa housing estate who had lived in Kampala for more than twelve years. Heynen found in Mwanza (Tanzania) that only 15% of the population had spent their lives in the town; 13% had been there for three to four years; and 25% had been there for only one year.

Swantz maintained that 20% of Dar-es-Salaam's inhabitants changes every year. Morgan states that for Africans in Nairobi the farm in the homeland is the focus for their existence and not their town dwelling. People come to town to make money, and when this is not forthcoming they drift back to the country-side. The European and Asian populations of African towns are much more stable and may even enjoy a greater proportionate increase than the African population though, of course, their absolute numbers are small. West Africa, with its longer tradition of town dwelling, tends to have more stable town populations than elsewhere.

Another indication of transience is the sex-ratio. African men strongly outnumber African women in town. In Nairobi there are 40 African women for every 100 African men, compared to 94 European women to every 100 European men and 86 Asian women to every 100 Asian men. Of the working-age-group in Kampala 63% are men and only 36% women, but in Uganda as a whole 48% are men and 51% women. In Zambia, town-dwelling African males account for 21% of the males in the whole country, and town-dwelling African females account for only 12% in the whole country. Leslie has written that 'a wife in town is a hostage to financial misfortune and is not prepared to put up with as much in hard times as a single man'.[9] On a practical basis, the only way that African women can assert equality with men in the city is to repudiate ties of marriage and set up as an independent woman, practising prostitution, or running a lodging house which is often a house of ill fame. Town girls have a bad reputation and men are slow to marry in town. They prefer casual unions until they can marry a girl from the country. The country wife will, of course, exert pressure on her husband to return to the country. In town, few people marry before the age of 25 and by middle-age half of the adult population has had four or five living-partners. A new study by Dr Lamousé-Smith of towns in Tanzania shows that Christian marriages are more stable than non-Christian ones.[10] Parkin found that, out of a sample of 166 couples in Kampala, 26 unions were regarded as temporary and 133 of the 140 permanent unions were marriages with girls from the tribal homeland. Transience, marriage and tribal affiliation, therefore, are related social facts.

Another indication of transience is the ratio of children to adults. Dr Lamousé-Smith found that 78% of town-dwellers were under 30 years of age, and 30% were between 15 and 20. Small children, however, tend to be few in the African population. In Nairobi there were 47 children for every 100 African adults in 1962, but there were 83 Asian children for every 100 Asian adults. The reason for the absence of children in African towns is because parents often send their growing children to be brought up by rural-dwelling relatives. This strengthens the ties between town and tribal homeland.

The word 'detribalization', as we have seen, is sometimes used in connection with urbanization and social change. It usually implies the naïve assumption that the African who moves to the town is free from all the restraints on his conduct among which he grew up. Detribalization was welcomed by people who emphasized the importance of a European type of education, but lamented by those who praised the simple virtues of the countryside, while deploring the corruption of the city. Missionaries were often among the latter group, and the missions in general tended to avoid the towns. In fact, of course, urbanization does not mean the end of tribal cultures, although it may affect them profoundly. Urbanization is a continuous process, and there is a continuous interaction between town and tribal homeland. There is no sudden break with the tribe. Rather, the transformation of the tribe is a continuous process in which urbanization plays its part. As Professor Southall has written, 'the African townsman brings a lot of cultural and tribal baggage with him to town, on the strength of which he fabricates new relationships to meet new urban needs'.[11]

Africans approach the industrial age with basically different ethnic and kinship presuppositions from the Westerner. This does not mean that the African is less adaptable to urban society, but it does mean that he will manipulate urban society rather differently from the European or American townsman. African values are surprisingly resilient in town.

African cultural values are typically community values and much of the pessimism about their survival in town is based on a popular—but outmoded—thesis that urbanization is essentially inimical to community life and the working of the extended family. It is said that town life necessarily engenders loneliness and individualism, and encourages the individual to form separated relationships in a grid or network, rather than in a group. While the emphasis on grid and group may vary in different situations, they are both compatible aspects of social life and always co-exist. Close-knit communities survive even in Western towns and there may be strong patterns of ethnic or racial segregation. The smallest and most tightly bound inter-marrying units were discovered in Paris and the large urban centres of France. Marris discovered that the working-class people of Bethnal Green in London belonged to cohesive and widespread kin-groups with a strong sense of community, even after 150 years of industrialization.[12] In Africa, the super-city favours tribal cleavages and is the ideal milieu for the formation of tribal 'villages'.

Although the traditional family is subjected to strong pressures in town and may, in certain areas and instances, give place to the higher-income nuclear family, it can also function well as an economic unit. This is as true of family commercial, financial, or industrial companies in Europe, as it is of the African extended family in town, with its system of mutual expectations depending on trust as a basis for credit. Leslie could write of Dar-es-Salaam :

'The basic unit in town is the kinship group of cousins, uncles, nephews; it is on relations of this degree of nearness that a stranger to town depends until he can fend for himself. Very few come to Dar-es-Salaam without a relative to go to, and most, particularly of the more numerous communities, have a positive web of kinship ties criss-crossing the town.' [13]

Nevertheless, it is true to say that both the background of the African townsman and the conditions he meets in the town encourage him to have one foot in the tribal homeland.

In rural areas people take their tribal affiliation for granted, but in town tribes may have an even greater importance. Tribal influences are strong in nearly all decisions taken by townsmen. Benevolent associations are set up on a tribal basis, and the 'joking-partnerships' that exist between some tribes enable the smaller tribal groupings to collaborate with others. The menfolk mix with people of other tribes at work and on the way to and from work, but at their house or lodging they tend to consort with their fellow-tribesmen. The womenfolk are of their own tribe and remain at home during the day, gossiping with neighbours who also speak the tribal language.

For most Africans, town life differs little from rural life in all that concerns the domestic-technical and the deeper cultural elements. African cities have their 'rural' areas. In Dar-es-Salaam, people farm the land in the river valleys which divide one section of the city from the other. Of the land in Nairobi scheduled as 'industrial area' 34% is under allotment cultivation or is undeveloped. In Kampala the interstitial spaces between the hills—the swamps and valleys—have become low-income areas where people live on a rural pattern and indulge in market trading rather than in shop trading. Banana plantations may be found and even herds of cattle or goats. Housing is not so much a form of slum as traditional housing transported to town.

The tribal composition of the town usually takes the form of one major host tribe and a variety of other migrant tribes. Thus in Kampala the host tribe is the Ganda, who frequently commute between town and farm in the nearby homeland. Morgan found a similar situation in Nairobi, where the host-tribe was Kikuyu and the second largest tribe Kamba. The farm outside the city, not the city itself, is the focus of existence for the Kikuyu.

In Dar-es-Salaam, Swantz found that the host-tribe, the Zaramo, accounted for 60% of the African population. During planting- and harvesting-time Zaramo women were absent from town for many weeks. When people were asked, 'Where is your home?', the majority gave as answer the name of a Zaramo village or country area. Of Zaramo mothers, 38% went to a rural area to have their babies. Of the urban Zaramo, 43% secluded their girls at puberty according to custom and 58% still sent their boys to circumcision camps. Of the married Zaramo, 71% were married in the countryside and only 17% were married to non-Zaramo. The majority of the Zaramo are still buried in rural areas. Swantz interviewed people who had left the city and one in eighty thought life in the city better than life in the country. Host tribes have an even stronger influence in many West African towns, because the tribes are numerically much bigger.

In some cases, where there is no dominant host tribe, a migrant tribe may take the place of the host tribe. This happened in the towns of the Zambian copperbelt where the declining Bemba tribe found new life in the towns. The Bemba soon dominated the towns and most national institutions through the power phenomenon of the city.

Tribal factors influence urban politics. William and Judith Hanna found that in Mbale (Uganda) welfare and co-operative ventures were set up on a tribal basis between the Bagisu and the people of the Bukedi District.[14] Both parties had their own district offices in town, and there was strong rivalry, and even discrimination, between the two groups for control of the municipality. The Indian community acted as a kind of buffer. Antagonism was sharpened by job competition in a free market.

The so-called 'target-worker' is a contributing factor to the phenomenon of transience. He comes to town to achieve a target—to earn a specified amount of cash which will be spent on a particular project at home: for example, bridewealth, improving a farm, or acquiring storable wealth of one kind or another which has prestige value. For some young men, coming to town is a kind of 'initiation rite' which will make them eligible to marry and prove to the girls that they are men of the world.

But the fundamental fact which makes the African town-dweller different from the Western town-dweller is that he comes to town as a landed farmer, and not as a wage-earning labourer. African farms are not bought and sold. The farmer cannot alienate his land and he gets no compensation for vacating it. What a man earns in town is inevitably only a part of the extended family's whole income, most of which is based on farming. The young committed townsman with good salary and assured pension, content to place his security in a nuclear rather than extended family, is still over most of Africa.

Bad conditions, job competition and tribalism heighten social tensions in the town. Such tensions and enmity are worked out in the traditional manner, through witchcraft accusation and the consultation of diviners. Swantz reckons that there are 700 full-time diviners or medicine-men in Dar-es-Salaam, and that about 10,000 people consult all these diviners daily. Of the cases brought to the diviners, 56% concern witchcraft accusation.

The purpose of this section on urbanization has been to show how it is an area of both change and development on the one hand, and of continuity and resilience of tradition on the other. However, it is an opportune moment to consider the courses of action open to the Church in this situation.

The Church is simply not organized to deal with the urban scene. The population of the cities is growing rapidly and the Church is unable, with her present structures, to keep pace with this growth. In Dar-es-Salaam, for example, about 30% of the population is Christian. In twenty years' time it will have increased to 50%. Swantz estimates that at the present rate of growth in Dar-es-Salaam, 14 churches or other places of worship would have to be built each year for the next twenty years to keep the present ratio of pastors to congregations.

In any case, the Church is unable to reach the urban Christians through present structures. Out of the 80,000 Christion in Dar-es-Salaam, for example, between 10,000 and 15,000 are not registered with their Churches, or brought into a Christian community. Noirhomme estimated that only 12% of the Catholics in Kinshasa were practising their religion at the end of 1959.[15] What is the criterion of 'practising' and 'non-practising'? The majority of these new Christian townsmen come from out-station communities where the eucharist is seldom celebrated, and it is difficult for them to become immediately accustomed to the concept of regular Sunday celebration in a town parish.

It has to be recognised that the urban parish does not correspond to any real 'natural' community. Usually the only stable element it serves is that of a few committed townsmen with high salaries. One solution would be to introduce the out-station principle into town, treating the location as the basic community. For ethnic reasons, people are probably more committed to their place of residence than to their place of work. However, machinery would have to be devised to overcome ethnic barriers —through 'umbrella' parish councils, for example. Pastor Swantz has advocated the 'house-church' idea. This would be a small Christian community or cell which could be visited by the clergy in rotation. In a city like Dar-es-Salaam, 100 or 200 little communities could cater for the whole Christian body.

Another suggestion is for the priest to be permanently resident in a location. This would work in the smaller town. Mwanza (Tanzania) has been divided into three sections, and a few years ago one of the parish clergy began to live in two rooms of an ordinary house rented for him by the Christians of one of these sections. However, something has to be done, in every solution that is tried, to break down the hierarchy of neighbourhoods and the socio-economic barriers as well as the ethnic ones. In this connection, another idea is to set up a 'super-parish' with a pool of priests.

To deal effectively with the problem of bad conditions and transience, the Church's community-building has to spring from social action, and from the multiplication of her channels of service to the town. The Church must diversify her functions according to specialized milieux : hospitals, prisons, universities, barracks, and so on. Accent should ultimately be placed upon worship and centres of worship, not on the building of costly churches. The most should be made of existing churches by sharing them between denominations. Priests and layworkers should be carefully selected for work in towns. Special urban catechists should be trained to carry out the work of community formation and organization, and priests should receive a specialized training in the realities of African city life. Finally, pastoral planning should be carried out, with the help of experts if need be.

Notes

1. The first part of this chapter is based on a number of works, including Cohen, R and Middleton, J (eds), *From Tribe to Nation in Africa*, Scranton Pa 1970; Southall, A (ed), *Social Change in Modern Africa*, Oxford 1961; Gutkind, P C W (ed), *The Passing of Tribal Man in Africa*, Leiden 1970; and Gulliver, P H (ed), *Tradition and Transformation in East Africa*, London 1969.
2. Southall, A 'The Illusion of Tribe' in Gutkind *op. cit.*, p. 28.
3. La Fontaine, J S, 'Tribalism among the Gisu' (1969) in Gulliver *op cit.*, p. 188.
4. Some ideas on mass media of communication have been taken from Jarvie, I C, *Towards a Sociology of the Cinema*, London 1970, and Larsen, O N, *Violence and the Mass Media*, New York 1968.
5. I owe this scheme of levels in the cultural personality to Dr Donald Jacobs of the Mennonite Church in East Africa.
6. This section on African Socialism is based very largely on Friedland, W and Roseberg, C (eds), *African Socialism*, Oxford 1964; and Onuoha, B, *The Elements of African Socialism*, London 1965; as well as on the works and speeches of African statesmen themselves.
7. Friedland and Roseberg, *op. cit.*, p. 2.
8. This section on urbanization is largely based on Miner, H (ed), *The City in Modern Africa*, London 1965; Leslie, J A K, *A Survey of Dar-es-Salaam*, London 1963; Parkin, D, *Neighbours and Nationals in an African City Ward*, London 1969. Reference is made to Morgan, W T W, *Nairobi City and Region*, London 1967, and to unpublished papers by Lloyd Swantz.
9. Leslie, *op. cit.*, p. 14.
10. Quoted by Lloyd Swantz in 'The Migrant and the Church', *Sharing* (a publication of the Pastoral Institute of Eastern Africa, Gaba) 1970, Vol 2 no 6, pp. 5–7.
11. Southall, A, 'Kampala-Mengo' in Miner *op. cit.*, p. 331.
12. Marris, P, 'Motives and Methods: Reflections on a Study in Lagos' in Miner *op. cit.*, pp. 40–41.
13. Leslie, *op. cit.*, p. 3.
14. Hanna, W J and J L, 'The Political Structure of Urban-Centred African Communities', in Miner, *op. cit.*, pp. 151–84.
15. Noirhomme, cited by Houtart, F and Rémy, J in *Milieu Urbain et Communauté Chrétienne*, Tournai 1968, p. 126.

Suggested further reading

Cohen, R and Middleton, J (eds), *From Tribe to Nation in Africa*, Scranton Pa 1970.
Friedland, W and Roseberg, C (eds), *African Socialism*, Oxford 1964.
Kaunda, K D, *A Humanist in Africa*, London 1966.
Miner, H (ed), *The City in Modern Africa*, London 1965.
Nyerere, J K, *Ujamaa, Essays on Socialism*, Nairobi 1968.
Onuoha, B, *The Elements of African Socialism*, London 1965.
Senghor, L S, *On African Socialism*, London 1964.
Southall, A (ed), *Social Change in Modern Africa*, Oxford 1961.

3 African Religious Ideas and the Encounter with Christianity

TYLOR defined religion as 'the worship of spiritual beings'. This is not really an adequate definition of religion, because one can discuss the meaning of the word 'worship' and question whether it is always addressed to 'spiritual beings', or at any rate to spiritual beings conceived as persons.

Even though some of them are not believers, social scientists do not question the existence of religion as a social fact relating to a specific experience identified by definite criteria. Durkheim so far stressed the sociological importance of religion that he called it 'the soul of society'. However, he and several later writers tended to believe that the sociological explanation of religion was an adequate explanation. Today sociologists accept people's religious beliefs and practices as important to them for what they purport to be, and they are inclined to attribute as much autonomy to religious motivation as they do to other kinds of motivation.

Religion is 'a response to ultimate reality', and we shall discuss what precisely we mean by 'ultimate reality' later in this chapter. Here let us note four points:[1]

Firstly, religion is conceived as response. The initiative is thought to lie with ultimate reality itself. There are different degrees of awareness of ultimate reality, but the relationship between the believer and ultimate reality is a dynamic one. Most important of all, the awareness and the response do not spring from the psychology of the individual alone. Religious belief does not spring from a sense of awe which a believer feels when confronted by the mystery of life, or the impressive phenomena of nature. This may be part of his experience, but religion cannot be reduced to this fact alone. The religious response springs from the individual's reaction to social facts, to a common cultural, historical and ecological context.

Secondly, religious experience involves the whole person. Being a social phenomenon, it cannot be reduced to the emotions, to the intellect or to the will of individuals alone. Early anthropologists, especially the Evolutionists, had too individual and too intellectual an approach to religion. They thought that monotheistic belief was the product of a long process of philosophical speculation in so-called civilized societies. They therefore found it difficult to believe that Africans, for example, could have an idea of God and a well-developed religion. Indeed, Sir Samuel Baker, the explorer, believed that the Northern Nilotes of Sudan had no religion at all.

'Without any exception, they are without a belief in a Supreme Being, neither have they any form of worship or idolatry; nor is the darkness of their minds enlightened by even a ray of superstition' (Baker, 'The Races of the Nile Basin', *Transactions of the Ethnological Society of London,* NS, V, 1891, i, 423–4).

In spite of this *obiter dictum*, the religion of the Northern Nilotes has been the subject of two recent and very full accounts which prove them to be among the most deeply religious people of the world! Religious experience is the product of intuition in the life experience of ordinary members of society. This intuition is achieved and expressed, not through intellectual formulations, but rather through more subtle, symbolical means.

Thirdly, religious experience differs in intensity. Some writers on the psychology of religion (for example, Rudolph Otto) base their conclusions on the most intense religious states, but religion is seldom experienced at high degrees of intensity, even though it is actually the most profound of human experiences. Much religious practice appears to be very matter of fact, but its influence is nevertheless great. Moreover, the religious sense can be developed, and this depends to a great extent upon social factors.

Finally, religion does not remain at the level of contemplation or speculation. It has to be translated into action, and applied to ordinary life, by means of a ritual phase. Religion demands action, and society determines the expression of this demand and the shape of the ritual, ritual being essentially a social fact.

Man identifies as sacred the ultimate, implied by his own experience. He realizes that his knowledge and control of reality are partial, and that he is essentially dependent upon something outside his experience. He is ignorant of all the consequences and repercussions of his very successes and achievements. He knows he is contributing to a movement he cannot comprehend. However, he also believes that this movement not only has an ultimate meaning but also possesses an ultimate autonomy and control. This ultimate ground of reality he conceives as a person like himself—a 'super-person'. It is a mysterious intuition of the sacred in terms of his own everyday experience. Like the little fishes' idea of heaven, it is an enlarged projection of his own world :

> '. . . somewhere, beyond space and time,
> Is wetter water, slimier slime.
> And there (they trust) there swimmeth One
> Who swam ere rivers were begun,
> Immense of fishy form and mind,
> Squamous, omnipotent and kind;
> And under that almighty fin
> The littlest fish may enter in.'
>
> (Rupert Brooke)

Man describes the sacred from both a negative and a positive point of view. It is at once utterly unlike his own experience, and at the same time it is the perfection of that experience.

The sacred is totally 'other'. It is 'set apart', holy, hedged round with prohibitions and taboos. It inspires fear. On the other hand, the sacred is the ideal. It is complete purity, wholeness, integrity, cleanness, order. It attracts and fascinates, it invites restless man to undertake a continual search for development and perfection and assures him that this search is worth while. It is blessing, prosperity and fullness of life.

If the sacred represents integrity and order, in so far as these are ultimately incomprehensible to man and beyond his control, the secular represents integrity and order in the world in so far as man is able to comprehend them and control them. Sacred and secular are not opposed, however. They are two ways of looking at the same reality. If man imagines that he enjoys ultimate control over reality, or that his growing control renders the idea of the sacred more and more obsolete, he is limiting the scope of his development, and robbing it of its fundamental impetus. This deviation is called secularism. If man's preoccupation with the sacred is such that it prejudices the material well-being of the human community, and impedes man's control over his environment, this is another form of alienation from reality. This deviation we call sacralism. Secularism deprives the secular of meaning; sacralism deprives the sacred of relevance. If sacred and secular are to be useful concepts, they have to balance and complement each other.

Rudolph Otto's definition of the sacred as *mysterium tremendum et fascinans* is not inexact. It is a mystery because it represents the incomprehensible, the 'other'. It is fear inspiring because it is surrounded with prohibitions and taboos, to emphasize its 'otherness'. It is fascinating because it leads man on to fulfilment in his everyday life. It is the source of blessing and order.

The words 'secularization' and 'sacralization' have positive content. As Fr Greeley points out, man transcends the merely secular by sacralizing it—not, of course, deifying it.[2] However, he discovers the relevance of the sacred by secularizing it. Secularization is not, therefore, desacralization.

There are a number of erroneous ideas about the sacred and the secular. Durkheim, for one, believed that sacred and secular (profane) were two absolute, opposed and mutually exclusive categories into which people classified everything real and ideal. This idea has been taken up by other writers, particularly by Mircea Eliade.[3] It is probably based on modern Western, secularist thinking which strongly opposes the secular to the sacred.

In fact, sacred and secular are relative concepts. Persons, places, actions or things may all be sacred at one time and secular at another. There are also degrees according to which they may be more sacred or more secular and less sacred or less secular. What is sacred for one category of persons may be secular for another. You cannot set limits to either the sacred or the secular. They are concerned with the same reality.

It was another error of Durkheim to believe that the sole criterion for the sacred was its being surrounded by taboos. It is, of course, true that this is one of the criteria, but taboos apply also to the concept of uncleanness which is opposed both to sacred and secular.[4] Durkheim and his followers have fallen into the contradictory assertion that the unclean is sacred. Uncleanness, however, means the opposite of order and integrity (wholeness). The notions of order and integrity depend on the ways in which people classify their experience. The sacred is described through systems of symbolic classification. For example, there is the common African colour classification.[5] White represents light, spirit power, purity, fertility, health; red represents blood, shed in war, in menstruation, in childbirth, and in witchcraft—therefore danger; black is the ambivalent colour of sorrow, night, evil, death, sexual desire, but also of rain-clouds and the blessing of rain. In such a system, white symbolizes order and cleanness, red disorder and uncleanness. Both, at times, may be surrounded by taboos. Experiences, objects, animals which defy order, or classification, are often regarded as unclean—the chameleon and the hyena, for example. So also are things which are tainted, blemished or deformed.

Uncleanness, with reference to the secular, means what is opposed to man-made order, or man-discovered order. For example, dirty shoes are all right in the garden, but not on the tablecloth. The unclean is what is unhygienic, opposed to scientific ideas about hygiene. These things are also the subject of social prohibitions and restrictions.

There is an opinion common to many modern writers, of whom Harvey Cox is typical, that mankind is evolving historically from a period of sacralism to one of secularism, as a result of scientific progress and the growth of towns.[6] For such people secularism is a modern problem, the solution of which lies in the future. A balanced view of sacred and secular, according to this opinion, is the term of the evolution. In fact, the sacralist and secularist mentalities are the product of social experience, as Dr Mary Douglas points out :

'Secularization is often treated as a modern trend, attributable to the growth of cities or the prestige of science, or just to the breakdown of social forms. But . . . it is an age-old cosmological type, a product of definable social experience, which need have nothing to do with urban life or modern science. . . . The contrast of secular with religious has nothing whatever to do with the contrast of modern with traditional or primitive. The idea that primitive man is by nature deeply religious is nonsense. The truth is that all the varieties of scepticism, materialism and spiritual fervour are to be found in the range of tribal societies' (*Natural Symbols,* London 1970, pp. ix–x).[7]

It is often said that Africans are 'notoriously religious'. This does not mean that secularism and scepticism were foreign to traditional Africa; nor does it mean, as Harvey Cox and others claim, that African traditional religion is necessarily sacralist and opposed to technical development. A balanced synthesis of sacred and secular has been achieved at many times and in many places in the history of mankind, and, more often than not, has typified African traditional religion. Such syntheses can take place at different levels of technical development in which man works out satisfactory solutions for the problems of living, without being necessarily committed to the need for continual mechanical invention. The modern Western world is secularist because it places the highest value on mechanical ingenuity and material success. This provides a spur to continuous technical innovation. It is not, however, the process of innovation in itself which can satisfy man, but the degree to which the technical changes are made meaningful to him and serve his happiness. Modern African countries may be infected with Western secularism as a result of technological development and Western-type education. The latter may also serve a pre-existing understanding of the sacred.

The religion of traditional Africa is often caricatured by evolutionist writers about secularity as being opposed to the material well-being of the people or as being basically unscientific.[8] Traditional religion, they say, was an alienation in which man felt himself unable to dominate his environment, in the grip of ghosts and demons, under the spell of the awe-inspiring phenomena of nature, a prey to imaginary magical forces or cruel and capricious spirits. Without denying that deviations have taken place, it is blatantly false to assert that people in traditional societies did not ever have a genuine view of the sacred, or a genuine religious experience.

We shall deal later with the question of symbolism, and we

49

shall see that natural objects and situations are capable of symbolic reference—that is, of being given a conventional significance which refers to a genuine human experience. Symbolism is the only satisfactory way of expressing and communicating the experience of ultimate reality (the sacred) or, indeed, of making the whole of reality intelligible to ourselves. Symbols are not scientific statements. They may even be scientifically erroneous, but they refer to genuine experience and cannot be opposed to science. In some African societies the sun was a symbol of God. Men knew the sun as an inaccessible source of light, a perfectly adequate symbol of the transcendence of God. The modern scientist knows the sun as a thing, a giant thermo-nuclear furnace which transforms hydrogen into helium, possesses a temperature of fourteen million degrees centigrade, and loses four million tons of weight through radiation each second. These scientific facts are not symbolically useful, and it is clear that the sun-worshipper is not worshipping the object known to science but the transcendent God whom the sun signifies and of whom he has had intuitive experience by looking at the sun.

Joseph Wood Krutch, the American naturalist, has dealt with the same problem with reference to ordinary perception :

'The table before which we sit may be, as the scientist maintains, composed of dancing atoms, but it does not reveal itself to us as anything of the kind, and it is not with dancing atoms but a solid motionless object that we live. So remote is the 'real' table—and most of the other 'realities' with which science deals—that it cannot be discussed in terms which have any human value, and though it may receive our purely intellectual credence, it cannot be woven into the pattern of life as it is led, in contradistinction to life as we attempt to think about it. Vibrations in the ether are so totally unlike, let us say, the colour purple that the gulf between them cannot be bridged, and they are, to all intents and purposes, not one but two separate things of which the second and less real must be the most significant for us. And just as the sensation which led us to attribute an objective reality to a nonexistent thing which we call 'purple' is more important for human life than the conception of a vibration of a certain frequency, so too the belief in God, however ill founded, has been more important in the life of man than the germ theory of decay, however true the latter may be' (*The Modern Temper*, New York 1929, p. 49).

We shall deal later on with the practice of magic. Magic is not a religious phenomenon. In religious contexts it can even be the very perversion of religious worship. It is the manipulation of symbolism as a technique for controlling one's environment. As a technique it can co-exist with religious belief; or else it can be the focus for a completely secular outlook. Both instances are recorded for African traditional societies, although it is, perhaps, more common for magic to co-exist peaceably with religious belief and practice.

There is a well-known encounter with an African rain-doctor recorded by Livingstone, in which the explorer misunderstood (a) that magic could be regarded as a technique compatible with religious belief, like any other technique, and (b) that man's experience cannot be departmentalized into areas of human control and divine control—that is to say, into exclusive categories of secular and sacred. Livingstone's God was a 'God of the gaps', retreating before the progress of science. It is ironical that man can now make rain scientifically by seeding clouds.

Livingstone accused the rain-doctor of waiting for the rain clouds before using his magic, and then taking the credit for the rain. The rain doctor replied

'. . . we are both doctors and not deceivers. You give a patient medicine. Sometimes God is pleased to heal him by means of your medicine. Sometimes not—he dies. When he is cured, you take the credit for what God does. I do the same. Some-times God grants us rain, sometimes not. When he does, we take the credit of the charm. When a patient dies, you don't give up trust in your medicine. Neither do I when no rain falls. . . .'

The medical doctor answered

'I give medicine to living creatures within my reach, and can see the effect though no cure follows. . . . God alone can command the clouds. Only try and wait patiently. God will give us rain without your medicines.'

To this the rain-doctor replied

> 'Well, I always thought white people were wise until this morning. Whoever thought of making a trial of starvation? Is death pleasant then?' (*Missionary Travels*, quoted by R G Lienhardt in *Social Anthropology*, Oxford 1964, pp. 176–7.)

Just as the sacred is sometimes characterized as sacralist by writers with a modern, secularist background, so theologians who accept the categories of sacred and profane as rigidly exclusive accuse the traditional religions, in which the balance is held between sacred and secular, of being anthropocentric, man-centred, and secular. These religions are not 'spiritual' enough, they say. They are not 'other-worldly'. They are not interested in ethics. Such accusations spring from a traditional (often Protestant) theology in which matter is exclusively opposed to spirit, natural to supernatural, secular to sacred.

Professor John Mbiti is one who frequently accuses African traditional religion of being too man-centred. This, of course, is the reverse of Harvey Cox's indictment of traditional religion.

> 'To live here and now is the most important concern of African religious activities and beliefs. There is little, if any, concern with the distinctly spiritual welfare of man apart from his physical life. No line is drawn between the spiritual and the physical. Even life hereafter is conceived in materialistic and physical terms. There is neither paradise to be hoped for nor hell to be feared in the hereafter. The soul of man does not long for spiritual redemption, or for closer contact with God in the next world. . . . God comes into the picture as an explanation of man's contact with time. There is no messianic hope or apocalyptic vision of God stepping in at some future moment to bring about a radical reversal of man's normal life. God is not pictured in an ethical-spiritual relationship with man. Man's acts of worship and turning to God are pragmatic and utilitarian rather than spiritual or mystical' (*African Religions and Philosophy*, London 1969, pp. 4–5).

> 'Man in some ways considers himself to be the centre of the universe, and this egocentrism makes him interpret that

universe both anthropocentrically and anthropomorphically.
. . . African ontology is firmly anthropocentric; and this makes
man look at God and nature from the point of his relationship with them. We find, therefore, many expressions which
attribute human nature to God' (*Ibid.*, p. 48).

These passages are an indictment of African traditional religion.
They almost rob it of all religious content. However, they are
based on the assumption that sacred and secular can and must
be separated and opposed. The reverse is true. Religion *has* to
be man-centred. Both the Old Testament and the New Testament show this. The prophets and Christ himself continually
condemned the formal worship which alienated man from the
human community and made him antisocial. 'The Sabbath was
made for man, not man for the Sabbath.' True religion has to
be centred on the needs and interests of mankind, otherwise
it is irrelevant. Natural and supernatural are simply abstractions
made from a single, actual reality.

Ultimate reality in Africa is usually conceived as a super-
person, or supreme being, associated with the sky (*Deus coelestis*).
His absolute character is expressed through ideas of creation,
ownership and control.[9] Creation is conceived as 'manufacture'
or 'moulding'; or else as 'life-begetting', in which case God is
represented as the first ancestor.

The natural phenomena of the sky are the obvious symbols
used by Africans to express God's sublimity and transcendence :
height, light, sun, moon, stars, sky, rainbow, wind, breath, spirit,
lightning, thunder. Nearly all the common African names for
the supreme being are traceable to sky symbolism or ideas of
creation. The following are some examples of names widely
used in East, Central, Southern and West Africa.

Mungu, Mulungu, Mu'ungu

Generic Bantu words for spirit in East and Central Africa, but
possibly derived from the root—*lungu*, meaning 'clan'. They
emphasize the idea of begetting life, and are applied both to the
supreme being and to lesser spirits.

Jok, Juok, Kwoth

Generic Nilotic words for spirit in the Sudan and Eastern Africa,
applied to the supreme being and to lesser spirits. They mean
'spirit' or 'power'. The Dinka also use the word *Nhialic*, 'the

sky' or 'the above', to refer to God. The name *Akuj*, used by the Turkana, Karimojong and Teso, has the same meaning of 'sky'.

Rua, Ijua, Izuva, Yuva, Ilyuva, Lyoba, Zyoba
Names for God deriving from the word for 'sun' in many Bantu languages of East Africa. In West Africa, the Tallensi of Ghana, the Mossi of Upper Volta, and the Basa of Nigeria are all examples of peoples who use names for God which literally mean 'sun'. *Nyame*, 'shining one' is widely used among the Akan peoples of Ghana, the Ashanti, and the Fanti.

Nzambi, Njambi, Tsambi, Yambe, Dzambi, Zam, Monzam
Words applied to the supreme being in many Bantu languages of Central Africa, possibly derived from the root-*amba*, 'speak', 'act', 'create'.

Lesa, Ileesa, Leza
Words applied to the supreme being in some Bantu languages of East and Central Africa, and which refer to lightning or thunderbolt.

Chiuta, Chauta, Cuta
'Rainbow', applied to the supreme being in Central Africa, because of its association with the sky and because it encircles the world.

Mu'umba, Mwumba, Kabumba
From the root-*umba*, 'to mould'. A frequent Bantu name for 'creator' in Eastern and Central Africa.

Matunda, Umatunda, Katonda
From-*tunda*, 'to create'. Another frequent Bantu name for 'creator' in East Africa. In the Nyamwezi languages and dialects the name is given the plural prefix *ma-*, and in some cases the personal initial vowel *u-* as well. This indicates the richness and inscrutability of God, besides his personal character.

Besides the names for God in everyday use, there are other names or symbols for God which can be found in the oral literature of African peoples, particularly in their prayers. These names reveal varying attributes, as well as varying ethical relationships with God. One cannot generalize about a single African concept of God. Each concept is part of a system of classification particular to a certain society.

One who saves   Watcher of everything   One with long

ears   Central roof-pole   Great eye   He who is every-
where   Chief   He who bends down even majesties
He who roars so that nations are struck with terror   Ruler
Giver   Almighty   Doer of all   One who clears the
forest   One who fills everything   Restorer   Great,
great one   Seeing one   One with very long arms
The   Unknown   Fire lighter   The unexplainable
Head   He who came into being of himself   Everlasting
one of the forest   One who controls   Thunderer
Marvel of marvels   Pure King   Sky   Owner of all
things   Deliverer of those in trouble   One who fills the
rivers   Fathomless spirit   Immovable rock that never
dies   One who saves (helps or steers)   One who makes
things rot   Father   Giver of life   Big-faced one
One who increases life   Bearer of burdens   Big doctor
Reaper   The one who is there   Protector   Winnower
Benefactor   There is a saviour   Winnowing tray
One who arranges things   Ever-ready shooter   Lord of
magic power   Distributor   Days   Wise one   One
who gives recompense   Founder   Transformer   One
stronger than an army   Educator   Worker of prodigies
Guardian   Possessor   The impenetrable   Insatiable
one   Overseer   Father of men   One without an
equal   The unsurpassed   Piler-up of rocks   One who
needs nobody   Knower of all things   Grandfather
Seer of all things   Hearer of all things   Lion   The
faithful one   The invulnerable   Mother chicken   The
herder   Preserver   Lifter   Healer   Reverend
elder   Friend in this village   Leopard   Elephant
Great Mother

The attributes of God are also revealed in the personal names
given to human beings. For example

He may come when he likes   Do not overlook the one with
hands outstretched to receive   He acts in his judgment
Only he can mock successfully   Only God matters   The
wicked curse and he watches like a herder   Only God truly
makes a choice   Only God saves   May they respect
him   Only God is truly committed to the task   It is
he who acts   God who really knows   Only God truly

loves   Their true vessel is God   Only God is truly the
good herdsman   He watches everything   Only God truly
gratifies   He alone is worthy of supplication   Only God
truly governs   God's portion   He alone causes things
to flourish   That which he gives me   God truly bestows
a name   Let everything pass through his will   He does
as he likes   His gift is in a trial   Upheld by him   He
sees me   Oh God   He outstrips battalions   Do as he
wishes   He who created this lovely little boy   Do as he
does   He makes me live   Only God exists   Darling
of God   Only God truly sees   Thanks to God   God
truly creates   I saw God there   I see him there   I
conclude that he saves me   God is enough   Gift of God

Professor John Mbiti, who has collected names for God from
more than 270 African peoples, finds the following attributes
represented

Omniscience   Omnipresence   Omnipotence   Trans-
cendence   Immanence   Self-existence   Pre-eminence
First and Last Cause   Spirituality   Invisibility   In-
comprehensibility   Eternity, Infinity   Immutability
Unity and Plurality   Pity, Mercy, Kindness   Love
Comfort   Faithfulness   Goodness   Anger   Will
Justice   Holiness   Creator   Providence   Protector
Controller   Nurse   Healer   Saviour   Ruler
Master   Judge   Leader in war   Friendship   Father-
hood   Motherhood   Source of death   Source of
misfortunes

To these one might add

Indefectibility   Recompense   Freedom

These attributes are even more numerous than those found in
standard textbooks of Christian theology.

The concept of God in African traditional societies can be
found anywhere along a spectrum that runs from extreme theism
to extreme deism.

Theism is the experience of God as multiple and overwhelming, and the acknowledgement of his direct and effective influence on man in his daily life. He owns and conserves every-

thing, and is at hand to punish man's faults when creation is abused. His presence is felt to be close even though it takes no tangible or lasting form. He is apprehended in moral and inter-personal relationships, and in the good and bad use of created things. This type of belief is typical of unspecialized hunter-gatherers and shifting cultivators, as well as of pastoralists —all of these being types of economy which are largely passive to the environment. The pastoralist in Africa is traditionally a kind of parasite on his herd, rather than an active stock-breeder. Theism corresponds (as does deism) to a specific social experience.

Deism, according to Diderot's definition, is 'a concept of God which has no religious reality—that is to say, the supreme being is acknowledged but plays no explicit role in religious life, in the daily life of individuals, or even in the collective rituals of the group. However, deism is characterized by a highly developed theology and a complex system of world order which sets the supreme being outside man's world. Often there are elaborate series of 'heavens', or orders of intermediaries which separate God from man. There are also elaborate mythologies. Guilt is generalized and unspecific. God is the ultimate controller of life and only intervenes in life-or-death situations. Deism is most commonly found among settled cultivators.

The so-called *Deus otiosus*, or 'lazy God' who is not interested in his creatures, is a familiar concept in the writings of anthropologists with agnostic tendencies, or with a concern to underline the differences between so-called 'primitive religion' and developed world religions. It refers either to the deistic situation, or to a theism in which mediators play an important role. Theism is certainly more common in Africa than deism, and the idea of *Deus otiosus* can be misleading. Scholars are inclined to avoid this term today.

Mediation is a familiar concept in Africa which enhances the importance of the one addressed. In many parts of Africa chiefs cannot be addressed directly, but have to be addressed indirectly through spokesmen, or with faces averted, or the mouth covered. The same idea is applied to prayer. God is addressed indirectly in the third person, or he is approached through mediators. These mediators may be spirits, or they may be human beings, chiefs or important men to whom the worship of the supreme being is restricted. Very often in African tradition religious beliefs and practices were departmentalized, according to the different levels of the social structure : family spirits, clan spirits, and the supreme being at the level of the nation itself. This does not mean that all these cults were not the property of the tribe as a whole. This is shown by the constant mention of the supreme being in everyday situations, proverbs, riddles, oaths, curses, and different forms of oral literature. It is also shown by the fact that the supreme being was mentioned in prayer to family spirits as the ultimate addressee of the prayer, or as witness that the prayer has been offered correctly.

On the other hand, in the deistic situation spirits can easily become semi-independent heroes who have practically no relation to each other, let alone to the supreme being. Instead of mediators they tend to become barriers to communication with the supreme being, each concerned with his special province. When assessing the compatibility of the African belief in spirits with Christian beliefs, one has to judge how far a relationship between them and the supreme being is affirmed or denied, and how far they are the objects of worship. We shall deal with this more fully when treating the question of religious rituals.

Because Africans believe in spirits, they are sometimes called 'animists'. It is best to avoid this misleading term, because it is unfair to emphasize the belief in spirits to the exclusion of the supreme being. One could call Roman Catholics 'animists' too. The term 'animism' is also associated with a theory about the origin of belief in spirits propounded by Sir Edwin Tylor. He believed that it arose from the recognition of the existence of souls (*anima, -ae*).

The spirit mediators in African traditional religion take many forms. The Earth Mother, Wife of God, or Moon Goddess, satisfies the desire for a 'feminine touch' in the concept of God. She also represents the receptive or passive principle by which God makes the earth fertile, and ensures the continuance of life on its surface. It is very much a belief of agricultural peoples.

The master of the animals was originally a hypostasis or aspect of the supreme being among hunter-gatherers. It was the personification of animal beauty, often equated with the sun, the splendid hero of the sky. In societies where hunting is a specialization restricted to relatively few people, the master of the animals becomes a nature spirit with a personality separate from that of the supreme being. It is a fantastic animal or giant, often belching fire, and having many heads. It plays tricks on hunters. It appears and disappears mysteriously, and is associated with the wind, whirlwinds and dust-whirls. It causes hunters and travellers to be lost in the forest or bush, and seizes children, especially girls. It is capricious and dangerous, but possesses great wealth and knows many secrets. It is often conceived as many, one for each herd. If the hunter knows how to behave —especially how to make the right offerings of tobacco or Indian hemp—the master of the animals will protect him and make him prosper in the hunt, and may even impart some of his secret knowledge to him. The master of the animals is a constant theme in African oral literature, especially in myths of salvation, which describe the rescue of a child from his clutches.

Nature spirits tend to represent the unfamiliar world of bush, mountain, lake, and so forth, in societies of settled cultivators. Unlike the hunter-gatherers and the pastoralists, settled cultivators do not have a wide knowledge of natural phenomena; moreover, their familiar world is restricted to the village and farm. Bush, forest, mountain and lake are dangerous and disturbing places, and the experience of them is personalized in the shape of malevolent, but not necessarily evil, spirits. Personalized experiences, even though they are deemed to have an objective existence of their own, are not necessarily the objects of religious worship. Belief in them and transactions with them can, from a Christian point of view, be merely vain observances or superstitions analagous to belief in fairies or leprechauns.

Sedentary peoples bury their dead in or near their settlements as a rule. They are also able to have more elaborate funeral rites and to build permanent shrines. Their ancestors are still with them and the soil still belongs to them. Hence there is a cult of the dead. Ancestors may be thought to be revengeful, and vindictive on occasion, but they have a right to be in order to punish men's sins, especially those of filial impiety. In general they are more familiar and benevolent than nature spirits, though some peoples (like the Baganda) believe that lineage spirits can be manipulated through magical techniques and made to afflict a man's enemies at his own whim (*mayembe*, horns).

If God is the creator of the world, the ancestors are the creators of society and are thought to be in a permanent relationship with the living. In fact they form one community with them. Some writers use the phrase 'living dead' to refer to lineage spirits who are remembered as individuals. This conveys the idea of their vitality and active interest in their descendants. They are the real rulers of the lineage and owners of its property. They are aware of the actions and even of the thoughts of their descendants, who must keep faith with the dead and show them piety. Lineage spirits are revered because of their success and power. This is not strictly related to ethical behaviour. Thus a wicked and cruel man's spirit may be very greatly revered, as much as that of a generous and kind man; while a good young man who dies without marrying or having children may not be revered at all. These spirits are spirits of successful men who sired children to continue the lineage. However, their memory can be cherished as an ethical ideal, and people may imitate them consciously and call upon them to be their guardians and models. In general, the relationship with the ancestors is one of love rather than of fear.

People bear the names of their ancestors and this is sometimes referred to as 'nominal reincarnation'. The bearers of the names are thought to have a very close relationship to their namesakes, but reincarnation, strictly so-called, is rare. The living need the favour of their ancestors, but the ancestors are also in the debt of their descendants. Some peoples, like the Shona of Rhodesia, hold that the dead are doomed to eternal wandering unless they are called home to the lineage in a special ceremony. Others, like the Chagga, believe that the very existence and happiness of the dead is in some way dependent on their having had children, and on their continuing to receive oblations and requests from these children.

That the ancestors are mediators is scarcely in doubt. Although they may be thought, from one point of view, to inhabit a place of their own, they are also often said to be 'with God'. Some peoples even say that they 'are' God, although they recognize well enough that they are created by him. The ancestors are usually associated with hills, the sky and high places. All of this is a symbolic way of explaining the close relationship which the ancestors have with God, that they are somehow one with him, and that God is somehow 'all in all'. The Bemba of Zambia even whisper messages into the ears of corpses, so that they can take them to the spirit world.

Birago Diop's poem 'Breath' is a fine summary of African feeling about lineage spirits or ancestors :

'Those who are dead have never gone away,
They are at the breast of the wife,
They are in the child's cry of dismay
And the firebrand bursting into life.
The dead are not under the ground,
They are in the fire that burns low. . . .
The dead are never dead.'

In the chapter on religious ritual, we shall discuss the compatibility of prayers and offerings to ancestors with Christian belief and practice. Some authors achieve this compatibility by rejecting the religious character of beliefs and practices about ancestors. They emphasize that they are concerned with 'veneration', rather than 'worship', and that the dead are simply respected and fed in the same way that elderly members of the lineage are respected and fed. This is a fallacious argument, since no one imagines that death does not make a difference to social relationships. The dead are known to be spirits, and not the same as living people. Undoubtedly African beliefs about their ancestors can enrich the development of the Christian doctrine on the vital relationship between living and dead, the communion of saints, and can render it more dynamic and two-sided; nevertheless certain traditional Christian positions about the relationship between living and dead have to be safeguarded. The basis of the respect for ancestors has to be purified, and the relationship of immortality to fecundity demands a more subtle, and less literal, interpretation. People can be creators of society and builders of the community in other ways than siring or bearing children.

Totemism is basically a form of classification by which a society orders its own relationships. Social groupings are identified by an emblem or totem, which is often also a food avoidance, sometimes reinforced by magical sanctions. Symbolic stories, or myths, may be told about the totem, especially if it is an animal, and it may be seen as a mythical 'ancestor'. Generally totemism is not a religious phenomenon, but in some societies it is a personalization of a group's relationship with God or with another spirit, and may be the object of worship.

In African traditional societies, morality is seen to be in an intimate relationship with the ontological order of the universe. This order is 'given', if not explicitly 'God-given', and it is expressed in the system of symbolic classification current in society. Any infraction of this order is a contradiction in life itself and brings about a physical disorder which reveals the fault.

In the sacralist situation, and in the Christian reaction to Western secularism, God is often pictured as extrinsic to mankind and the world. He is pictured as a human lawgiver, and morality is seen as a code of positive law, with sins as transgressions of a law. In the secularist situation, human law cuts loose from morality itself, and a distinction is made between crime and sin. In African tradition this is not the case. Faults are not transgressions of a 'law', but factual contradictions of established order. However, a distinction can be observed between sins which offend and invite punishment from God and spiritual beings, and faults which bring about a physical disorder by themselves. These latter are violations, as it were, of the laws of life, neither ethically good nor bad—merely dangerous. Such might be the breaking of minor taboos, or conventions, or disregard for magical power. Although the faults may be anti-social in character—for example, the breaking of avoidance customs between in-laws—they are thought, in this case, to harm those who commit them, rather than to offend others. In so far as faults really do harm to others (jealousy, envy, theft, anger, injury, murder, rape, adultery, incest) and involve the ill-will of one person towards another, they more or less explicitly involve the spirits who are the guardians of social order. Ritual faults and omissions which are direct affronts offered to spiritual beings involve society also in the retribution which they bring. Faults which affect the relationship between men and spiritual beings are sins, and tend to be collective in their implications.

This is not to say that Africans do not also feel that they can offend against individual persons. Society is structured. It is not only the experience of the group, but also of the 'grid', the network of inter-personal relationships centred on ego. In educating children to morality, appeals are made both to statuses in the group ('a boy does not do that', 'a Kikuyu does not do that', 'a married woman should do that') and to personal values ('that will make your father angry', 'if you do that, it will hurt your mother', 'your little sister needs to be helped', and so on). However, in Africa, it is fair to say that group-orientated appeals are stronger than person-orientated appeals in moral education.

The charge is frequently made that Africans did not traditionally know of offences against God himself, nor of offences involving punishment in another world. There are documented instances of the belief that certain actions offend God directly— for example, disobedience to authority in Rwanda, or theft in Ukimbu (Southern Tanzania)—but even if most offences against spiritual beings involve the ancestors rather than God one is still dealing with the phenomenon of sin. The idea of retribution after death is not unknown, although it may be bound up with the reactions of those left alive, and their concern to perpetuate the memory of the good rather than the wicked.[10] In any case, one should not expect to find retribution in an afterlife when no clear distinctions are drawn between this world and 'another world'.

Sin is thought to be a reality and not, as some anthropologists have suggested, merely the fear of a punishment which society believes is attached to certain actions. Africans are conscious of sin as a state, and rites of purification and reconciliation are attempts to get rid of a state, not just (as Frazer and Pettazoni thought) a question of taking practical precautions to avoid the consequences of a fault. This is true even when sin is referred to by the name of the consequent disaster, as for example 'sickness', 'barrenness', 'wasting away', 'death'. It is shown in the symbolism of the rites of purification when blood is let and thrown into the air, when water is blown out of the mouth, when firewood is thrown away, or when the sin and its consequences are passed on to a sacrificial animal.

Various images are used for sin which help us to understand what it means to those who use them. Besides heat, shadow, and uncleanness, there are two other important symbols for sin: destruction and the breaking of a covenant.[11]

Destruction conveys the idea that sin is the negation of existence. It brings about the annihilation of a whole lineage, and blots people out forever. An example of this idea is found among the Lugbara of Uganda, where *nyoka* is the punishment of annihilation sent by the supreme being and *ezata* ('destruction') is the name given to sin.

The covenant is largely implicit in that men are assumed to be in a mutual relationship with God and the spirits until the bond is violated. It is then that the former existence of the covenant is appealed to in prayer. This covenant is usually seen as a loving family relationship and the plaint raised in prayer is 'Why are you doing this to us? We are your children'. Sacrifices, as we shall see later when dealing with ritual, have the characteristic of a pact, or *quid pro quo* with God and the spirits. This expresses the renewal of the relationship of dependence upon, and service of, the spiritual beings who are the objects of worship. Healing the breach of the covenant necessarily involves an appeal to God or the spirits to restore the relationship.

It has sometimes been said by anthropologists and missionaries that Africans have no internalized guilt-feelings. This is because it is common in Africa to extrapolate or externalize on to some person, object or symbol, one's internal feelings, fears and expectations.[12] People express themselves as passive to experience, but this does not mean that the experience itself is non-existent. Thus Africans tend to say 'The stone tripped me', rather than 'I tripped on a stone', and African languages have constructions which favour this extrapolation of experience.

Extrapolation is also used in the confession of sin or the admission of guilt. This does not mean that those who use it are simply exculpating themselves: exculpation is as common in Africa as in other parts of the world, but it is not always implied in extrapolation. It is more often a conventional means of expressing guilt. However, extrapolation is an indication that the external and social characteristics of sin are important. Sin is present when it becomes manifest or externalized. For example, being drunk may not be thought sinful, until the drunkard injures someone; or having illicit relations with a girl might not be thought very sinful, until she is made pregnant. Internal states such as anger, envy and ill-will are recognized, however, as sins, and they are seen as exerting a bad influence on social relations, or as prejudicing the performance of social rituals.

It is at these moments that they have to be confessed, and their rejection externalized in symbolic action.

In Africa, guilt is seen more as shame than as the breaking of a law. Shame is the sense of inadequacy and failure that one feels at having let oneself and others down. A man is cast for a role within a particular social milieu, and he is ashamed of himself for having failed to fulfil that role. Such shame has nothing to do with self-pity.

Most African societies have myths which purport to explain the experience men have of sin. These myths usually explain how God withdrew from the world because of a sin of greed or curiosity. The woman is usually associated with the original sin because in the symbolic classification of male-dominated societies women represent the qualities of weakness and fickleness! A myth told by the Dinka of Sudan recounts how God allowed men to plant one grain of millet a day. Woman was greedy and took a long hoe to plant more. In doing so she struck God, who withdrew in anger from the world.

The Ashanti of Ghana tell how woman was greedy and filled her mortar too full with yams. In pounding the yams the pestle struck God, who withdrew angrily from the world. The Ituri pygmies of Zaire say that man and woman came every day to feed God, who was living in a clearing in the forest. They were not allowed to stay and see him take the food. Woman was curious and stayed to see God come out of his hut. God was angry and retired from the world.

Mention has already been made of salvation myths in which people, and particularly children, are rescued from the master of the animals conceived as a forest monster. In some versions of these stories the monster swallows the whole human race. When the monster is killed and cut open all the people come out. The saviour is often a 'wonderchild' or innocent child, and the value of the myth is clearly the triumph of innocence over iniquity, and the salvation from the consequences of sin.

Moral ideals in African traditional religion often appear very human. For example, among the Shilluk of Sudan the ideal is cunning and worldly success; among the Ashanti of Ghana it is magnanimity and material prosperity; among the Nyakyusa of Tanzania it is the same ideal expressed as 'heaviness'. Longevity and riches are often seen as a sign of virtue. These ideals are similar to the Old Testament ideals of the ancient Jews. Although they are focused on a material world, it is, as we have seen, a world in which spiritual and moral values are held in high esteem. African moral ideals are not to be condemned outright: they are capable of development and purification.

As we have seen, individuals experience society as a bounded group or social unit, and also as a grid or network of relationships on an ego-centred basis. In different societies the relative strengths of group and grid vary. We then find different emphases on the sacred and secular, and differences in the form of religious beliefs, according to the types we have just examined. These can be arranged in a diagram[13] such as Fig. 2.

The four societies A, B, C, D, are the product of combinations of: strong group—personal, regulative, self-subordinated cosmology; weak group—impersonal, non-regulative, self-exalted cosmology; strong grid—affirmation of the value of material things; weak grid—affirmation of spiritual joys, asceticism.

Societies A and B are complementary opposites, which would meet in the ideal, perfectly balanced society. Society B tends to be a sub-culture, or parasite group on society A, unable to exist in a permanently unstructured condition. Societies C and D are the deviations of secularism and sacralism.

Dr Douglas offers some examples of the four types. Society A: Dinka (Sudan), Nuer (Sudan), Mandari (Sudan); society B: pygmies (Congo), modern hippies (Europe and America), Christian religious congregations in their first fervour; society C: Hadza (Tanzania), modern Europe and America; society D: Anuak (Sudan), some Central African peoples, American McCarthy-ists.

There is no Christian value which is not first of all a human value expressed in a specific cultural form. Christianity cannot exist except as incarnate in a culture. In the missionary situation, Christianity is preached first of all in terms of a culture foreign to the people who receive the message. Some missionaries have been content with this situation, in which the newly converted Africans obey the Church's regulations and attend Mass and the sacraments without really understanding what is going on. In fact, many African Christians interpret what they do not understand in their own way, and the result is a juxtaposition of two cultures and two religions. This is the situation which

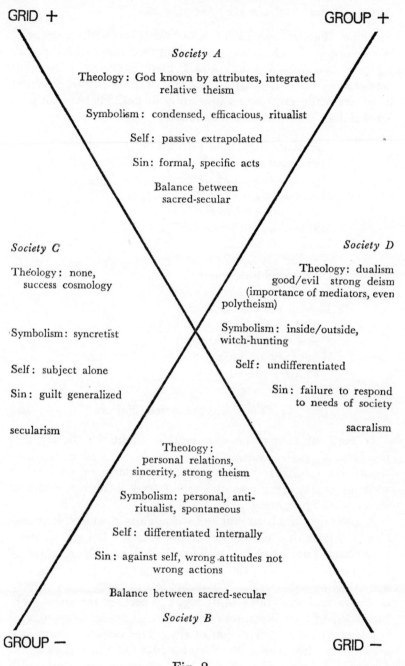

GRID +   GROUP +

Society A

Theology: God known by attributes, integrated relative theism

Symbolism: condensed, efficacious, ritualist

Self: passive extrapolated

Sin: formal, specific acts

Balance between sacred-secular

Society C

Theology: none, success cosmology

Symbolism: syncretist

Self: subject alone

Sin: guilt generalized

secularism

Society D

Theology: dualism good/evil strong deism (importance of mediators, even polytheism)

Symbolism: inside/outside, witch-hunting

Self: undifferentiated

Sin: failure to respond to needs of society

sacralism

Theology: personal relations, sincerity, strong theism

Symbolism: personal, anti-ritualist, spontaneous

Self: differentiated internally

Sin: against self, wrong attitudes not wrong actions

Balance between sacred-secular

Society B

GROUP −   GRID −

Fig. 2

Professor Tanner has called a 'working misunderstanding'.[14] But does it work? Obviously, we cannot be content with a purely legalistic Christian practice; and if there is no communication between teacher and taught, the former cannot say whether the latter are really professing Christianity or not. The African poet Okot p'Bitek has satirized this situation :

'The things they shout I do not understand,
They shout anyhow,
They shout like mad people.
The padre shouts words
You cannot understand,
And he does not seem
To care in the least
Whether his hearers
Understand him or not.
A strange language they speak
The Christian diviner-priests,
And the white nuns
Think the girls understand
What they are saying,
And are annoyed
When they laugh.'

(*The Song of Lawino*, Nairobi 1967, p. 116.)

It may, of course, be that certain traditional beliefs and practices are perfectly compatible with the profession of Christianity, but this has to be demonstrated. It is no good the Church winking at, or being unconsciously forced to accept, practices she does not understand.

A great deal has been said and written about liturgical adaptation in Africa, but adaptation of the message is logically more important. The Word has to be preached and the response of faith elicited before it can take full expression in sacramental action. Moreover, African rituals are less enduring than African concepts and categories of thought. There is therefore more likelihood of an adaptation of the message being accepted, and being of use, than adaptation of rites. This does not mean that rites can be dispensed with. Very far from it! But it does mean, probably, that the Church will have to create new rites which are in harmony with the African mentality, rather than attempt to take over and adapt ancient pagan rites.

In subsequent chapters, we shall examine concepts and values in African oral tradition, in African rituals and in African social institutions, in order to see how they are discovered by analysis, and to what extent they are useful for teachers of Christianity, and for Christian worship. In this chapter we shall consider only the principles.

'Adaptation' is a misnomer because it suggests that Christianity somehow adapts itself. In fact, since it is not in itself a culture, Christianity cannot adapt itself without betraying itself. The term 'adaptation' derives from the preconciliar mission theology in which Christianity was seen as a cultural tradition. What really happens is that Christianity in one cultural dress encounters a non-Christian culture, and then tries to incarnate itself in the new culture. In doing this it challenges and transforms the culture. Two processes are involved: the 'undressing' of Christianity from the foreign culture, and the 'dressing' of Christianity in the indigenous culture. These processes, however, are simultaneous, since Christianity cannot exist without some dress or other. You cannot have a 'culturally naked Christianity'.

The great difficulty is that in this encounter or 'adaptation' one must work inwards from two separate starting points. One must start with the indigenous culture itself, to discover what its authentic human values are, and how far these values are already Christian values, or can be developed as 'seeds of the Gospel' into Christian values. One must never begin with a Christian doctrine—for example, the Holy Trinity—and then look for similarities in an African tradition. This is an entirely superficial adaptation, which turns it into a gimmick for making Christianity acceptable.

Secondly, one must have the total picture of the Christian message in mind when looking for the 'seeds of the Gospel', otherwise one will not recognize them. Moreover, the Christian message must not be limited to the mere area of overlap between Christianity and African traditional religion as this would impoverish it completely. Innovation may be necessary, and perhaps even the preservation of foreign cultural forms for concepts and values that are completely foreign to the indigenous culture, but these must be well integrated and articulated within

69

the new Christian culture. In teaching the doctrine of the Trinity, for example, one might begin with the indigenous idea of the richness of God, expressed, let us say, in a plural term for the supreme being. But can one ultimately dispense with the three persons, described by the symbols inherited from the Jewish culture, in which the Trinity was revealed, as 'Father', 'Son' and 'Spirit'? Obviously not. In the doctrine of the Trinity, the indigenous idea of God must be developed and given even an entirely new dimension.

Sacred scripture has a privileged place in the Christian tradition. It was within the Jewish culture that the mystery of Christ was revealed to mankind, and the very first essay in adaptation was made by the New Testament writers who tried to express concepts and values, first described in terms of the Jewish culture, in terms of the newly dominant Greek culture. These are historical facts and Christianity is a historical religion. To deny them would be to deny Christianity itself. It follows, therefore, that the Church can never dispense with the Bible in the form in which it was written. One cannot, for example, replace scripture by an anthology of African myths. Strictly speaking, there is no African 'Old Testament' or 'African scripture', because the Jewish scriptures are indispensable to all Christians. However, they can and must be expounded in terms of African culture. The same is true of the various historic conciliar and papal pronouncements. The African Christian cannot pretend that these pronouncements were never made, or that they are only of interest to Western Christians. Nevertheless, he has to understand them and receive them on his own cultural terms. In the light of the scriptures and of the Church's understanding of the scriptures, the African can understand his non-Christian cultural tradition as a preparation for the Gospel. In this sense alone can one speak of 'Africa's Old Testament'.

It has never been the intention of the Church to oppose everything in the ancient culture. Nonetheless, the impression was given more often than not that everything was entirely forbidden. The missionaries forbade or discouraged beliefs and practices either because they thought they were bad or because they were uncertain about their moral value. The first generation of catechists and faithful were often even more intransigent than the missionaries, likewise the first members of the African clergy.

It was thought, wrote Professor R E S Tanner of the Sukuma in Tanzania, that to be 'a good Christian, one had to be bad Sukuma'. Even nowadays one sometimes hears Christianity being preached in this negative way.

Christianity has an ambivalence towards non-Christian religions. This can be seen, for example, in the epistles of St Paul who, on the one hand, tells the Corinthians that 'you cannot drink the cup of the Lord and the cup of demons' and, on the other, tells the Romans that '. . . pagans who never heard of the law . . . are led by reason to do what the law commands. . . . They can point to the substance of the law engraved on their hearts. . . .' (1 Cor 10:21 and Rom 2:14–15.) In other words, as we have said, Christianity comes both to complete and to challenge what traditional religion teaches. We cannot condemn traditional religion out of hand; it was a means of grace. But we cannot approve all its practices indiscriminately. We must be discerning. Before Vatican II Catholics tended to stress the negative side. Since the Council they are stressing the more positive side of what Christianity has in common with traditional religion.

Some people speak as if the Church had nothing to do in mission lands but ratify the traditional beliefs and practices of the people. This, as we have just seen, is wide of the mark. If we did this, the explicit witness of the Christian community would simply disappear. The Church has to be a visible sign of the unity of mankind to be achieved in Christ. It also has to be an effective sign of that unity, helping to bring it about and bearing explicit witness to it. The Church must also call others to join its witnessing community. It has something of its own to bring, and it has to transcend the needs and wishes of non-Christians. While remaining in the traditional culture, the Church has to introduce a new spirit and spark off a new development.

Another school of thought stresses the dangers of contamination from non-Christian religions. The non-Christian tradition must die, it is said, before it can rise to life in the Church. Missionaries must wait until the non-Christian tradition ceases to be a living force before it is safe to use it. This position raises several unanswerable questions :

What happens if it does not die?

Have we any right to wish for the death of a non-Christian tradition, when Vatican II tells us to 'acknowledge, preserve and promote' the moral good in non-Christian religions?

Is it any use adapting Christianity to a dead tradition?

Should not the Church have a dialogue or encounter with living traditions?

Is it not better to risk abuses in a genuine attempt at adaptation than never to make the attempt?

Yet another school of thought maintains that any adaptation we make now will be obsolete before it has been introduced, because of the rapidity of present social change in Africa. It says that adaptation will always result in 'archaism' or 'folklore'. On the other hand, one cannot adapt to a future situation which may never be verified. The implicit conclusion is simply that we must do nothing at all! In any process of social change there are elements of continuity. The Church must look for these stable factors and adapt to them. In the past the Church has kept human values and cultural forms alive. It kept the classical culture of ancient Greece and Rome alive during the Dark Ages, and it later flowered into the renaissances of the 12th and 16th centuries. The Church was justified, as it turned out. There are signs that the African élite is taking an increasing interest in its own culture. It is no use adapting either to a past which cannot be revived, or to a future that is uncertain. One must adapt to values which are meaningful here and now, and which are likely to survive.

The 'take-over bid' is rarely a modern temptation, but early missionaries considered it their duty to take over a whole tribe or society and adapt all its institutions forcibly. Cardinal Lavigerie's 'Christian kingdom' idea in Uganda was modelled on the success of St Augustine in the Kingdom of Kent and St Rémy in the Kingdom of the Franks. We know now that Christianity does not make it its first aim to take over an entire society through its structures and institutions, but rather to be an effective presence within society so that society transforms itself. Christians cannot use any pressure, physical or moral, to take over non-Christian institutions.

Another form of adaptation has been the attempt to imitate a well-established traditional practice without forcing a Christian monopoly of it in the hope that, for Christians, it will replace the traditional practice. In so far as this can be done without it being construed as rivalry with the existing institution it can be successful, but there are obvious dangers. An example of the kind of complications that can arise is provided by the attempt to Christianize the *jando*, or boys' circumcision in Masasi and Nachingwea, Tanzania. The Anglican missionaries deplored the obscene and immoral character of the traditional rites and resolved to start their own *jando*. The first Christian jando was held in 1919. The *lupanda* tree, one of the central symbols of the *jando*, was replaced by the cross; and the invocation of the ancestors was replaced by the invocation of the Christian saints. In African eyes, this impoverished the symbolism of the ceremony and weakened its relevance to social life in the area. When the Catholic missionaries joined the Anglicans in the area, they attempted the same adaptation. The result was a series of *jandos* —Anglican, Catholic and pagan—over which the missionaries never really gained control.

Positive tolerance, another solution, is the situation in which certain practices are construed not only as not being opposed to Christianity but as being capable of a positive Christian interpretation and development when Christians perform them. This was the basis of Matteo Ricci's approval of Christians participating in ancestor rites in seventeenth-century China.

The Christian sacraments are *sui generis*, and therefore it is natural to assume that most adaptation of rites will take the form of constructing entirely new rites to give expression to authentically Christian ideas and purposes. These, however, should be rooted in local symbols. Elements taken from traditional practices will help to make the new rite comprehensible and relevant to the people, in so far as the symbols and elements are compatible with Christian belief and practice. The Second Vatican Council explicitly recommends this kind of adaptation : 'In mission lands initiation rites are found in use among individual people. Elements from these, when capable of being adapted to Christian rituals, may be admitted along with those already found in Christian tradition.' (*Sacrosanctum Concilium* 65). This is by far the commonest and most successful form of adaptation, and it is the one which presents the least problems.

Account must be taken of the present situation of the liturgy in the areas in which we work. The Roman rite has been installed in Catholic Africa, and will, therefore, have to be the starting-point for liturgical renewal. When non-liturgical devotions of foreign origin are popular because they receive a local interpretation, they should be preserved. In many parts of Africa the Stations of the Cross are extremely popular because they are seen as a mourning rite for Christ.

Prayer and worship are essentially ritual in Africa, which is to say that they are accompanied by symbolic action. In Western countries there is a revolt against, even a contempt for, ritual. In an extreme form, such an attitude betrays a misunderstanding of the nature and importance of symbolism in religious experience and practice. It is sometimes said that ritual should be discouraged among African Christians because of the danger of a magical interpretation, but the same argument could be used against hospital medicines. In fact the need for symbolic action in African Christian worship far outweighs the danger of abuse. Sacramentals, rightly understood, should be encouraged.

Worship and catechesis must correspond to the interests of the people. Tanner found that the Sukuma of Tanzania were predominantly interested in the fertility of their wives, their cattle and their fields, but that Catholic teaching and worship had nothing to say about these subjects. People have social celebrations and seasonal rites which solemnize and give expression to their expectations and their experiences. The Church's ritual must perform this function also.

It goes without saying that for a missionary bare knowledge of the language is not enough; it may even be misleading. There must be more than a verbal adaptation. Expatriate and African priests and educators need to have a systematic knowledge of the local culture in order to form correct judgments about African beliefs and practices and determine their value for Christian worship and catechesis.

The tribal Church and the tribal liturgy must be avoided. On the other hand, the Church must find its place in living cultural traditions. In her adaptation the Church should encourage the exchange and mutual understanding by different ethnic groups of each other's heritage. Her assemblies should be open to other cultures, not rigidly closed to them. Areas of relative cultural homogeneity within which common solutions could be tried should be defined. These areas should be flexible enough to cross diocesan and even national frontiers where necessary. Whatever happens, adaptation must be made to real human and social situations and must cater for recognizable and legitimate variations. It must not relate to purely juridical entities.

Many traditional elements are peculiar to a restricted tradition. These should not be favoured. Elements with a wide or universal significance should be preferred. For example, the Sudanese Dinka epithet 'head carrying-ring of my father', as applied to a divinity, is hardly capable of extension, because it is so circumscribed by the psychology and sociology of the Dinka people. On the other hand, the Shona epithet 'piler-up of rocks' applied to Mwari, the supreme being, is intelligible to most people in Eastern Africa, where outcrops of rock are very common.

We conclude this chapter with some remarks on the sociology of conversion to Christianity. Conversion is an individual act, but it has social implications. It is a personal adhesion to values shared by a group—an adhesion, therefore, to social values. It springs from social influences and pressures. It entails new social roles, the making and breaking of social relationships.

Two mistakes are often made in discussing religious conversion. One is to treat it as a purely individual affair; the other is to represent it as a sudden crisis, or clear-cut choice between two irreconcilable alternatives. In fact neither is the case.

Conversion is adhesion to the values of a group, and it is therefore very much affected by the function of that group in society.[15] Secondly, conversion depends very much on previous social influences. These influences may have been at work on the individual for a very long time. Moreover, adhesion to a relatively new set of social values may not entail the explicit renunciation of previously held social values. Rightly or wrongly, the previously held values may be thought compatible with the new values.

Some writers give the impression that the function of religion is to be emotionally helpful to people at moments of stress or frustration. It is said to raise people's morale and to help them make a positive affirmation of faith in life. Conversions are well known to take place at moments of life-crisis—for example, adolescence and senescence—and to be more numerous among women. Although these facts cannot be denied, the function of religion in society cannot be limited merely to its usefulness at moments of crisis. A religious reaction to crisis may be, in fact, no more common than an irreligious reaction. Job's reaction to misfortune was to bless God : his wife's reaction was to curse God. Different reactions depend on the individual's background. Sociologists have shown that the individual is less likely to experience religious conversion when there has been a total absence of religious education or previous religious experience than he is when there has been such a background. Religious needs are culturally learned needs.

Conversion can be a very gradual process which is impossible to pin-point. An individual can participate in a religious culture without belonging to it. He may identify himself consciously or unconsciously with a religious group and share its values without being officially a member. This is different from the religious awakening of a child or adolescent born within a particular religious culture because it entails a final, conscious adhesion to a set of values and a consequent change of status.

In so far as conversion is a reaction to crisis, it is not an index of a religious denomination's success; but, in the measure that conversions are gradual, it may be. The gradual conversion is likely to be more stable than the crisis conversion. In any case, conversion statistics have to be balanced by estimates of religious practice. Since the Second Vatican Council Catholics have become more aware of the dangers of nominal conversion, and missionary effort is no longer directed mainly towards the statistical increase of conversions, a policy formerly encouraged by the method of financing by which money was directed to areas where a numerical increase in membership was observed.

Conversions may be few and lasting, or they may be many and not lasting. In either case, practising Christians may be few because the Church is not socially relevant. Converts join a religious group which has a transient membership, or they join what is effectively a protest group at odds with society at large. The function of religion in society is therefore of great importance when considering the reasons for lasting conversions, or for the lack of them.

Religion integrates all aspects of culture, since every experience of man comes under its scrutiny. Every human interest can be seen as a religious interest. Religion provides support for the fundamental values of society. Religion acts as a binding link between different sections of society and explains the relationships : for example, family, lineage, village, chiefdom, larger political units, the cosmos. Religion provides a further basis for the interaction of these units. Religion introduces harmony, discipline and order into social activities. It provides leadership and gives purpose. It humanizes man's activities. Religion conserves values and institutions essential to society, such as the family system or the political system, by providing religious sanctions for them. It teaches filial piety and good citizenship.

Finally, religion is creative and helps to make society productive. It creates new qualities and teaches heroism. Through its 'forwardness of reach' and its adaptability, it is a mechanism for continuity in society. It has within itself the means for recreating itself and readapting itself to new conditions.

Religion, however, may also be a fossil in society, a rigid force for conservatism and reaction, stifling progress and creativity. It can frustrate the expectations of society. It can create or exacerbate divisions in society, by pitting sections or castes against each other. It can be a divisive force when outside pressures are threatening society and forcing greater integration and enlargement of social scale. It follows that conversion to missionary religions in an African society depends on the respective roles of these religions *vis-à-vis* each other and *vis-à-vis* the traditional religion and its social role.

Religion can be said to be centrally relevant to a society when it exhibits a focus of interest identical with that of society as a whole. This is possible for a missionary religion, no less than for a traditional religion.

Central relevance is positive when the approach to the common focus is positive, negative when the approach is negative. Thus the Protestant missionaries in Kikuyu-land (Kenya) had the same focus of interest as the traditional Kikuyu religion itself—female circumcision—but the Protestant approach to it was wholly negative while the traditional approach was completely positive. For a long time there were few conversions to Christianity because the Protestants felt it so important to condemn female circumcision. However, after the Mau-Mau crisis,

77

female circumcision ceased to have the same importance for the Kikuyu that it had formerly had. Their interest now shifted to purification and rehabilitation. In this field the Churches had a positive, central relevance and many conversions followed. Among the Ibo of Nigeria the Catholic mission seemed to offer many avenues of social advancement and this accounts for the very large number of conversions, in spite of the fact that no real encounter took place between Christian ideas and the Ibo spiritual world.

Religion is marginally relevant when it serves as a vehicle of protest for a marginal or minority group, or for an immigrant community. It is also marginal when it serves a community with a transient membership. For example, in Sukumaland (Tanzania) conversions are more numerous among the immigrant cotton growers of Geita district than among the 'hard-core' cattle-owning Sukuma of Shinyanga and Maswa. In the latter areas, the Sukuma far outnumber the immigrants and relatively few conversions are made. An example of a transient community would be the school community. In many places the majority of conversions take place in school to a type of religion which is adapted to the school community but which does not have any relevance to society as a whole.

It is obvious that missionary religion can be a revolutionary religion, central to the interests of people in a changed social situation, whereas traditional religion can become marginally relevant or completely irrelevant.

In unitary societies there is one religion which is coterminous with a single, unified socio-political structure. Unitary societies are either centralized or stratified.

In centralized traditional societies, such as Buganda or Ankole in Uganda or Rwanda and Burundi, missionaries tried to make key converts, or to establish parties of converts at the king's court. Christianity became established very quickly in centralized kingdoms of this kind, but it was accepted precisely because of its foreign character, and this explains the religious conservatism and reluctance to carry out any adaptation in these areas. When the Christian missionaries arrived in Buganda in the second half of the nineteenth century, Ganda traditional religion was showing signs of strain as a force for integration in the country. Religion was essentially a clan phenomenon and although the Kabaka was head of all the clans he had no specifically royal cult which could give him spiritual ascendancy over the clan cults and clan leaders. In his search for a royal cult, Mutesa I turned to Islam, Protestantism and Catholicism one after the other. He found the missionary religions too strongly organized to yield themselves completely into his control. As a result, a series of chiefly parties formed, favouring the different religions. In the unitary situation the missionary religion is either totally accepted or rejected. It is accepted in its very strangeness and foreignness, because it is this character which gives it ascendancy over other cults. Its novelty and un-African-ness strengthens the monopoly which the chief or chiefly party has over it. Buganda accepted Christianity in exactly the form in which nineteenth-century Europe presented it, and has had little subsequent interest in adapting it to Ganda tradition.

In stratified tribes without chiefs—as in Kenya, the Kikuyu, Kalenjin, Masai—the whole society is organized in horizontal fashion, in age-grades which cut across the whole tribe and affect everybody in turn. Religious relationships between the grades have been traditionally worked out. In tribes like that of the Kenya Luo social organization is minimal and the whole tribe is 'atomized' into households of a few people. There are no intermediary units between the household and the ethnic group as a whole. In all these types of society there is no possibility of acquiring key converts or of exerting any influence from a centre. These types of society accept Christianity with greater difficulty, or else adapt it radically to their own way of life by setting up independent churches.

Over most of Africa there was never any religious pluralism in the strict sense. A person born into a particular tribe was taught the religion of that tribe along with the rest of the tribal culture. However, there were societies with a pluralistic type of socio-political organization which affected religion in practice. In multi-chiefdom societies or politically segmented societies there are not only the loyalties to lineage and chiefdom, dispersed clans and association of chiefdoms but also, cutting across these allegiances, are individual loyalties to societies and guilds which have a social basis and which operate for political or professional purposes, such as hunting, dancing, chiefly ritual and propaganda, medicine, and so on. These guilds subscribe to the religion and cosmology of the tribe as a whole, but they give them a diverse social expression and may even represent specializations within the religion. Examples are the Nyamwezi, Sukuma and other multi-chiefdom societies of central and western Tanzania, or the societies of West Africa which are made up of associations of villages.

In the pluralistic society the missionary Church is easily understood as one of many competing socio-religious communities. This impression is confirmed by the missionaries' attack on the guilds and by the fact that Christianity is itself divided and competing. The convert to Christianity may see his Church membership as compatible with other, traditional socio-religious loyalties, and the Church may be forced into a marginal role.

It is an essentially new situation for Africans to be able to choose to give their allegiance to one of a variety of immigrant religions or to remain in the religion of their tribe. Although the different religions may employ techniques of self-isolation and incapsulation, and may appear to be in conscious competition with each other, they may in fact be complementary. Not only will they influence each other's development, but each of them may cater for a different set of social or psychological needs and there may be considerable mobility of membership between the various denominations. Families may be split up between the denominations for this reason. Religious pluralism in the family is especially common in polygamous households where the influence of the different co-wives over their own children may result in their practising different religions.

Religious pluralism may be responsible for creating the social conditions in which secularism flourishes, especially where theology is irrelevant and where emphasis is placed upon the individual and his choice of religious allegiance. Secularism in Africa is not necessarily a product of science or modern conditions. The Christianity which was brought to Africa in the nineteenth century was a Christianity retreating before the advance of science, a 'God-of-the-gaps' Christianity. It appeared superior to traditional religion because it was preached by white men, was based on a book, and was expressed in a culture which was technically superior. In the way it was presented, however, it often appeared less socially relevant than the religion it displaced. The result in some areas has been to encourage secularism. Examples are the Lozi of Zambia, the Teso of Uganda, and the Ibo of Nigeria. Competing denominations have also confused the local people and lessened the value of Christian teaching. This, according to Professor A Ogot, has happened among the Jopadhola of Kenya/Uganda.

Conversion may be a rite of passage into a new and more desirable social identity. Consciously or unconsciously, it has replaced in some areas the traditional initiation of adolescents. School conversions are sometimes sparked off by the desire for a new name and status, and attendance at school itself often exempts children from the traditional initiation, even when it does not expressly forbid it. In so far as names alone are concerned, it is difficult to correlate the taking of new names with conversion because non-Christians can take Christian names without baptism and baptized Christians may revert to their African names. Adolescent conversion is clearly linked with the cultural setting of the school and with the desire for social advancement.

Schools and catechumenates may often be a means of escape, for girls who wish to avoid marrying a suitor they dislike, for parents of twins avoiding embarrassing twin rituals, for young men avoiding bride service, for widows and other women whose independence is threatened in a male-dominated society, for frustrated rivals such as co-wives in a polygamous household, for the psychologically deprived, for unsuccessful diviners, or for sorcerers and antisocial persons who wish to start a new life and avoid the consequences of their actions. The Church can offer the people a new form of security and a new identity.

To say that all these motivations exist is not to say that it is impossible to inculcate healthier motives, or that these converts cannot become exemplary Christians. However, they will only do this if the Church is centrally relevant to society, having a common focus with the people at large, and if there is a recognizable community into which the convert is initiated—a community that dovetails with, and animates, the wider, natural community.

Notes

[1] Much of this section is based on Wach, J, *The Comparative Study of Religions*, New York 1961, and on Evans-Pritchard, E E Y, *Theories of Primitive Religion*, Oxford 1965.

2 cf. Greeley, A, developing ideas of Mircea Eliade on the demise of ritual in *Strangers in the House*, Chicago 1967, p. 67.
3 cf. Eliade, M, *The Sacred and the Profane*, New York 1959.
4 For ideas on taboo and its relationship to sacred and unclean, I follow Steiner, F, *Taboo*, London 1956, and Douglas, M, *Purity and Danger*, London 1966.
5 cf. Turner, V W, 'Colour Classification in Ndembu Ritual', in Banton, M (ed), *Anthropological Approaches to Religion*, London 1965, pp. 47–84.
6 cf. Cox, Harvey, *The Secular City*, New York 1965.
7 Much of what follows here makes use of Douglas, M, *Natural Symbols*, London 1970.
8 Harvey Cox, *op. cit.*; Colin Williams, *Faith in a Secular Age*, London 1966; and even the 'Dutch' Catechism (*A New Catechism*, London 1967) frequently give this impression.
9 The section on African religious beliefs owes much to Goetz, J and Bergounioux, F, *Prehistoric and Primitive Religions*, London 1965; Mbiti, J, *African Religions and Philosophy*, London 1969; and Smith, E, *African Ideas of God*, London 1950.
10 cf. Pauwels, M, *Imana et le Culte des Manes au Rwanda*, Brussels 1957, pp. 39 and 40; my own fieldwork among the Kimbu of Tanzania provides another example of faults against the supreme being.
11 Some ideas on the symbolism of evil are taken here from Ricoeur, P, *Finitude et Culpabilité*, Paris 1960.
12 cf. Lienhardt, R G, *Divinity and Experience*, Oxford 1961, p. 151 ff.
13 The diagram and explanation given here are an adaptation of ideas found in Douglas, M, *Natural Symbols*, London 1970.
14 Tanner, R E S, *Transition in African Beliefs*, New York 1967, p. 122.
15 The section on conversion uses ideas from Carrier, H, *The Sociology of Religious Belonging*, London 1965; Pirouet, M L, 'A Comparison of the Response of Three Societies to Christianity', Makerere Institute of Social Research (mimeographed) 1968; Welbourn, F B, *East African Christian*, Oxford 1965; and Parsons, R T, *Religion in an African Society*, Leiden 1964. For information on the Ibo, I rely on a communication from Elizabeth Isichei.

Suggested further reading
Douglas, M, *Purity and Danger*, London 1966.
Forde, D (ed), *African Worlds*, London 1954.
Goetz, J and Bergounioux, F, *Prehistoric and Primitive Religions*, London 1965.
Maurier, H H, *The Other Covenant: A Theology of Paganism*, New York 1968.
Mbiti, J, *African Religions and Philosophy*, London 1969, and *Concepts of God in Africa*, London 1970.
Otto, R, *The Idea of the Holy*, London 1959.
Secretariat for Non-Christians, *Meeting the African Religions*, Rome 1969.
Smith, E, *African Ideas of God*, London 1950.
Tanner, R E S, *Transition in African Beliefs*, New York 1967.

4 African Values in Christian Catechesis

AFRICAN oral literature is a very important source for discovering African categories of thought, African values and African concepts of man, society, the world and God. Story-telling is the chief way that social and moral values are inculcated into children by parents and grandparents in the African home, and adults take a pride in the art of story-telling and recitation. Even though in modern Africa story-telling in the home is becoming less common than it was, Africans are still better orators, conversationalists and listeners than writers and readers. The art of oratory flourishes in formal gatherings, and the radio has given a new impetus to oral expression. Even the themes of traditional oral literature have been given a new lease of life in school readers and published collections of traditional stories, as well as in the works of modern African writers. The traditional literature of Africa is very important to the priest, catechist and religious educator for an understanding of the mind of those to whom he is transmitting the Christian message. It is therefore necessary to know something of the traditional literary forms and of the methods of analyzing them. Above all, it is necessary to understand the nature and power of symbols.

It is customary to distinguish in literature between poetry and prose, but this is rather difficult in African traditional literature.[1] The distinction rests on the degree of patterning in the composition. At one end of the scale is the rigidly metric poem; at the other, everyday conversational speech. Most African traditional literature is somewhere in between. Much of it is free narrative with a basic unchanging structure, with every now and then a rigid formula that must be recited by heart. The distinction between speech and song is, perhaps, more realistic in Africa than that between poetry and prose, since the learned formulae are very often, if not nearly always, songs. However, speech and song are interwoven, and one of the most popular literary forms is the story-song—a story punctuated by a refrain in which the audience joins. This refrain very often contains the key to the message of the story and is inserted at psychological moments with great effect. It is also a means of formalizing audience participation, an important element in African story-telling which itself is always a community celebration.

The following is a suggested list of African literary forms:

1. RITUAL FORMULAE
Prayers and *invocations, oaths, blessings, curses, magical spells.* These formulae usually follow a more or less fixed pattern, but with a certain amount of freedom for personal application and adaptation. They can, at times, be quite lengthy. We shall deal later and in greater depth with prayers, oaths, and magical spells.

2. DIDACTIC TEXTS
Proverbs. These are statements about life. They remain purely at the level of observation and experience. One must not expect to find real wisdom or valid moral judgements in proverbs. They may be purely descriptive:

'When the moon is shining the cripple becomes hungry for a walk' (Ibo, Nigeria).

Or they may often be purely cynical:

'If a child cries for a razor, give it to him' (Swahili, East Africa);

'Let a strong man pass' (Swahili, East Africa);

'For the brave man there is mourning, for the coward safety' (Kimbu, Tanzania).

Or proverbs are contradictory:

'Your neighbour's childbearing is your concern' (Sena, Malawi);

'Ask a favour from your neighbour's child only once, the second time its mother will insult you' (Sena, Malawi).

One has to be careful in handling proverbs. One cannot base a whole philosophy of life, or system of moral values, on proverbs alone.

Riddles. These are partly didactic, partly a game or amusement, and partly a mutual expression of loyalty to a cultural tradition. In so far as they are didactic they may teach observation and mental alertness; some teach history, or moral values. For example:

'My house has no mouth.'
Answer: 'An egg' (Sandawe, Tanzania);
'I have a hundred children and I support them all.'
Answer: 'Roof pole and rafters of a house' (Nandi, Kenya);
'The Chief of Wikangulu is sitting; the Chief of Kipembawe is squatting.'
Answer: 'Groundnuts and peanuts' (Kimbu, Tanzania);
(This refers not only to the way the plants grow, but also to the historical fact that the people of Kipembawe settled in territory belonging to the people of Wikangulu.)
'My father and I went on a journey and we were lodging in a house that was all doors and windows.'
Answer: 'A fishing net' (Kono, Sierra Leone).

Instructional Formulae. These are songs, often highly symbolical, used to teach people values and give people advice, especially in initiation ceremonies or other rituals. They usually accompany ritual and provide the explanation for what is done. For example:

'The monkey eats everything that bears freely. That is why he climbs the mukolobondo tree.' (Bemba girls' initiation song, Zambia).
Explanation: The girls climb the tree and imitate the monkey; like the monkey they must find food for their families wherever they can.[2]
'I am striking you with my foot. Take hold of my foot—become like me' (Ga, birth ceremony, Ghana).
Explanation: the godfather uses an idiom which means that he is impressing his character on the child.[3]

Children's songs and rhymes. These are songs or sayings taught to children. Some may imitate the noises made by animals or the cries of birds, and may unconsciously reflect cultural values or social preoccupations. For example, the cry made by the dove or pigeon:

'*Gu-gu, pita xuntili; Gu-gu, pita xuntili.*'
'Gu-gu, go to the beer party; Gu-gu, go to the beer party'
(Kimbu, Tanzania).
There are also lullabies, songs that accompany games, tongue-twisters and trick-rhymes. Many of them contain a moral.

3 ETIOLOGICAL STORIES

On the surface these are popular explanations of how things have come to be as they are now—how animals have acquired certain characteristics, how groups of people came to acquire a name, why certain social practices take place, and so on. They are 'Just-So' stories or 'Why' stories. In fact the explanation given in the story need not be taken too seriously, and the stories usually have an underlying moral theme or purpose. Often these stories are a means of teaching etiquette or home morals.

4. FOLK TALES

These may be difficult to distinguish from other literary forms but, broadly speaking, they are stories told for their own sake. Listeners enjoy them because of the intricate structure of the story, or because of the cleverness of the characterization, the power of description and homely detail. In general, the trickster stories belong to this category—the clever exploits of hare, tortoise, chameleon or spider. Animals in the stories have human characteristics and there is usually a value or moral. This value, however, is secondary to the technique of the story itself.

5. MYTHS

All African literary forms employ symbols, and all can be called 'myth' in this sense. However, some stories are more obscurely symbolical than others. This is because they represent archaic traditions. These stories have a general or universal theme, often religious or cosmological, about creation or the withdrawal of God from the world. The values taught by these stories are usually profound and important.

6. HEROIC RECITATIONS AND PRAISE POEMS (Panegryric)

These are long pieces of free verse, like the heroic recitations of the Bahima of Ankole, the *Oriki* poems of the Yoruba, and the praise poems of the Tswana chiefs. Celebration and praise are the main sentiments, and there is a great deal of description and even exaggeration.

7. OCCASIONAL POETRY

There are many occasions which require a poem or song : lyrics or love songs; elegiac songs or songs of sorrow; songs for hunting, working, and welfare. Religious songs and poems will be treated later in the section on prayer.

8. HISTORICAL NARRATIVES

These narratives are straightforward accounts of events in the recent past, perhaps remembered over two or three generations. The narratives are factual, but the human element is emphasized and the story is often made to yield a moral. However, this does not usually affect its veracity. The interpretation is biased but not necessarily the presentation of the facts.

Having seen the various forms oral literature can take in Africa, we must now examine the notion of symbolism on which all literature, and African oral literature in particular, is built. A symbol is one of the categories of sign; we must therefore first consider the different kinds of sign.[4]

A sign, in general, is anything which suggests something else. Man is able to know himself and the phenomena of his experience because the images he apprehends are signs. Some of these images are, by themselves, signs. Others are made into signs by man.

A natural sign is an image which suggests something else—an idea—by itself. For example, smoke suggests the idea of fire, a patch of colour of a certain shape and size suggests the idea of a table, a candle suggests the idea of light. Natural signs are signals which spark off a reaction in the beholder. This is the most basic level of communication and it applies to animals as well as to human beings. Even a dog who sees the colour and shape of a chair is told by what he sees that it promises comfort if he jumps and sits on it.

A conventional sign is an image made arbitrarily into a sign by man himself. In this kind of sign there is no connection or necessary congruity between the image used and the idea signified by the image. The most perfect example of conventional signs is in language. In language a sound image is attached to an idea by convention, and different languages use different sound images to convey the same idea. Thus we have :

house	English
maison	French
Haus	German
casa	Italian
nyumba	Swahili
*ka*ₗ	Nandi
ng'anda	Bemba

Conventional signs must be taught and learned. Explanations of them must be given. For example, the significance of national flags is conventional. In the Tanzanian flag green signifies the mainland, blue signifies the ocean and the islands, black signifies the people, gold signifies mineral wealth. One cannot know of this significance merely by looking at the flag. An explanation must be given first.

Metaphors are conventional signs, because they are images attached to ideas with either no congruity or a very low degree of congruity. If you say 'I am up to my neck in hot water' or 'He has kicked the bucket', you are not making statements about hot water or buckets, and there is no need for the listener to visualize them in order to understand the meaning of the metaphor. These images are simply taking the place of ordinary sound images. One could have said 'I am in serious trouble, and 'He is dead' instead of using the metaphors, and the message conveyed would have been the same. As we shall see, it is possible for a symbol that has become hackneyed to turn into a metaphor. Metaphors are dead symbols.

Conventional signs are a useful means of instruction and communication, even if they do not have the peculiar power of symbols. For example the Adinkra signs of Ghana, which are stamped with calabash dye stamps onto cotton cloth, each have their own deep signification which requires explanation. Or again, the carved motifs on the lintels and door posts of old houses in towns on the East African coast all have their individual significance. But, like the Adinkra signs, they are formalized to the extent that they need explanation. For example, the palm-tree stem motif signifies prosperity. All over Africa signs are painted on the walls of houses, caves, and rock-shelters, or carved and painted on objects and utensils. Very frequent signs are the series of concentric circles and the spiral or coil design, both of which refer to the solar representation of God, the first in his aspect of omnipresence, the second in his aspect of zenith and inaccessibility.

A symbol is a conventional sign founded in a natural sign. The image, which is the natural sign, conveys first of all its natural signification, but, because it occurs in a specific existential context, it also conveys a conventional signification. Symbols are not usually explained. They speak by themselves through their existential context, appealing to the observer's own experience, to his sense and to the very life processes which he feels are a part of himself. Symbolic thinking is not pure reasoning, nor is it fully conscious thought. Men are not fully in control of symbols because, to a great extent, they are given them by the facts of their experience. You cannot just 'create' a symbol, as you can 'create' a sign. For this reason symbolic thinking has been called 'committed thought' or 'semi-incarnate thought' (Gusdorf) and 'objectified thought' or 'the science of the concrete' (Lévi-Strauss).[5]

The following are some examples of symbols :

A candle signifies light dispelling darkness. This is its natural signification. On Easter night we commemorate the resurrection of Christ and we sing of 'the light of Christ'. This is the existential context. A lighted candle carried into the church on Easter night signifies the risen Christ giving light to men. This is the conventional signification.

At girls' puberty rites among the Kimbu of Tanzania, the following song is sung : *umukeela mpingu andovile* (the maker of bead necklaces is pleasing to me). It is an instructional song which tells the girl that she must marry a virile husband. How does it come to mean this? Girls love the makers of bead necklaces because they want bead necklaces very much. This is the natural signification. At puberty rites girls are preparing to be the mothers of children. This is the existential context. The love for makers of bead necklaces, when mentioned at girls' puberty rites, makes them think how they must love virile men who can give them the children they want so much. This is the conventional signification.

A Chewa proverb from Malawi runs *safunsa anadya phula* (the one who did not ask ate wax). Eating wax betrays ignorance of how to separate honey from the comb. This is the natural signification. 'The one who did not ask' is the premise or starting-point of the proverb, and therefore the existential context. Eating wax when you did not ask signifies that ignorance will not be dispelled unless you ask. This is the conventional signification. We are dealing here mainly with word images which are symbols, but real objects and actions can be symbols, as, for example, the Paschal candle. We call symbolic action 'ritual'.

Symbols can have more than one conventional significance. They may operate at several levels—the physical and the social, for instance. The colour red may signify the blood of childbirth or menstruation, and also danger or ritual prohibition. Symbols appeal to the experience of individuals, and each individual, in any case, makes his own application.

Symbols do not exhaust all the truth about what they signify. They refer to something relatively unkown, or to an experience which is relatively indefinable. They are an invitation to further personal discovery.

Symbols are part of experience, because everything that exists is a natural sign and can become a symbol. Symbols are not pure abstractions from reality. They are known through experience and reflection on experience.

Symbols are not allegorical (literally, 'speaking about something else') but tautegorical (literally 'speaking about the same thing'). This means that, in order to understand the conventional significance of a symbol, one has to see first how it operates as a natural sign. The words 'allegory' and 'allegorical' usually refer to conventional signs, especially to stories in which each event or element is a conventional sign. Allegories cannot be symbols.

The explanation of the symbol is provided by the context in which the symbol exists. There are, however, different frames or levels of explanation, and different degrees of context.[6] The exegetical explanation is the explanation offered by the one using the symbol—the story-teller, for example. However, he may not be able to give a reasoned explanation because his understanding of the symbol may not be fully conscious, and because symbols are by definition largely indefinable. They are experienced, not explained. The exegesis of a symbol is often, itself, a symbolic exegesis.

The operational explanation is obtained when the observer or listener makes an analysis of how the symbol operates in its immediate context—for instance, in its relation to the situation in which it is used, its relation to other elements in a single text, and so on.

The positional explanation is obtained by referring the symbol to its remote context, to other situations in which the image is used, and by observing any regularity. This will then help us to understand what resonance the symbol may have in a given context at the start of the process. It supposes, of course, a widespread knowledge of the people's culture as a whole.

There are also different kinds of symbol which cater for different levels of meaning. Some symbols can easily be translated into abstract ideas because people can become fully conscious of their meaning. We can easily appreciate the meaning of the Virgin Birth, but quite apart from the question of its historicity, the fact of the Virgin Birth is a symbol of the greatness of the event of the Incarnation. Such symbols possess a manifest meaning. They are symbols behind which we can see.[7]

Other symbols can be partially translated into abstract ideas because people can become semi-conscious of their meaning. The meaning of the symbol may be completely hidden at first, but one may become gradually and partially aware of its meaning. One can speak of 'the hand of God', and explain this as the way God, as an efficient cause, brings about events to fulfil his own purposes. But this is not sufficient as an explanation because the image makes people feel God's action more vividly by evoking the experience of a hand, touching. Such symbols possess a latent meaning: they are symbols behind which we *think* we can see.

Finally there are symbols which relate to fundamental life processes, or to psychological experiences basic to every human being. They are so much a part of ourselves that they can never be explained in terms of abstract ideas. For example, we know what love is and we know what fear is. We may be able to talk about them in terms of physical reactions, but we cannot explain them. Still less can we explain our experience of the love of God, or of fearing God. Love and fear are symbols for something indefinable in our relationship with God, something which we shall not fully comprehend even when we enjoy the beatific vision. These symbols have a hidden meaning. They are symbols behind which we can never see.

The word 'myth' is sometimes used to refer to symbolism in general as well as to a symbolic story in particular. Myth is often treated as if it was opposed to history. This is far from the case. Nor is the difference between myth and history related to truth or falsehood. The aim of history is to establish facts by an appeal to evidence. The aim of a myth, in this sense, is to teach a truth—possibly even a historical truth—by means of symbols. Myths are not historical narratives, and they do not pretend to appeal to evidence in support of what they teach. Myths may teach an untruth, just as a historical narrative may in fact be untrue, and the evidence on which it rests false. Nevertheless, true or false, the aims and methods of myth and history are different and should not be confused. This remains so even when myth employs historical figures and events as types and symbols for its own symbolic teaching : Abraham Lincoln is both a historical person and a symbol. Magna Carta is both a historical document and a symbol.

Human beings cannot exist without symbolism but they can refuse to admit the fact. They can also refuse to know symbols except as translated into ideas. In the Western world, symbols may be consciously accepted in certain fields, such as psychiatry, literature and art, but in ordinary life Westerners become conscious of their symbols only in translating them, or attempting to translate them, into abstract ideas. They are not content to leave symbols as they are. They are not on the mythical wavelength. This is because of the immense prestige of science and conceptual analysis.

Hence the continual urge in the Western world to analyze and rationalize symbols. With recent advances in audio-visual communications and advertising psychology, there are signs that the rationalist approach is being abandoned in some quarters, but it still remains a strong force. We notice it often in attempts to renew the liturgy. There is a concern to find a rational meaning for everything done in church—if there is no 'reason' for a gesture or a rite, it should be abandoned. This is a bad criterion, since symbols communicate their message at the semi-conscious and even the unconscious level. The value of a liturgy can only be proved by experience; it cannot be reasoned out.

The only adequate way of speaking about God is through symbols, appealing to man's religious experience. Consequently scripture and theology employ symbols. Some people have thought that myth or symbolism is a kind of 'cake of carbon' which has formed on the engine of rational thought about God, and that all one has to do is 'decarbonize', or, as they put it, 'demythologize'. The assumption is that when one has extracted the rational content in myth one has got the essential message. As we have seen, it is impossible to reduce all symbols to rational terms. In so doing they are impoverished beyond recognition. Demythologizing is like peeling an onion; when you have finished you are left with nothing except tears in the eyes! What we should be doing is not demythologizing theology or the Bible, but *re*mythologizing ourselves—which means getting used to the idea that theology and scripture are not necessarily appealing to historical evidence, but are purposely employing symbols to speak about God.[8] This is not to say that reasoning has no place in theology or Bible studies, but we must not make it our sole aim to rationalize their message.

The word 'symbol' takes its origin from the Greek word *symballein*, 'to recognize a legitimate guest'. The symbol was originally a kind of invitation-card made of two parts—of a ring, of a staff, or of a tablet. If the two parts fitted, the guest was recognized as legitimate. The etymology is apt for the symbols we have been speaking about, since the image has to recognized by the observer and 'fitted into his experience' before it can be understood.

The word 'symbol' came also to be applied to the creeds of the Christian Church because they were a recognition of, and response to, the Word of God, and a sign of who was and who was not a real believer. Creeds refer to the truths of revelation expressed in the symbolic language in which they have been revealed to us.

Without wishing in any way to rob him of the glory of having first taught scholars to take African categories of thought seriously and to study them systematically, it must be admitted that Fr Placide Tempels in his *Bantu Philosophy* is guilty of demythologizing. Fr Tempels has attempted to replace the dynamic symbols in which Africans traditionally express themselves by abstract formulations: vital force, Bantu ontology, Bantu criteriology, Bantu psychology, Bantu ethics, and so on. He has built up a Western-type philosophy on certain demythologized African concepts. It is a legitimate exercise to analyze African symbols for their rational content, but it is dangerous to assume that this process is an accurate translation of Bantu thought. It is also dangerous to base the study, as many African 'philosophers' do, on the linguistic analysis of Bantu prefixes, or on the analysis of one section of traditional literature, such as proverbs, and to imagine that the whole of African wisdom is contained therein.

Symbolism plays a very important role in scripture as well as in texts with a greater or lesser historical content and texts employing other instructional techniques, such as allegories. The words 'sign' and 'symbol' are used loosely by commentators, but it is fair to say that the Jews preferred symbols to signs (in the sense in which we are using the words). Every event was regarded as a symbol of the presence and purpose of God. They were not bare signs—external proofs of God's power or purpose—nor the effects of a remote divine cause ruling the world indirectly through 'natural law'. God was seen to be personally and constantly active in all events. As Chesterton remarked, for the Jews the sun did not rise by natural law but because God said 'Get up, and do it again'.

In the New Testament, Christ preferred the technique of the symbol in his instructions. The parable is essentially a symbol: an appeal to the experience of the listeners. Jesus was reluctant to offer explanations: 'He who has ears to hear, let him hear.' He wanted the hearer to feel the meaning of the symbol by drawing on his own experience. The parable is concentrated on a certain psychological moment which is the climax of a story, like the net full of good and worthless fish, the seed growing secretly, the fire cast upon the earth, the finding of the lost coin, and so forth. The existential context is provided by the context of the discourse: 'The kingdom of heaven is like. . . .' It remains for the hearers to explore their experience and to discover in what this likeness consists. It is an invitation to the believer. As the stories are retold in the Church, new applications, new depths of meaning are discovered in the parable. You cannot put God in your pocket.

Allegorical explanations of the parables are sometimes found in the New Testament itself (almost certainly not given by Christ), but extra-biblical allegorical explanations became very popular in the first centuries of the Church. Allegories cannot replace symbols, but they may complement them, if they are faithful to the value expressed originally by the symbol. It must be borne in mind, however, that symbol is one thing and allegory (conventional sign) another. In a famous passage, St Augustine of Hippo finds a conventional sign in each detail of the Parable of the Good Samaritan. The Samaritan is Christ; the man who fell among thieves is Adam; the Inn-keeper is the Apostle Paul; the inn is the Church; the Priest and Levite are the priesthood and ministry of the Old Testament which avail nothing, and so on. All of this is excellent teaching, but the parable by itself teaches the hearer that he must have a dynamic view of his neighbour. The neighbour is the one whom a man approaches in love.[9]

Karl Rahner has built up a theology of the symbol based on the fact that all beings are in one way or another symbols. As symbols, all beings are both one and many.[10] In this they mirror the organic unity of the Trinity itself which is the starting point of creation. The Second Person of the Trinity is the *imago patris*, the symbol of the Father, who in the incarnation was not simply masquerading in human nature, but really made human nature a symbol of God.

The symbol of the Incarnation explicitly reveals how all beings point, as symbols, to God. The Church continues the symbolic function of Christ. It is the sacrament (symbol) of the world operating through a series of sacraments (symbols). The sacrament is even more effective than the ordinary symbol, because it reproduces, or prolongs, the historic action of Christ.

In the past, scholastic theologians attempted to explain the working of the symbol by means of an intellectualist theory of analogy. They asked: How can you say anything about God at all? God is so different. For example, what do we mean when we talk of the 'wisdom of God'? If we say that divine wisdom is totally different from human wisdom, then you cannot know anything about God at all. On the other hand, if you believe that divine wisdom is of the same order as human wisdom, then you are reducing God to the human level. The Thomists answered the dilemma by the 'analogy of proportion' which maintains that, although divine wisdom is different from human wisdom, there is a 'proportion' between them. Divine wisdom (whatever it is) is to God what human wisdom is to man. The facts may be different but the proportion is the same.

The followers of Scotus answered : What is the use of saying God is wise if you do not mean the same thing that you mean when you say man is wise? In answer, the Thomists accused the Scotists of anthropomorphism. The controversy has raged among scholastics and neo-scholastics into our own century. There is, of course, no answer to the dilemma on a purely intellectual level, because the scholastics were dealing with symbols and the symbol is not a purely intellectual phenomenon. Somehow, man experiences God through symbolic perception, not through reasoning. Reasoning may strengthen belief, but it is not the foundation of belief.

Another intellectualist explanation of the symbol was that of Lévy-Bruhl. Lucien Lévy-Bruhl (1857–1939) was a French anthropologist with philosophical training.[11] He came to believe that the world was divided into two camps : Europe and North America where people reason scientifically, and the rest of the world where people employ symbols. This in itself was a gross oversimplification, but it remains true that symbols receive less emphasis in the Western world than in other areas.

Lévy-Bruhl went on to formulate the 'law of mystical participation of symbols' by which, in the mind of so-called 'primitive' man, symbols actually participate in the reality they symbolize. This type of thinking, he said, was 'pre-logical'. This did not mean that men who use symbols cannot think logically, but that the belief in mystical participation is incompatible with a critical and scientific view of reality. Lévy-Bruhl wrongly believed that when men use symbolic shorthand, such as saying 'I am a red parrot' instead of 'I belong to the red parrot clan', they are making the mistake of thinking there is a physical connection. He condemned 'primitive' man for perceiving things as symbols, before seeing them as real objects.

Shortly before his death, Lévy-Bruhl retracted the word 'pre-logical' and replaced his '*law* of mystical participation' by a 'sentiment of mystical participation'. He was beginning to realize that reasoning and symbolism are not incompatible but complementary, and that all beings are symbolic. Being *is* participating. Symbolism is not pure thought, and consequently one cannot formulate intellectual laws for it.

What are the functions of symbolism in African society? Symbolism explains and makes articulate certain deeply felt and shared experiences of the present. Symbolism also helps people to classify—'to humanize'—their experience, integrating themselves into society and the world. Symbolism validates social institutions and norms of conduct in society. It also sanctions and supports authority in society. Finally, valuable information is transmitted through symbolism, from generation to generation or from one human group to another. For these reasons the Church cannot afford to neglect African symbolism. Symbolism is a point of contact with the people and their mentality, a means of reprogramming the Christian message, a means of locating points of conflict between African thought and Christian thought, a means of locating felt needs, a source of information to the heralds of the Gospel, and a means of Gospel penetration without the danger of syncretism.[12]

The symbol is designed to teach a message, but we should not imagine that this message is readily discernible from the story or piece of literature viewed as a whole. Short sayings or songs, such as proverbs and instruction songs, may be built on a single symbol, but longer texts are made up of several symbolic elements. These elements do not have to be considered in the order in which they occur in the text. As Lévi-Strauss has pointed out, symbolic stories should be read like a musical score, with several voices or parts combining simultaneously to produce a given effect, to convey a given message.

Following the usage of Lévi-Strauss, we speak of the armature as the combination of a number of given symbols or symbolic elements.[13] The armature may be the same in a series of different stories. The code is the arrangement of these symbols or symbolic elements. Thus two stories may have the same armature, but different codes. Finally, the message is the teaching or meaning of the code. It is, of course, quite possible for two stories with different codes to be giving the same message.

Here is an example of the analysis of a symbolic story. It is the myth charter of a chiefdom in West Central Tanzania called Kipembawe chiefdom :

A man of the Sagara tribe, called Mulingula, came to Kipembawe and married Igongo, daughter of the Chief Ikili Ntondo Mutikilwa. In those days, Kipembawe was not called

Kipembawe but Mpanda, and the people who lived there were brothers of the Nyisamba people. The Sagara stranger brought with him pumpkin seeds and told the people of Mpanda to plant them. He then returned to Sagara land, telling the people to eat the pumpkins if they liked, but to keep their seeds for him to plant another year. While he was away, there was a famine at Mpanda and the people were very hungry—so hungry that they ate all the pumpkins entire and did not keep any seeds. When the Sagara traveller returned he asked for his seeds, but they had none. They offered him goats, cows, ivory, slaves, one after the other, but he refused all offers of compensation. Finally, in contempt and desperation, the chief took up dust from the earth and said 'Here, take that!' Surprisingly Mulingula accepted. Once more, Mulingula travelled back to Sagara land, met his elder brother Molova, and said 'I have planted seed in the earth where I got married, and the earth now belongs to us'. So they returned together to Mpanda and divided up the country between them. Molova ruled Kipembawe and Mulingula ruled Igunda. Chief Ikili departed towards the west and the name of Mpanda died.

The story is quite factual in outline. It describes a forced change of dynasty by a relation through marriage, but most of the story is taken up by the seemingly unimportant dispute over pumpkin seeds. This suggests symbolism, and the suggestion is borne out, in fact, by positional analysis.

The word 'earth' used in the story also means 'country' or 'chiefdom' and it is customarily applied to the chief's dynasty and its members. A chief's son is called 'son of the earth', and a kinsman of the chief is called 'kinsman of the earth'. The ruler himself is sometimes called 'the one of the earth', and the chief's principal emblem, the ghost-horn, is called 'the honour of the earth'.

The phrase 'planting seed in the earth' is often loosely used by people in this area to refer to a man marrying a woman (who is symbolically associated with 'mother earth'), but more specifically the phrase means marrying a woman of the chief's family. In this area, the chief's family is matrilineal, while all other families are patrilineal, and chiefs are elected from among the sons of sisters of former chiefs. This means that any commoner could become father of a chief, and that the chief's family needs commoners to make it fruitful.

It is at once clear that the planting of the Sagara stranger's pumpkin seeds in the earth of Mpanda is a symbolic parallel to his marrying a woman of the chief's family. So much for positional analysis.

The next stage is operational analysis, in which we see how the symbol is used in the text itself. The seeds which the stranger demanded are his offspring, since they are the fruit of his 'planting the earth'—that is, marrying a chief's daughter. In a matrilineal system the offspring belong to the mother's family, not to the father's. The stranger claims the offspring, but is denied them. 'The seeds have been eaten.' To 'eat' something frequently means to take something over completely, even to steal something. The symbol of 'earth', however, is multivocal, referring both to the chiefdom and to the dynasty which rules it. In refusing the offspring of the marriage, the chief and people of Mpanda have inadvertently given the stranger a right to rule the chiefdom. This is the explicit interpretation of Mulingula himself. It is worth noting, in support of the positional interpretation of 'planting the earth' referring to marriage with a chief's daughter, that at the operational level of the story itself the girl is called Igongo, which means 'lineage'.

Conclusion : *the armature* consists of the elements of pumpkin seeds, planting, earth, eating, taking up dust. *The code* consists in the arrangement of the elements of planting seeds in the earth, eating the seeds from the new crop, taking up dust from the earth. *The message* is that the Sagara stranger had a right to rule the chiefdom if the chief's family took his children.

In many if not most cases, the message of a text refers to a value belonging to the traditional culture. When this value recurs frequently, we may say that it is a theme in the traditional literature of an area. The following is an attempt to list dominant themes, based on a fairly wide examination of collections of oral literature from the whole of sub-Saharan Africa. We give the dominant symbol in a characteristic form or forms, followed by the value associated with it. This study is obviously more impressionistic than thoroughly scientific. It would be a very large undertaking to analyze each and every text from every point of view in each and every published collection.[14]

Creation of world/mankind : *absolute mastery of God*

Withdrawal of God from mankind : *human inadequacy* (curiosity, pride, greed)

Origin of death due to hatred : (life = love)

Origin of death due to killing of God's messenger : *recognition of God present in world*

Oracle condemns girl to be sacrificed; one who tries to carry out the sentence dies instead : *mercy rather than sacrifice*

Girl insists on choosing her husband and finally makes a bad match : *realism, acceptance*

Trickster (hare, tortoise, spider, chameleon, jackal, trickster man/men) : *cunning, success*

Trickster who fails : *cunning success is not the ultimate value*

Hunter who is rescued by his dogs : *dependence on inferiors*

Giant / ogre / monster / elephant / djinn / talking skull / outsize pumpkin / who swallows everyone and is finally overcome : *salvation*

Wonder-child/orphan/cripple/blind child/who becomes a saviour : *triumph of innocence/power of the weak*

Children that turn into animals/pumpkins/calabashes; *home ethics, obedience/tolerance*

Nature's revenge : *responsibility for created things*

Disobedience that leads to disaster : *obedience*

Irredeemable fool/slow girl who is easily tricked : *common sense, practical loyalty*

Girl who could not keep a secret and lost a treasure : *practical loyalty*

Downfall of the boaster : *humility*

Lion with bone in his throat/or with frog/rat in his belly : *weakness of the strong*

People saved by watchman who stayed awake : *alertness*

Children who are searching for their parents : *home ethics, parental responsibility*

Friends/lovers who dispute about their love : *love is not rivalry*

Origin of chiefship = reward for endurance : *authority is a burden*

Theft by God of drum/girl, attempt by spider to get it/her back : *inscrutability/mastery of God*

It should be noted that a single text may refer to more than one theme.

It is obvious that where traditional stories are still enjoyed (which is not the same thing as saying that they are still told in the home) the catechist, religion teacher or preacher can use them as material for catechesis. The more general adaptation of general themes presents few problems, it being often enough simply to allude to the theme during the course of an ordinary sermon or instruction. A more radical adaptation takes place when there is an attempt not only to use the theme but to adapt the sermon or instruction to the traditional literary form which contains the theme. The following examples both try to do this.

The experiment of a catechesis adapted in this manner was made by Fr B Mangematin WF, of Nigeria, and was published in 1963. It is an attempt at catechesis through prayer using the symbolism and the form of a Yoruba praise poem, an *Oriki* in praise of a god or a person. The aim of the catechesis was to teach the holiness of God. Symbols such as the prostration of the animals before the 'lord of the forest' (lord of the animals) are developed into biblical symbols (the prostration of Moses before the burning bush), the message of 'awe before a great power' being preserved and built upon.[15]

When the guinea fowl wakes up in the morning
It must prostrate to the Lord of the Forest.
If it fails to greet him thus,
It will be killed by the hunter.
He will carry it home on his back.
He will sell it in the market,
And use the money to make charms.
If the antelope wakes up in the morning
And does not bow to the lord of the forest
The hunter will come and eat its head with pounded yam.
Most Holy God, Creator of Heaven and Earth,
I prostrate to you every morning.
Before I set out to do anything.
God is holy. God is holy like fire, like a burning fire.
His face is like the sun
When it shines in full strength. (Apoc 1:16)
Moses in the wilderness facing the burning bush,

And God said to Moses :
Do not come nearer.
Take the shoes from thy feet;
The place where you stand is holy ground.
And Moses hid his face.
Most holy God you are like lightning.
He rides fire like a horse.
Lightning with what kind of cloth do you cover your body?

With the cloth of death.
Lord of Hosts, swift and sharp like the sword.
Thy word is more piercing than a two-edged sword,
Reaching to the division of the soul and the spirit,
Of the very joints and marrow,
Disentangling the inmost thought and intention of heart.
                                        (Heb. 4:12)

The terrible rumbling one,
The leopard that devours the liar,
The Lord of the house of fire (*Onile-ina*).
Noonday fire,
The pure king,
The King without blemish,
Gleaming white, snow white.
White and pure like the light, the morning light.
God said : Let there be light.
And God separated the light from the darkness. (Gen 1:3–4)
O God, Creator of the Light of the First Day,
O God Light-bearer, fire-bearer.
The one clothed in white robes, who dwells above,
Terror of the infernal darkness.
Awake sleeper,
Rise from the dead,
And Christ will enlighten thee. (Eph. 5:14)
God is holy like the eyes of a child,
Sparkling with life, intelligence and pure love.
If you have dirt in and or under your nails,
Who cares?
If you have dirt in your eyes
Please, you say, come quick, help me to rub it away.
The lamp of the body is the eye. (Mt 6:22)

I am the Way the Truth and the Light. (Jn 8:12; 13:6)
O God, Father Most Holy,
You are the eye of the blind man
   the feet of the lame
   the father of the poor. (Job 29:16)
But there are those who shun the light,
Who rebel against the light,
They do not know its ways.
They do not abide in its paths.
It is dark when the murderer rises
To kill the poor and the needy.
The eye of the adulterer watches for twilight;
He says : No eye will see me.
In the night the thief roams about,
And puts a mask over his face.

Thy face, O Lord, is like the morning sun !
God is holy like the eyes of a child.
Blessed are the pure of heart;
They shall have eyes to see God. (Mt 5:9)
God is holy like the fire,
And we are but dust and ashes. (Ps 144:4)
Like the wind we go, like a shadow our days pass.
Our Father who art in heaven,
Holy be thy name.
Praise the Lord our God
And bow down before his footstool,
For he is most holy, (Ps 99:5)
And we are poor sinners :
Pray for us sinners, now and at the last hour.
His dwelling is in unapproachable light (1 Tim 6:16)
And we are sitting in the shadow of death.
But the light has shone in the darkness.
He has considered the lowliness of his handmaid.
The Almighty has done great things for us,
Holy his name.
He has taken us from the land of sin and slavery,
He has saved us from the land of Egypt.
The waters saw thee, O Lord, and shuddered.
They ran away, the very depths were troubled (Ps 77:17)

You led your peoples like a flock (Mt 7:21)
To the promised land, to the holy land, heaven.

Our Father who art in heaven,
Holy be thy name, thy kingdom come!
Holy, Holy, Holy is the Lord of Hosts (Is 6:3)
Alas I must keep silent;
My lips and the lips of all my countrymen are polluted with
  sin. (Is 6:5)
Blessed are those who wash their robes in the blood of the
  lamb,
That they may enter the gates of the Holy City. Amen.
                                                    (Apoc 22:14)

The second example is a sermon, one of a series preached experimentally in a rural area of Tanzania in 1968–9 and published in 1969.[16] The sermon is based on a traditional story-song which employs two themes: salvation from the monster or ogre and the triumph of innocence. An attempt was made to preserve the story-song form by introducing a refrain, alluding to the message during the course of the sermon.

Among the stories of our people there are many stories about a girl called Chali, and in all these stories Chali offended her parents by disobeying them and running away to the forest. When she reached the forest, however, she became lost and fell into the clutches of that fantastic animal, the wicked giant Idimungala. Chali's parents and all her relatives looked for her in vain; she was not to be found. One day (so one of the stories goes) two travellers met Chali in the forest and told her father about it when they got home. Chali's father sent several men to look for her and bring her back, but they were unable to save her. She was under a spell, and each time they came upon her she disappeared from their sight. A second time Chali's father sent some men to save her, and a second time they failed. Finally he sent some small children to look for her and bring her back, and these children were successful. They saved Chali from Idimungala and returned her to her father.

(Refrain) *The Child Jesus has saved us.*
The meaning of this story is clear. It is this: to save someone

from evil, what is required is innocence, like the innocence of young children. Sinners and those who are guilty of faults are unable to save anyone. This story of Chali contains a truth. Simplicity, childlike innocence and humility bring salvation.

(Refrain) *The Child Jesus has saved us.*

Now we Christians have been saved by a child. God made himself into a child in order to save us. God has no sin. There is no fault whatever in him. He alone is able to save us, and the symbol of his sinlessness is that he was born of a human mother and became a tiny child.

(Refrain) *The Child Jesus has saved us.*

Jesus was born at Bethlehem in the country of Palestine, an obscure little town in a small and insignificant country. He was not born rich. He was born poor. He was not even born in a proper house. He had no worldly power. His great power was the almighty power of God, the God in whom there is no sin.

(Refrain) *The Child Jesus has saved us.*

Like Chali in the story, we human beings have sinned. We have been disobedient. We were lost in the forest—that is to say, we were in a state of sin. We had fallen into the hands of that wicked giant, Satan.

(Refrain) *The Child Jesus has saved us.*

Many prophets were sent to look for us, but every time they were unable to make us come out. People did not want to listen to them. In the end it was a child who was sent, and he was successful.

(Refrain) *The Child Jesus has saved us.*

Now the Child Jesus has saved us and has set us an example. He has told us: become like little children. 'If any man does not receive the kingdom of God like a little child, he will never be able to enter it.' We must therefore have the humility, the lowliness and innocence of the tiny child. In this way we shall safeguard the salvation we have been given by Jesus.

(Refrain) *The Child Jesus has saved us.*

But if we disobey again, if we offend God, our Father, we shall fall again into the hands of our enemy in the forest. We shall again be in the state of sin. So, beloved Christians, let me wish you all a happy and blessed Christmas; but above all, let me wish you the happiness this Christmas of following the example of the child of Bethlehem in his gentleness, his humility and his innocence. Amen.

(Refrain) *The Child Jesus has saved us.*

This sermon develops the traditional themes of salvation and innocence into the Christian biblical themes of Christ's birth and teaching about spiritual childhood. Part of the sermon, however, is an allegorical adaptation of the original story, in which the latter is applied in its various details to the history of salvation. This is legitimate, since it does no violence to the original story and serves the themes of the original story.

Let us now turn to subject of prayer in African tradition.[17] One frequently hears it said that traditional Africa knew only one kind of prayer, the prayer of petition. Such an accusation can only be born of ignorance, for careful study reveals an extremely rich prayer tradition among the peoples of Africa. Petition plays its part in spoken prose, but poetry and song lend themselves more easily to the sentiments of praise and thanksgiving. This fact, it seems, may explain why such sentiments are commonly overlooked. A study of traditional prayers in Africa must include religious panegyric and hymns.

Hence we shall look at the structures and content of traditional African prayers in all their forms recorded by ethnographers; and notice some of the problems that they pose for the Christian theologian and liturgist. The hope is that these prayers may become better known and better understood, so that they can provide material for a creative African Christian liturgy.

Obviously the meaning or content of African prayers depends very much on the concept which those who use them have of God. This concept varies from one culture to another, although ideas of God were always wider than ordinary ethnic and language boundaries. Over and above differences in the concept of God, the prayers employed a symbolism which drew its inspiration from differing geographical environments and differing historical experiences. Prayer is common to all African societies, and, generally speaking, the providence, omniscience and omnipresence of God are vital realities expressed in the prayer texts, even if prayer to the Creator was sometimes socially structured and the practical necessity of human mediation or vicarious praying was accepted.

There are three main forms taken by traditional prayer: the litanic form, the panegyric or praise poem, and the stylized ejaculation or short invocation. The litanic form, as its name implies, is the form of call and response so popular in the speech and song of traditional Africa. The following example is taken from the Kikuyu people of Kenya.[18]

> Say ye, elders may have wisdom and speak with one voice.
>> Praise ye Ngai, peace be with us
> Say ye, the country may have tranquillity and the people may continue to increase.
>> Praise ye Ngai, peace be with us.
> Say ye, the people and the flocks and herds may be free from illness.
>> Praise ye Ngai, peace be with us.
> Say ye, the fields may bear much fruit and the land may continue to be fertile.
>> Praise ye Ngai, peace be with us.

The praise poem (or hymn) is usually of some length whether it is concerned with the exploits of God, spirits or men. The following fine example, taken from the Shona of Rhodesia, contains a short petition towards the end, although the main burden of the prayer is decidedly one of praise and confidence.

Anyone with a knowledge of the Rhodesian landscape will recognize the images used in this prayer.

> Great Spirit,
> Piler-up of rocks into towering mountains!
> When thou stampest on the stone,
> The dust rises and fills the land,
> Hardness of the precipice;
> Waters of the pool that turn
> Into misty rain when stirred.
> Vessel overflowing with oil!
> Father of Runji,
> Who seweth the heavens like a cloth:
> Let him knit together that which is below.
> Caller-forth of the branching trees:

Thou bringest forth the shoots
That they stand erect.
Thou hast filled the land with mankind,
The dust rises on high, O Lord!
Wonderful one, thou livest
In the midst of the sheltering rocks;
Thou givest of rain to mankind :
We pray to thee,
Hear us, Lord!
Show mercy when we beseech thee, Lord.
Thou art on high with the spirits of the great.
Thou raisest the grass-covered hills
Above the earth and createst the rivers,
Glorious one.[19]

The stylized ejaculation is extremely common, and usually accompanies religious ritual. The following example is taken from the Nupe of Nigeria.

May the whole town have health;
May it have to eat,
May it have to drink;
May the whole town have health.[20]

Prayer-formulae and phrases tend to be stereotyped in Africa, but there is considerable freedom for adaptation and application to the immediate situation and needs of those offering the prayer.

Times of prayer relate to the symbolism of the various times of day. For example, the hours of sunrise, midday and sunset may refer to sun symbolism in the worship of the Creator. Geographical features such as mountains may also be related to religious symbolism, and may direct the posture that must be adopted. In Kikuyu and in Uchagga, the worshipper may be expected to face the sacred mountains of Kenya and Kilimanjaro, the abode of God. The journey to the sacred place may also be an integral part of serious, formal prayer in Africa. Standing, squatting, prostration are variously demanded by custom, and the sacred dance also has its place. Although purely vocal worship was known, African prayer traditionally accompanied symbolic action or ritual on most occasions. The occasion of prayer was very often that of a disaster or misfortune affecting the individual or the group. This, however, did not necessarily denote a 'God-of-the-gaps' mentality, because misfortune and its removal was often consciously related to confession of sin and salvation from sin. Very often also prayers of urgent petition were accompanied by a spirit of real praise and acceptance. Moreover, prayers were often recited on joyful and festal occasions, such as weddings and initiations. Private prayer was known, but community prayer was, perhaps, more popular and more typical. In any case, it was expected that the man who prays should associate himself in prayer with his kinsmen and neighbours, and with the dead whose world of relationships was often conceived as a mirror of our own. The ancestors pray and share with the living in worship.

Mediation is a familiar concept in Africa and one which enhances the importance of the person addressed. In many places chiefs could not be addressed directly, but had to be approached through mediators or spokesmen, or with the face averted, or the mouth covered. Sometimes, too, the third person singular was employed in direct conversation with the great. Such ideas have been carried over into prayer, and explain the roles of spiritual beings such as the Earth Mother, Moon Goddess, 'Wife' of God, Master of the Animals, nature spirits and ancestral spirits. They also explain why worship was so often departmentalized, as it were, in traditional Africa; and why it varied both in degree and kind according to the different levels of the social and political structure.

Generally speaking, entry into prayer took two basic forms: presentation and invitation. In the first case, the worshipper presents himself with his family or community to God and the spirits with such phrases as, 'Here we are!', 'Your children are before you', 'We come to you', 'We have come to your place'. As was remarked above, the last phrase might be literally true: a pilgrimage may have taken place. In the second form, the worshipper invites God or the spirits to come and be present: 'Let the great ones gather!', 'You, Divinity, I call you in my invocation', 'Our Liberator . . . we have heard him, he has come'. The basic condition of prayer is the attitude of confidence or dependence by which the worshipper places himself in the hands of the powers, to receive from them whatever is just. The worshipper therefore humbles himself. He and his fellows are 'children', addressing their 'father', 'grandfather', 'elder'. Perhaps the most extreme example of self-abasement is to be found in the Dinka phrase 'children of the ants'. Often, however, the worshipper's humility is expressed by a certain diffidence and a pretence of ignorance. 'Whether or not I know how to make this sacrifice', say the Kono of Sierra Leone, 'you will trouble the one who does not know. . . .'[21]

It has already been noted that petition is not the only purpose of traditional African prayer, but petition is, of course, extremely common. However, it is far from being selfish petition. Prayer was said for the family, children, harvests, rain, peace, victory, health, national prosperity, etc. Moreover, petition was often made in a spirit of *do ut des*, as in the Old Testament. The favour sought was seen as the response on the part of God and the spirits to an act of praise or hope made by the worshipper. Thus a typical petition structure is :

(a) Presentation of the problem in a time of trouble.
(b) Petition itself which expresses human dependence but does not exclude human action.
(c) Honour rendered in the confident hope that the powers will act.

The order can be varied, but the elements of the structure are usually present. Thus, in the following Nuer prayer of petition on behalf of a boy wounded in a spear fight :

> Friend, God who is in this village,
> As you are very great,
> We tell you about this wound,
> For you are God of our home in very truth.
> We tell you about the fight of this lad.
> Let the wound heal,
> Let it be ransomed.[22]

Analysis reveals *presentation* ('We tell you about this wound', 'We tell you about the fight of this lad'), *petition* ('Let the wound heal, let it be ransomed'), and *honour/confidence* ('Friend, God who is in this village, as you are very great', 'For you are God of our home in very truth').

If petition is linked to praise and hope, it is also often linked to contrition, since the worshipper recognizes that misfortune comes upon him as the result of sin, and that he needs salvation both from the state of sin and its punishment. The following is a Dinka example :

> Children of the ants, we have suffered from dryness.
> Why am I without cattle? Why am I without grain?
> That is what I ask, ee!
> I am a man that boasted of himself.
> I slaughtered in greed my major ox.
> Children of Aghok, my father, the children of the ants are forsaken?
> (Yet) my father, the creator indeed created men.
> We honour our lord that he may look in upon us.[23]

This is a clear act of contrition for pride and greed, and the penitent prays for God's favour as a response to the honour he renders. Going even beyond such sentiments of repentance, there is the feeling that misfortune somehow brings God closer to men. God shares in man's sufferings. Again, the Dinka of Sudan afford us a good example :

> . . . You, Divinity, you are called by my words, because you look after all people, and are greater than anyone, and all people are your children. And if evil has befallen them, then you are called to come and join with them in it also. . . .[24]

Another important sentiment in traditional African prayer is that of thanksgiving, and there can be no finer example of gratitude and personal commitment than the prayer attributed by Kikuyu to their first ancestor, the founder of their people :

> O my Father, Great Elder, I have no words to thank you, but with your deep wisdom I am sure that you can see how I value your glorious gift. O my Father, when I look upon your greatness, I am confounded with awe. A great Elder, ruler of all things earthly and heavenly, I am your warrior, ready to act in accordance with your will.[25]

The fact that Africans have preserved prayer-texts traditionally ascribed to their ancestors and to heroes of the past is a reminder of the importance of anamnesis in African prayer. There is a strong consciouness of the necessity of continuity and tradition. Prayer and worship are effective because they are part of this tradition, and it is therefore important to worship in the way the ancestors worshipped, to be at one with them in prayer. The following are examples of this characteristic; taken from Kikuyu and Dinka :

> We praise you in the same way as our forefathers used to praise you, under this same tree, and you heard them and brought them rain.[26]
> And you my prayer, and you prayer of the long distant past, prayer of my ancestors, you are spoken now.[27]

It might be thought that contemplation was altogether too sophisticated a form of prayer for traditional Africa. Once again, the doubting Thomas is proved wrong. Silence played an important part in sacrifice and religious ritual on occasion. The pygmies of Zaire, for example, traditionally carried out their first-fruits offering to the Creator in silence, and the Kimbu (Tanzania) chief silently and motionlessly communed with his ancestors while the elders went to the graves to make sacrifice. Michel Kayoya expresses the sentiment behind the prayer of silence very well in the words he puts into his father's mouth when the latter is rebuked by his son for not taking part in vocal prayer :

> My son, you are under a delusion. You think we have to use formulae when we pray to Imana our God. When I contemplate the work Imana has accomplished in my house, I have no need to tell him about it. Before him I keep silence, and I offer him in silence the house over which he has made me the head.[28]

It would be misleading to give the impression that there are no problems for the Christian theologian or liturgist when confronted by the traditional prayer of Africa; there are problems a-plenty. Let us look at three perennial problems.

The first is that of scolding prayers, or prayers of complaint. Vehement complaint in prayer could be a sign that prayer is becoming a technique for making God do what one wants—a form of idolatry, in fact—and that the spirit of humble dependence which is the essence of true prayer has been abandoned. On the other hand, scolding, complaining and bargaining may simply be human responses to the inscrutability of God's action

and have to be set against the implicit, and even explicit, acceptance of God's will as the outcome.

Related to this problem is that of the infallibility of prayer,
the feeling that if worship has been carried out correctly in all
its details then the powers are bound to grant what is asked.
If they do not, there is a mistake somewhere. Usually the mistake
is attributed to the worshipper, but in some instances the mistake
may be attributed to God. An example is that of the Ngombe
(Zaire) hunter who prayed for a successful hunt, but who only
killed his quarry after some initial failure. His prayer of thanksgiving therefore went as follows :

> Our God, we rejoice,
> We thought you had make a mistake![29]

Once again, it would have to be decided from the context of
worship and the mentality of the worshipper, whether this was
idolatry or whether it was an understandable anthropomorphism.

Finally, there is the problem of built-in divination in prayer.
The worshipper may expect an answer to prayer, or a sign that
the prayer is to be answered in the very act of worship itself.
This is divinatory prayer. The worshipper may expect the sacrificial animal to urinate, for example; his maize-flour offering to
be disturbed during the night; or, if he is praying for rain, he
may even expect the rain to begin to fall before his prayer is
over. Human beings, even Christians, are often tempted to look
for a sign of divine approval, but it has to be remembered that
the degree to which we impose conditions on God is the degree
in which our prayer is lacking in the spirit of openness and
dependence, and therefore less a prayer.

Social anthropologists have usually made it their business to
study religious beliefs and practices in Africa, at least as part
of their general ethnography. Consequently, their works contain
numbers of texts of traditional prayers. Further individual
research can add to the collection. For Christians who are com-
posing prayers for African use, such collections of traditional
prayers should be a normal source of inspiration for forms,
images and sentiments.

However, let us not be content with a too localized or tribal
approach, but, in this time of emerging national cultures in
Africa, let us explore and share the heritage of each ethnic

group and make use of such ideas and symbols as have a universal resonance. There is considerable scope already in Christian worship for extemporisation and creativity. With regard to the eucharistic texts, Catholics are at present bound to verbal translations of texts composed in Europe, although instructions emanating from Rome have indicated that creation, rather than translation, may be the final goal of the present liturgical renewal.[30]

The following is an attempt to create an African eucharistic prayer, inspired by African traditional prayer texts and modelled on the essential elements of a eucharistic prayer : thanksgiving, epiclesis, anamnesis, narrative of institution, acclamations, intercessions, doxology. The symbols it employs are sufficiently general to be comprehensible to Africans everywhere.[31]

Thanksgiving

Principal :	God, Father of our ancestors,
	friend in our midst,
	your children come before you.
	Here is your food !
	Here is your drink !
	These things are yours before they are ours.
	Now we are making a feast,
	but it is a thanksgiving;
	we are thanking God.
Concelebrants :	O God, we and our ancestors
	thank you and rejoice.
	This food—
	we shall eat it in your honour.
	This drink—
	we shall drink it in your honour.
Principal :	We thank you for giving us life,
All :	we thank you !
Principal :	We thank you for giving us freedom,
All :	we thank you !
Principal :	We thank you for bringing us peace,
All :	we thank you !
Principal :	We thank you for him who bears the punishment which is our due,

All :	we thank you !
Principal :	For him on whom fell the punishment which brought us peace
All :	we thank you !

Epiclesis

Concelebrants :	Father, send the Spirit of life, the Spirit of power and fruitfulness. With his breath, speak your Word into these things; make them the living body and the lifeblood of Jesus our brother. Give us who eat and drink in your presence Life and power and fruitfulness of heart and body. Give us true brotherhood with your Son.

Narrative of Institution

Concelebrants :	On the night of his suffering he gave thanks for the bread which he held in his hands. This bread he shared among his followers, saying : all of you, take this, eat this : It is my body which will be handed over for you.
All :	It is the body !
Concelebrants :	Then he shared drink with them, saying : all of you, take this, drink this : It is my blood, the blood of the pact of brotherhood which begins now and lasts forever. This blood will be poured out for you and all men so that sins may be taken away. Do this and remember me.
All :	It is the blood !

Acclamations

Principal :	Let us proclaim the mystery of faith :

115

All :   Hail, hail, hail,
              death, resurrection
              and return,
              may happiness come!

Anamnesis
Concelebrants :   Lord, you are resurrection and life.
                  You, crucifixion, are here!
                  You, resurrection, are here!
                  You, ascension, are here!
                  You, spirit-medicine of life, are here!

Intercessions
Concelebrant :   Father, bring us life;
                  give us kinship and brotherhood
                  with all the sons of God,
                  with the elders and fathers of your people,
                  with the living
                  and with the living-dead,
                  with children yet unborn,
                  in Jesus, who was anointed with the medicine
                  of life.

Doxology
All :   And you our prayer,
                  prayer of the long distant past,
                  you, ancient Word, spoken by the Father,
                  you whose breath is the Spirit,
                  prayer of the ancestors,
                  you are spoken now!
                  Amen.

Promissory and declaratory oaths played an important part
in traditional African society. They usually called God or the
spirits to witness a declaration or promise, and the oath was
taken in the presence of symbols related to the supreme values
of society. It was also a community act. Some oaths were secular
in that they appealed to a magical sanction and not to God or
spiritual beings. Oaths were frequently administered in judicial
ordeals, for example :

   (holding a piece of wood) 'If I have stolen, may I become
   dead like this wood' (Nandi, Kenya).[32]

'If I have not spoken the truth, I will never again see the green grass spring up; a spear will kill me before the rains start' (passing naked between two rows of spears—Elgeyo, Kenya).[33]

Oaths were taken at initiation rites, in covenants, blood-pacts, in settlement of land disputes, and so on. The peculiar efficacy of traditional African oaths derived from three elements: an immediate mystical sanction (religious or magical), eventual community sanction, and use of an explicit and powerful symbolism which appealed to people's experience.

If Christian vows, oaths and religious undertakings appear to be less binding than traditional African oaths, it may be because in the minds of those who take them they lack these elements.

To conclude this chapter, let us take a brief look at modern African writers. A great many Africans are writing in English today. Their works include autobiographies, plays, novels, literary criticism, political science, and poetry. It is mainly in the novel that their importance lies. The novel has always been one of the most important vehicles of ideas and values in a literate society, and there is evidence that the African novel is making an impact on the African élite. Its importance to the Christian educator and theologian cannot be emphasized too strongly, for the following reasons: African novels reveal what attitudes are being taken by thinking Africans towards the old and new social orders and to the process of social change; African novels reveal the depths of certain human problems and social situations; African novels point to new values emerging in contemporary society. African novels indicate the degree of understanding of religion and its role that educated people in Africa have today.[34]

In West Africa, urbanization is the all-absorbing problem; so are the materialism and hedonism which it entails. Traditional societies boasted highly developed material cultures, but these are visibly undermined by the new urban materialism. West African writers are preoccupied by the clash between cultures and by the new materialism.

In South Africa, the overriding problem is that of racial discrimination and the relations between the races. The independence of other African countries aggravates the tensions of South Africans, and their written works are concerned with the struggle for the basic human freedoms. The most usual theme is that of the common humanity which unites all races.

East and Central Africa present a more complex situation. Some authors are almost untouched in their thinking by Western values. Other writers go to the point of extreme Western sophistication, while still other writers ridicule them for this. One or two writers have managed to achieve a synthesis at a more subtle, even spiritual, level.

Some African writers are simply oral story-tellers putting their stories into print. Amos Tutuola of Nigeria is an example. His stories are simply Yoruba folktales, but they are creative and up to date—part of a still living tradition. Peter Palangyo of Tanzania uses the novelist's style, but his material is essentially traditional. In his novel *Dying in the Sun*, the hero, Ntanya, is an African Job, an innocent sufferer, who receives no answer to his complaints, but who finally comes to accept his suffering as a mystery.

Chinua Achebe of Nigeria, one of the finest literary craftsmen among African writers, is nevertheless passive and even fatalistic in his description of the conscious and unconscious break-up of traditional Ibo society. He offers no solution for the dilemma of the clash of cultures. Okot p'Bitek, the Ugandan poet, is also a passive observer. Okot, however, is a biting satirist, poking fun at the superficial sophistication of Westernized Africans, lamenting the passing of traditional values, but offering no programme of positive synthesis.

Ferdinand Oyono of Cameroon portrays the disillusionment of Africans betrayed by whites; and John Munyonye of Nigeria, although more optimistic, does not analyze very deeply the Christian solutions exemplified by some of his heroes.

Cyprian Ekwensi, one of the earliest Nigerian writers, believes that African values can be lived in the modern African city and that a synthesis of African and Western values can take place. Unlike Chinua Achebe, he sees the present, not the past, as the golden age. Initiatives, he believes, must be taken now. Ekwensi does not think it an easy task but, for him, virtue untested is no virtue.

James Ngugi of Kenya is also positive, but he achieves his synthesis at a higher level. He is the African writer with a mentality that comes nearest to that of the New Testament.

He writes about the Kikuyu experience of Mau-Mau, and there is a messianic streak in his stories. The people look to a messiah who will restore the hopes for which they fought. Ngugi has come through the Mau-Mau crisis spiritually enriched. He depicts the people as disappointed with their independence; it is not what they fought for. Ngugi wants a spiritual freedom that serves the highest human qualities. His hero, Mugo (in *A Grain of Wheat*) has the courage to confess that he is a murderer and a traitor just when he is about to be hailed as a great leader and patriot. He prefers death to living a lie. Robert Serumaga from Uganda also presents us with characters who rediscover and deepen their humanity in a time of crisis.

Ezekiel Mphalele writes about the subtleties and complexities of South African race-relations. He is interested in the problems of all races, and in the casualties of a discriminatory system. Peter Abrahams, however, goes deeper into human psychology. For him, there is no black and white. Man must be accepted as man. In *Mine Boy*, the black man and white man stand together and suffer together for the cause of humanity. Lewis Nkosi and Alex Laguma treat a similar theme in a different way.

In Malawi, Aubrey Kachingwe, in his book *No Easy Task*, tells us the story of the struggle for independence both at national and individual levels, but in fact it betrays a pragmatic paternalism. The hero is content to work for a newspaper which does not represent public opinion. The African political leaders are conformist and submissive. England, not Africa, is the promised land. From England come all the good things that assure Africa's future. Africans do not win independence : it comes to them from England. On the final page, the hero sets off for further studies in England! Eneriko Seruma of Uganda exemplifies the class of disorientated Africans, blindly following vague ideals of sexual success.

African writers are often very religious in their outlook. They tend to idealize the religious values of the African past, but few, if any, have a New Testament mentality. Few have an accurate idea of the tenets of Christianity. Organized Christianity is for them at worst a hostile force in Africa, at best a harmless expedient for acquiring education or medical services. African writers have not, for the most part, seen any deep concordance between Christianity, African tradition, and the aspirations of modern Africa. The only clear example is, perhaps, Fr Michel Kayoya, a Murundi priest, writing in French.[35]

In the following chapter we shall turn from literary forms and symbols and examine ritual or symbolism in action.

Notes

1. This discussion of traditional African literary forms owes something to the late W H Whiteley's Introduction to his *A Selection of African Prose*, Oxford 1964, Vol 1, as well as to Ruth Finnegan's *Oral Literature in Africa*, Oxford 1970. However, it remains basically my own classification.
2. Richards, A I, *Chisungu*, London 1956, p. 72.
3. Field, M J, *Religion and Medicine of the Ga People*, Oxford 1937, p. 173.
4. This section on symbolism draws from many sources, the chief ones being Bevan, E, *Symbolism and Belief*, London 1962; Gusdorf, G, *Mythe et Métaphysique*, Paris 1953; Lévi-Strauss, C, *The Savage Mind*, London 1962, *Structural Anthropology*, London 1968, *The Raw and the Cooked*, London 1970; Turner, V W, *The Ritual Process*, London 1969, *Schism and Continuity in an African Society*, Manchester 1957, *The Drums of Affliction*, Oxford 1968; and Whitehead, A N, *Symbolism, its Meaning and Effect*, Cambridge 1958.
5. cf. Gusdorf, *op. cit.*, and Lévi-Strauss, *The Savage Mind* (*op. cit.*).
6. cf. works of V W Turner.
7. These categories of meaning are identified by both Bevan and Turner. I have used the terminologies of both.
8. cf. Hill, E, 'Remythologizing: the Key to the Bible', *Scripture*, Vol XVI, no 35, July 1964, pp. 65–75.
9. cf. Dodd, C H, *The Parables of the Kingdom* (3rd ed), London 1965, p. 13.
10. Rahner, K, 'The Theology of Symbol' in *Theological Investigations*, Vol IV, London 1966, pp. 221–45.
11. Lévy-Bruhl, L, *How Natives Think*, New York 1926.
12. The functions of myth, as presented here, are based on a trilogy of articles by J A Loewen in *Practical Anthropology*, Vol 16, no 3, 1969, pp. 147–9.
13. Ideas for the analysis of myths have been taken from Lévi-Strauss, cf. works cited above, note 4.
14. These themes have been culled from collections made by a number of authors from all over Africa. They include Grace Ogot, Clare Omanga, Pamela Ogot, Osenath Odaga, Joel Makumi, Anne Matindi, J Ibongia and Stephen Gichuru. Anthropological collections such as the Oxford Library of African Literature have also been used.
15. I am grateful to the Editor of *The African Ecclesiastical Review* for allowing me to re-publish here Fr B Mangematin's Oriki, which appeared in Jan 1963, Vol V, no 1, pp. 50–54.
16. The homily quoted here was one of several printed in the article, Shorter, A, 'Form and Content in the African Sermon', which appeared in *The African Ecclesiastical Review*, Vol XI, no 3, 1969, pp. 265–79.

[17] This section appeared (with a few changes) in *The African Ecclesiastical Review* as 'Prayer in African Tradition', Vol XII, no 1, 1972, pp. 11–17.

[18] Kenyatta, J, *Facing Mount Kenya*, London 1938, p. 239.

[19] Smith, E W, *African Ideas of God*, London 1950, p. 127.

[20] Nadel, S F, *Nupe Religion*, London 1954, p. 76.

[21] Parsons, R T, *Religion in an African Society*, Leiden 1964, p. 74.

[22] Evans-Pritchard, E E Y, *Nuer Religion*, Oxford, 1962, p. 112.

[23] Lienhardt, R G, *Divinity and Experience*, Oxford 1961, p. 243.

[24] Lienhardt, *ibid.*, p. 230.

[25] Kenyatta, J, *My People of Kikuyu*, Oxford 1966, p. 3.

[26] Kenyatta, *Facing Mount Kenya*, p. 247.

[27] Lienhardt, *op. cit.*, p. 221.

[28] Kayoya, M, *Sur les Traces de Mon Père*, Bujumbura 1968, p. 46 (translation from a forthcoming English edition to be published by East African Publishing House).

[29] Smith, *op. cit.*, p. 172. (The name for God used in the original is Akongo).

[30] cf. *Notitiae*, 44 (1969), p. 12, Instruction on Liturgical Texts.

[31] This Eucharistic Prayer appeared, first of all, in *The African Ecclesiastical Review*, Vol XI, no 2, 1970, pp. 143–8. The version given here has several changes and additions.

[32] Huntingford, G W B, *The Nandi of Kenya*, London 1953, p. 117.

[33] Massam, J A, *The Cliff Dwellers of Kenya*, London 1968, p. 76.

[34] A seminar at the Pastoral Institute, Gaba, in 1970 studied African writers. Some of the ideas here are taken from the report of that seminar, edited by Fr Charles Imokhai of Nigeria.

[35] Kayoya, *op. cit.*

Suggested further reading

Beier, U, *An Introduction to African Literature*, London 1967.

Bevan, E, *Symbolism and Belief*, London 1962.

Finnegan, R, *Oral Literature in Africa*, Oxford 1970.

Lévi-Strauss, C, *The Savage Mind*, London 1962 (especially pp. 1–47); *Structural Anthropology*, London 1968; *The Raw and the Cooked*, London, 1970.

Turner, V W, *Schism and Continuity in an African Society*, Manchester 1957; *The Drums of Affliction*, Oxford 1968.

5 African and Christian Ritual

WE HAVE been dealing up to now with literary or verbal symbols. In Africa such symbols are usually joined to symbolic action, known to anthropologists as 'ritual'. Everywhere, human beings have a fundamental need to dramatize or celebrate their experiences or expectations through symbolic action. This was shown in the Soviet Union where, in 1919, funeral ceremonies were forbidden. The dead were to be disposed of as unceremoniously as possible. By 1934 funeral ceremonies were back again, and government grants were even given for them. Russian funerals today include embalming, viewing, civil or religious services, and elaborate memorials. It is clear that death is such an important event that human beings need to make it intelligible to themselves through symbolic action.

Lévi-Strauss called ritual 'a favoured game'.[1] It is favoured because it is not like competitive sport in which one side wins. It is like the play-acting of children, in which the participants each take a role—father and mother, cops and robbers, cowboys and Indians. All the participants get satisfaction from the game. It introduces harmony, not competition. Like the acting of children, it dramatizes experiences and expectations, or ideal story-book situations.

Victor Turner, on the other hand, sees ritual as a *gestalt* or dialectic—the meeting point of conflicting interests. In rituals men act out the tensions they experience and bring about a tensed unity once more. Ritual, in Turner's view, is a kind of safety valve.[2]

Whichever view is taken, ritual is highly important. In the words of Monica Wilson, it is 'the key to an understanding of the essential constitution of human societies'.[3] We have seen that symbolism is an appeal to experience—that it is 'committed' or 'semi-incarnate'. It is natural therefore for literary or verbal symbolism to overflow into symbolic action, thus linking symbols to real life. Ritual stands as a bridge between verbal symbols and man's daily activity, and participates in the nature of both. It is symbolic, on the one hand; but it is also a high point of human activity, on the other. Through ritual man makes his experience intelligible; he humanizes and gives purpose to his activity. Ritual reinserts man into reality, and helps him restore order to society.

Rituals can be divided from the point of view of how far they make an appeal to spiritual beings, or ultimate reality. Rituals which do not make such a direct appeal may be called secular; those which do may be called religious. Obviously, many rituals combine both secular and religious elements and are hard to classify; however, it can be said that certain rituals tend more to the secular and others more to the religious.

Rituals of redress operate to redress a calamity or affliction in the affairs of the social group. This may be a natural disaster which affects every member of the group, such as a drought, or it may be a sickness or affliction that has befallen an individual who thereupon becomes the symbol of the tensions within the community. The first stage in ritual is divination, which attempts to discover which factors are involved and what are the appropriate rituals to be performed. The ritual which then takes place is designed to make the hidden tensions of society explicit, and to restore the *status quo ante*.

Rituals of life crisis, or rites of passage,[4] concern an individual, or group of individuals, passing from one state of life to another state of life, or from one status to another status. The ritual helps the individual to accept the claims of society in the new state. The individual can express his conflicts and tensions through the ritual, and resolve them. Life-crisis ritual provides emotional support for the social structure.

The term rite of passage refers to the individual's passage from one state to another, and this is expressed by three phases of ritual: rite of separation (from the previous state); rite of incorporation (into the new state); liminal (or threshold) period between the two.

Liminal rituals are rituals in which the attempt is made to prolong, or repeat the experience of the liminal period. They are a development of the life-crisis rituals.

'Liminality' has a social significance. It provides a counter-balance to the rigidity of social structures. It is 'anti-structure'. It recalls society to the basic experiences of humanity. Inferiors in the structure can achieve symbolic superiority, and superiors in the structure can rediscover their humanity. Such rituals are those of secret societies and mask societies.

Turner even goes so far as to say that there are 'liminal' periods of history, when people are passing rapidly from one social order to another. Such periods are characterized by liminal rituals which are cultural hybrids, taking elements both from the old and the new. Such are millennarian movements, and movements of witch-eradication.

Liminality can be a spontaneous experience, a 'happening', or it can be institutionalized or normative. It can also be ideological in the sense of an unattainable Utopia. Such Utopias flourish in societies where liminal ritual is too strongly institutionalized.

Much of what has been said earlier about the analysis of literary symbols also applies to ritual. However, ritual is an even more complex phenomenon to analyze, since, in addition to the symbolic structure, there are other structures. Firstly there is the symbolic structure. Ritual is an aggregation of symbols, in Victor Turner's phrase 'a bunch of keys'—keys to the understanding of society. They have to be analyzed according to the method outlined in the last chapter for literary symbols, but there will be a multiplicity of symbols, codes and messages in a ritual, besides an interplay between verbal symbols and symbols in action.

As we have seen, corresponding to the symbol are messages about values. Ritual is an authoritative communication about crucial social values and the relationship of values to each other, the value system. It is therefore said to have a value structure. It also has a structure of purpose. Ritual is a system of ends and means which consists in the manufacture of certain key symbols which are designed to have an effect on people. This effect may be achieved by a non-rational-technical process such as magic or sorcery, or it may be achieved by the religious appeal to ultra-human agencies.

Finally, there is the role structure. Ritual is the product of the interaction of different human actors who represent different social categories. Ritual is a process—a configuration of changing and developing elements. It is a micro-history, and to study a ritual one must study the whole field context.

Some rituals are merely or mainly expressive. They appear only to be giving expression to human feelings or expectations. They are 'saying' something about events, rather than 'doing' something about them. They are celebrating them, or making a statement about them. Secular rituals are often merely expressive.

Other rituals are instrumental. They appear to be trying to influence events, make events happen, prevent them happening. These we call instrumental. Rituals can be socially instrumental, but this is not because of the nature of the rituals themselves, so much as because of social sanctions. Thus people may be prevented from planting or harvesting until the rituals have taken place. Among the Nandi of Kenya, where there is a four-year initiation period every fifteen years, it is possible for a boy to just miss the ceremonies because he is slightly too young, and have to wait until his early twenties for initiation. Physically he is mature, but socially he is still a child. Again, in the Western world, the marriage ceremony is a legal instrument which not only makes a statement about marriage but is regarded as bringing marriage into existence legally.

Rituals can be physically and psychically instrumental because they not only symbolize the effect desired but may actually bring it about through physical or psychical laws. Thus a certain medicine may be symbolic, but at the same time it may possess curative properties.

In so far as ritual makes no explicit or direct appeal to God or spiritual beings to make it instrumental, it is secular ritual; but this secular ritual may still be intended to influence events without explicit or direct appeal to known physical or psychical laws. We then call this secular instrumental ritual 'magic'. Magic may, in fact, operate instrumentally through physical and psychical laws unknown to those who make it. We still call it magic, however, because its very character consists in its being an instrumental symbol which is thought to 'work by itself'.

When ritual makes an appeal to God or spiritual beings, we call it religious ritual. By definition, therefore, religious ritual

125

is never merely expressive, but always instrumental, because it is always an appeal to spiritual beings who influence events. On the other hand, religious ritual is typically communitarian, as opposed to magic which is an individualistic ritual of power.

Among secular expressive rituals we find, firstly, the seasonal rituals, planting rites, fertility rites, harvest rites and some rain rites which are non-magical. These are festivals which celebrate the rhythmical structure of existence in the world. They render explicit the parallels between the biological cycles of women and those of plants and the phases of the moon. Often there are myths associated with these rites in which archetypes or hero/ heroine figures express the synthesis symbolically. The archetype often suffers, dies, is buried and rises again in the form of a plant. Symbols of life-death-life, impregnation, conception and childbirth are used. Fr J Goetz SJ has coined the word 'cosmo-biology' for these rituals to express the idea of a continuity between human life and the rhythms of nature.[5]

A very important group of expressive rituals are the life-crisis rituals or rites of passage. Some of these relate to a physical or territorial passage, such as rites for leaving on a journey and being welcomed home again, rites for leaving one country and entering another, rites for leaving one village or house and entering another village or house, rites for leaving profane places and entering sacred places. The archway or doorway, narthex or porch, is a physical expression of the idea of passage. It is the limen or threshold itself. Consequently it is frequently used in other rites of passage as a symbol. One finds triumphal arches, for example, or elaborate gate-houses in the palaces and compounds of African chiefs and kings.

Then there are rites of pregnancy and childbirth. At the onset of pregnancy, women are isolated in varying degrees in the various societies. They are surrounded with, and subject to, a great many taboos. At the birth of the child special ceremonies accompany the woman's reintegration with society as mother. Pregnancy coincides with the passage of the child into the world and into human society. This is another rite of passage. The child at birth is separated from its mother, and then secluded for several days (often for as long as it takes the umbilical cord to wither). Then the child is brought out of the house with ceremonies which symbolize its incorporation into society.

A very well-known rite of passage in Africa is that of initiation at puberty. Those to be initiated are separated from normal society, and normal obligations and rights are suspended. The candidates are secluded in a hut, or in a camp in the bush or forest. They are instructed in their future role as adults and potential parents. Finally, they are 'reborn' in their new status and incorporated into society. The cutting of the foreskin, labia or clitoris, or other body incisions and markings, are symbols of setting aside childhood and taking on a new personality. The initiate is 'changed'. We shall deal more fully with these rites when discussing preparation for marriage in a later chapter. In stratified societies, people pass from one grade to another—for example, from child to warrior, to married man, to young elder, to elder. There are initiation ceremonies for all these grades, which are similar to puberty initiation. They are known as age-set initiation.

There are, however, other forms of initiation, such as that into secret and other types of society or guild. These initiations follow the example of puberty rites very closely. There is usually a period of seclusion or transition, and the idea of death and rebirth is strongly suggested by the symbols. The candidate may pass through an arch backwards, or through a woman's legs. He may be naked and lie on a bed of thorns. He may be given a new name, sit on a 'mother's' lap, be given baby food and a new mother and father, and so on. All these are symbols of childbirth and the pains and experiences of childbirth.

The initiation of chiefs and office-holders also follows the puberty pattern to some extent. The candidate is separated from his previous status as a commoner. He may be beaten 'for the last time' for example. Then he is taken to a secluded place, or taken into a house, where he is instructed and invested with the insignia. Finally, he is brought out and shown to the people in his new status.

Sometimes betrothal and marriage form one continuous rite of passage; at other times they are distinct rites. During the betrothal period the bride may be subject to certain prohibitions. Often the bride is secluded before marriage, or the transition may be effected by the wedding procession, bringing the bride to the bridegroom's house or crossing his threshold. The period of bride-service undertaken by the groom in some societies may also be a period of transition, ending with the birth of the first child. Divorce rites are usually simple affairs, if they take place at all. Usually it is desertion ratified *post factum*, or just taken for granted when the woman is past childbearing. We shall deal with marriage rites in more detail when we consider marriage and the family.

Funeral and mourning rites are long and complex rites of passage for the living as well as for the dead. In some societies there is a first and second burial, as among the Chagga of Tanzania. There may also be a 'laying of the ghost' or calling of the dead person home, as among the Shona of Rhodesia. The transition of the dead person to the spirit world may be concurrent with the corruption of the body, with a process of embalming, with the washing and laying out of the corpse, or with the procession to the grave.

Mourning rites begin with the leave-taking by the living of the deceased, usually in the form of ceremonies at the burial itself : for example, throwing earth into the grave backwards, or anointing the corpse with eyes averted. There is a certain seclusion for the mourners, ordinary activities being suspended during that time. Mourners may shave their heads or paint their bodies. Relatives and friends come to share their grief and to perform household tasks for them. The end of the liminal period is celebrated with a ritual, often a ritual meal. Special rituals may exist, as among the Ga of Ghana, for the separation of husbands and wives from their deceased spouse. Inheritance rites follow upon the closure of mourning and often parallel initiation rites for chiefs and office-holders. The initiation of a chief is a particular form of inheritance rite.

Besides rites of passage there are other rituals for special occasions. An example of this is the twin ritual. Twin rituals are an adaptation of normal rituals of childbirth, but they emphasize the ambivalence of twins. In their numbers twins are both a blessing and a curse. They are a sign of fruitfulness, but they also imply the difficulty of carrying and breast-feeding two babies, a fact which often results in the death of one or both twins. The abnormality of the birth is symbolized by a formal obscenity. Obscene songs are sung, the twins' parents may have to go naked, and actions with overt sexual symbolism may be performed. This acts as a psychological release. Twins break the rules, so rules are broken in celebrating their birth. Non-identical (dual ova) twinning rates per 1000 maternities are higher for Negroes than for other races. In Great Britain the rate is 8.9%, in Italy 8.6% in Spain 5.9%; but in Ibadan, Nigeria, it is 39.9%, in Rhodesia 26.6%, in Kinshasa (Zaire) 18.7%.[6] Twin rituals are a common feature of African societies for this reason. There are many other rituals for other special occasions. We shall discuss friendship rituals and blood pacts in a later chapter.

We now turn to secular, instrumental rituals. Here we are dealing with techniques that can be taught and learned, bought and sold, bequeathed and inherited; we are not concerned with the belief that certain people have praeternatural, innate powers such as that of witchcraft. Secular instrumental ritual is called magic, and the belief is that the very expressivity of a symbolic rite is instrumental in itself, without an appeal to spiritual beings or to physical or psychical laws.

Africans do not necessarily distinguish between the magical properties and the physical properties or effects of a symbolic rite. Often emphasis is placed on the symbolic character of the rite when, in fact, physical and psychical laws are at work unbeknown to the participants in the ritual. That is why in African languages there is often no verbal distinction between 'magic' and 'medicine' or between 'sorcery' and 'poison'.

Objectively (from the anthropologist's point of view) one can distinguish 'good' and 'bad' magic or medicine. Good magic is designed to bring about good effects, to cure, to protect, to profit a person. Bad magic is designed to produce a bad effect, to harm or hinder a person. Writers sometimes speak of 'white' and 'black' magic, or of 'magic' and 'sorcery' when referring to these two types of magic.

Subjectively (from the African practitioner's point of view) 'good' magic includes ritual undertaken to harm someone whom the practitioner feels he has a right to harm, while 'bad' magic includes ritual which prospers a wicked or antisocial person. From the Christian point of view, of course, retaliatory magic against guilty persons is wrong, since it is a form of rendering evil for evil, at the very least in intention if not in fact.

An earlier generation of anthropologists was fond of the term 'magico-religious', implying that magic and religion were the same phenomenon. Although magic may be employed in religious contexts—and in the Christian view this is a perversion of religion—Africans know perfectly well that there is a distinction between them.

Christian writers, anxious to distinguish between the Christian sacraments and magic, have stressed the importance of dispositions for the sacraments as opposed to the automatic character of magic. This is an erroneous distinction. Magic is by no means automatic. Moreover, dispositions, especially the observance of taboos, may be regarded as necessary for the practice of magic. The difference between magic and the sacraments is that the latter appeal to the power of God through the historic acts of Christ while the former appeals only to the power of the symbol itself.

Let us take a look at some examples of magic and sorcery. The Sukuma of Tanzania compound a medicine out of the sanitary towel of a man's mother-in-law. This will make lions stay away from him. The explanation is that as a man must avoid his mother-in-law, so in the same way lions will avoid the man. The Nupe of Nigeria burn dead Kola leaves when the trees are in bloom in order to ensure a fruitful harvest of Kola nuts. Death and dryness are thus symbolically destroyed. The Nandi of Kenya 'catch the footprints' of a man they wish to injure, and among some other peoples a neighbour who wants to spoil the fields of another farmer spreads on them the excrement of a leper. Just as the flesh of the leper goes bad, so, it is thought, the fields will go bad.

All magic is 'sympathetic'—that is, it anticipates a desired effect symbolically in the belief that certain forms of anticipation are successful. Frazer distinguished two main forms of sympathetic magic : imitative and contagious. Imitative magic imitates the desired effect. Thus the Shona of Rhodesia use a medicine made from the sinew of a hare in order to make an athlete run more swiftly. Contagious magic anticipates the desired effect by contact rather than imitation. Thus a sorcerer will use grass from his victim's house, ash from his hearth, soil on which he has urinated, dirt from his clothing, his nails, his saliva and so on. What the sorcerer does to these objects which have had contact with his victim will, he hopes, also happen to the victim himself.

Sir James Frazer was one of those anthropologists who gave an intellectualist explanation of magic. He believed that magic was faulty science or mistaken reasoning. Practitioners of magic, he said, really believed that there was a physical connection between the symbol and the effect symbolized. It was a logical mistake. However, this is unlikely since millions of human beings could not be guilty of the same logical mistake; and people who practise magic do not make faulty deductions in empirical situations. It is not the likeness or the contact which brings about the effect, but the whole symbolic rite. Another group of anthropologists thought that people who practise magic believe they are operating an invisible magic force. They called this (mistakenly) by the Polynesian word *mana*. Mana was actually an abstract idea and had nothing to do with magic. In any case magic, by definition, does not appeal to physical or psychical laws.

There is such unquestioning belief in the efficacity of magic and such an interest in the marvellous among Africans that it is difficult to obtain well-documented, sound, scientific evidence for the efficaciousness of magic. The social scientist is, by profession, sceptical, but he should also preserve an open mind. He should be prepared to encounter irrefutable evidence that magic really works, and that the events anticipated in the symbolic rite really come about. However, it cannot be the case that they come about because of the symbolism alone. In terms of science that is impossible. The following are among the theories of how magic works—if it does.

Priests and religious have often attributed the efficacity of magic to the direct miraculous intervention of the Devil. The old argument rested on the fact that, in known scientific terms, there was no proportion between cause and effect. Therefore, when magic succeeded, the Devil was at work; when it did not, there was at least an implicit invocation of the Devil. This is a fallacious argument because traditional practitioners of magic in Africa did not know of a devil, and because magic, by definition, explicitly excluded an appeal to spiritual beings in its direct exercise. Indirectly, magic was perfectly compatible with belief in God and in good spirits, and Africans held that magic was part of God's creation. One could even pray to God to give one more success in one's magic, even though the magical rite was not itself a prayer.

It is difficult to prove when and where the Devil is working

miracles! Miracles worked among non-Christians could also be
attributable to God, and in any case certain phenomena such as
paranormal language (speaking of languages by people who
have never had an opportunity to learn them) which were regarded as criteria for diabolical possession are now known to
psychiatrists as symptoms of pathological or psychic conditions,
the content of which may be demonic or pentecostal or a mani-
festation of belief in other kinds of spirit. It is impossible to
observe the Devil at work, and he probably achieves more by
making people sin against love or justice than by making them
fall into pathological states!

At the very least, magic is effective by chance. Often no limit
is set for the fulfilment of the magic spell. The practitioner has
only to wait until he finally meets with success and then claim
that his magic was the cause. This does not mean that he is
cynical about it, nor does it mean that he cannot admit failure.
Failure is attributable to a defect in the magic and so reinforces
belief in the ritual. Magical rites have a thousand and one built-
in reasons for failure.

Magic may also be socially efficacious. The victim of a theft
goes to the diviner to discover the thief. The diviner announces
that, due to his magic, the culprit will soon be recognizable
because some misfortune will overtake him. For example, his
stomach will swell. This threat becomes known, and the thief
secretly returns the stolen goods rather than risk the misfortune.
This is a good example of the social sanction. The thief, when
he becomes known, will also be punished by society.

Another explanation for the efficacity of magic is psychophysiological. People go to traditional doctors to obtain remedies
both at the physical and the psychological level. It may be that
the psychical is more important than the physical in their minds.
The symbolical rite parallels and renders explicit the expectation
of a cure, or it may operate chiefly at the subconscious level.
It is effective in the same way that psychotherapy is effective.

In cases of sorcery the victim may become ill as a result of
the effects of grave fear. He may even die. Lévi-Strauss quotes
the following sequence of symptoms:[7]

The victim is convinced of the effectiveness of the sorcery.

The conviction of society confirms this and treats the victim
as endangered and dangerous.

The victim's fear affects his sympathetic nervous system.

This leads to a decrease in the volume of blood and a drop in blood pressure.

This causes damage to the circulatory organs.

As a consequence, the victim rejects food and drink.

Dehydration follows, which accentuates decrease of blood.

The capillary vessels become more and more permeable.

Death results and a *post mortem* reveals no lesions in the body.

How can sorcery or magic affect a person when the victim has no knowledge of the spell? Some people have used Jung's controversial theory of psychic forces and the collective unconscious to explain it. Such forces are not personal but collective. They are deep, instinctive forces which may be unleashed and be communicated from person to person unconsciously.

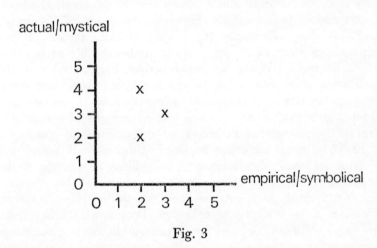

Fig. 3

A useful analogy for understanding the degree to which medicines operate on a physical or mystical level is to draw a graph in which the vertical plane represents the actual and the mystical, and the horizontal represents the empirical and the symbolical. On the vertical plane zero would represent, let us say, medicine designed to cure a cut finger here and now; at the top of the vertical plane would be a medicine designed to prevent a man ever cutting his finger again. On the horizontal plane zero would represent medicine with 100% physical properties, whereas the final figure would represent medicine which was 100% symbolical (magic). African medicines could therefore be plotted as co-ordinates of these two factors.[8]

Let us now look briefly at spirit possession. Spirit possession is essentially the belief that a spirit or spirits are possessing a person. Usually, however, this belief accompanies the psychic state known as mental dissociation. This is a condition which can be induced either naturally or artificially by drugs or mesmeric techniques. Dissociation gives the subject the impression that there is another person speaking through him or forcing him to speak without prior reflection. In this condition he usually speaks a foreign language (paranormal language is rare) or else he speaks an altered form of his usual everyday language. This is known as glossolalia, or speaking with tongues. Glossolalia is not productive but quickly becomes stereotyped.[9] The subject feels pains in his limbs and a constriction in the chest. His body shakes and he feels unsteady. He may even throw off his clothes and run away. Generally the subject is more restrained and experiences great clarity of perception, being able to marshal his facts quickly. When the trance is over, he feels relaxed and in a state of euphoria, but he quickly falls into a deep sleep. Dissociation can be pathological or hysterical, or it can be beneficial and a vehicle of true religious experience—for example, that of the Apostles at Pentecost, or of modern Pentecostals.

In Africa spirit possession is often institutionalized. Sometimes it is a religious phenomenon. The subject is thought to be possessed by the spirit of an ancestor to whom worship or sacrifice is addressed. At other times there is a spirit possession society which is a community of affliction. People who suffer from nervous complaints or who are already addicted to dissociation join together in the belief that certain neutral spirits are possessing them and are the cause of their illness. The aim of the rituals is to speak to the spirits and get them to co-operate. The spirits are 'talking germs or viruses'. There is no religious worship of, or religious attitude to, these spirits, who are comparable to fairies or leprechauns.

Psychologically, spirit possession may be a help, as psychotherapy is, to sick or deprived people. Sociologically, it may assist in status definition as a rite of passage to a more clearly defined status in society. A certain prestige attaches to spirit possession, and it may be a means for a wife to assert herself against her husband, or against her co-wives. It may also serve the general functions of liminal ritual.

Spirit possession has often been condemned by priests and religious educators as being possession by the Devil. This is improbable and incapable of proof, and it gives those who take part in it a bad conscience, if it does not cut them off altogether from the life of the Church for years. Even when the spirits are referred to by people using the word for the personage known to Christians as the Devil, it is unwise to assume that the spirits in question are seen as ethically bad, like the Devil. If spirit possession is a religious phenomenon, it may be a sin against the first commandment. If it is not, it may not be a sin at all. There is, however, a danger of losing control of dissociation, and finding that one has such a facility for falling into the state that it becomes an embarrassment. It may also act like a drug. Confessors should probably always counsel against it, but should take a more lenient view of those who have already experienced it. Above all, something should be done to create a meaningful liturgy of the sick, to help people who otherwise take part in spirit possession.

Divination, objectively speaking, is simply a magical rite intended to reveal hidden knowledge or to foretell events. The technique may be based on mere chance or it may be more or less under the diviner's control. For example, there is the rubbing-board, or the practice of rubbing hands, the termite oracle, and the poison oracle (administered to chickens, or inserted with maize flour in a ball of millet porridge to see if the flour changes colour). Such methods are largely subject to chance. Ventriloquism (talking pots, talking gourds and so on), mechanical devices, trances, interpretation of glossolalia, inspection of entrails of birds and animals, throwing pieces of leather, may be more subject to control by the diviner.

The oracle, or magical technique consulted by the diviner, is not necessarily infallible. Oracles may be contradictory, or there may be reasons for rejecting the verdict of an oracle or being sceptical about it. Appeal is possible from less powerful oracles to more powerful ones. Among the Azande of Sudan the poison oracle is asked a positive question and then a negative question. If the condition (sparing or killing the chicken) is fulfilled each time, the oracle is deemed to have revealed the truth. But the verdicts may be contradictory, in which case the consultation is said to be invalid.[10]

The diviner is not necessarily a cynical person. He may admit to trickery, but still believe that his tricks reveal the truth. Most answers given by oracles are simply incapable of being tested anyway. If an oracle declares that it is dangerous for a man to go hunting, or to travel on a certain day, it is certain that the man will not put the oracle to the test. If a man asks which ancestor is troubling him, or which of his enemies is practising witchcraft against him, it is impossible to test the oracle's verdict. It is anybody's guess which ancestor it is, just as witchcraft is by definition a secret and undemonstrable process. The client goes to the diviner with certain options or suspicions in mind. These are revealed in initial conversations with the diviner, or in the process of divination itself, and the result is that what the client hopes, fears, or expects will be revealed is revealed by the oracle. Some diviners seem to have powers of telepathy, because they appear to be able to tell the client facts about himself and the purpose of his visit at the very start of the interview. This is a means of creating confidence.

Sociologically, divination acts as a 'switchboard' : it switches the client on to the right level, religion, witchcraft, natural remedies and so on. The client then knows what ritual or course of action to follow, as a result of the consultation. Divination is a means of giving social approval to a course of action already decided upon by the client. It is also a form of exculpation when the client has to make retaliation.

In itself divination is a 'vain observance' and not very serious. The malice of divination derives from a bad intention or from the risk of harming others, either by accusing them of witchcraft or other crimes, or of providing grounds for retaliation against them. To consult a diviner about the best remedy for a light stomach-ache may not be very wrong, but to consult one about the cause of a death is an invitation to the diviner to make explicit the client's suspicion of witchcraft. The client, in the hands of the diviner, may be led on to make accusations in a form that he never consciously intended. Oracles consulted in the home, being in the control of the client himself, are less obnoxious. Factors to be taken into account, therefore, in judging the gravity of the fault are, whether the subject put himself into the hands of a professional diviner, and what the object of the divination was.

African societies have important individual specialists in medicines with physical properties, in magic, in divination, and in witch-finding. Such specialists often combine all these specialities, but they are usually called by a single term which means 'doctor'. The term 'witch-doctor', which emphasizes witch-finding, is misleading since it suggests to the uninitiated that the doctor is himself a witch. The doctor may deal in retaliatory magic (objective sorcery), but he would indignantly repudiate the suggestion that he was a witch. His task is to find witches. Most of these doctors see their role as essentially good, and they may have very extensive knowledge of the medical properties of herbs and roots. Some individuals may have the reputation of giving people bad medicine to make them come for cures, but this is probably rare in fact, and in any case is difficult to prove. These 'doctors' do not have a sense of vocation, in the sense that they feel an obligation to help people who cannot pay; on the other hand, they often only charge fees for good results. The traditional doctor is the pillar of belief in sorcery and witchcraft, although it is impossible to get people to appreciate this fact.

Missionaries in some areas sell medicines to villagers without adequate diagnosis. By doing this, they are encouraging a magical attitude to hospital medicines and are the allies of the witch-doctor.

Theologians have usually assumed that magic was irrational. However, as we have shown above, it is still possible that magic may be efficacious for psychological and psychophysiological reasons.

In the case of 'white' magic there is no moral problem. Sorcery is different, since there is the danger of harming some-one. There is also the question of the malice of the intention, even if the rite is not efficacious. Sorcery must therefore at least be judged to be morally wrong according to the gravity of the harm intended by the sorcerer.

The rituals of witch-finding and witch-eradication are not easy to classify, since they stand midway between secular and religious ritual. They are really the application of magical techniques to a belief in persons who have extraordinary or mystical power to harm others. Notice that we are not dealing with sorcery, the technique of harming others by means of symbolic ritual, but with an inherent power. Anyone can be a sorcerer, but not everyone can be a witch. Witchcraft belief is the standardized nightmare of a society. It is the product of a situation where group values are overstressed, at the expense of grid values. Witches are a threat to the group as a whole. They are human beings, more wonderful and more powerful than other human beings, but their power is essentially and implacably evil. The witch in traditional African belief is the nearest thing to the Christian personification of evil in the Devil.

Witchcraft beliefs vary in detail from one African society to another and, as we shall see, the variations reflect different types of social tension and social structure. However, there is a core of similarity. A witch is a human being who possesses a mysterious and inherent power to harm others by secret means either voluntarily or not. The power is inherent—that is to say, it is usually inherited. Witches are not thought to learn their trade or purchase their secrets. Sometimes, however, it is thought that witchcraft can enter into a person at the behest of another witch. Both men and women can be witches, but usually it is thought to be inherited through the female line only. The power is secret, and the witch operates at night. Witches attack people when they are asleep. They feed on the 'body-soul' of their victim and cause him to sicken and die. They lust for human flesh. They disinter the corpses of the dead and feed on them, or they resurrect them as spirits who work for them as servants. Witches dance naked on graves. They make themselves invisible. They turn themselves into animals. They travel on the backs of familiars, especially night animals like hyenas and screech-owls. They send wild animals to attack men. Their power is exercised involuntarily as well as voluntarily. A person can be a witch without knowing it. A baby, for example, can be a witch. That is why in some societies suspect-witches easily consent 'to cool their witchcraft' in a neutralizing rite. They are not necessarily responsible. The non-active witch is harmless, but measures have to be taken against the active witch.

Some societies, like the Azande of Sudan and the Nyakyusa of Tanzania, believe that there is a witchcraft organ or some sign in the witch's body which will be revealed by an autopsy after the witch's death. It is not known until the autopsy is performed, and the sign discovered, whether the deceased was a witch or not. If he was, fears are set at rest. Sometimes a witch can be identified exteriorly by some deformity, by red eyes, by ugly features, by his having cut the top teeth first as a baby and so on. Some people, like the Azande, believe that witchcraft emanates from the witch and is visible at night like a light.

We have seen that sorcery is destructive magic. We have also seen that Africans regard as sorcery only that destructive magic which lacks social approval, the illegitimate use of destructive magic. The rest is good, retaliatory magic. In English it is difficult to say that someone has been 'ensorcelled' by a sorcerer. Usually we say 'bewitched', but this suggests that a witch is involved, which is misleading. In many African societies sorcerers are thought to be witches as well, or people refer to both by a single term. Some anthropologists use the word 'wizard' to refer to both sorcerers and witches. This, again, can be misleading since in English usage 'wizard' refers only to a male witch. The word 'witch' in English normally refers to females, but can also be (and is increasingly) used of males. For our purposes, we shall use the word 'witch' of both males and females, and avoid the word 'wizard'.

In many African societies it is felt that only a witch would use destructive magic without social approval (i.e. be a sorcerer). There is therefore a practical equation between witch and sorcerer. Very often no distinction is made between the lethal physical properties of poison and its evil symbolism as bad medicine (sorcery). Poisoning is an activity attributed to witches because it is secret and anonymous, like witchcraft. Sorcery, therefore (especially in the form of poisoning) tends to be attributed to witches.

Although the witch is thought to retaliate against enemies, and motives of revenge and sordid personal gain are commonly attributed to witches, the latter are thought to act vindictively, rejoicing in the evil they do, when they are conscious of it. Witchcraft is by definition irrationally vindictive or inexplicably persistent. When misfortunes are overwhelming, inexplicable, irrational, they are attributed to witchcraft. A parent whose children die one after the other suspects a witch. Sudden illness in children, especially young children who cannot explain their symptoms, is attributed to witchcraft. The farmer who has inexplicable prosperity in a year when everyone else is starving must be a witch. The father who does an irrational thing, such as have incestuous relations with his daughter, is thought to be a witch. Although the revenge of a witch may be considered legitimate, the means taken is never thought to be legitimate : it is excessive and antisocial. Serious, secret crimes, the authors of which are unknown, are also attributed to witches.

Witchcraft accusation takes its origin partly in the psychological need to provide an outlet for repressed hostility, frustration and anxiety. It also provides a way to explain serious misfortunes and to render those who suffer them blameless in the eyes of society. In traditional African societies misfortune is linked with sin, impiety, and the breaking of taboos. Putting the blame on a witch is a method of exculpation. Witchcraft accusation dramatizes and reinforces the norms of social conduct by pointing to contrary antisocial conduct.

Because witchcraft is thought to be a mysterious power which operates inexplicably, an accusation can be made without any need for circumstantial evidence. Moreover, because witchcraft can be exercised unconsciously—in sleep for example—no account need be taken of the suspected witch's denial of guilt, or of any defence he or she may bring against the accusation. All the advantages lie with the accuser. Witchcraft being mysterious, the magical technique of divination through oracles must be used to discover the truth of one's suspicions. Suspicion falls on those who have motive, those who are the enemies of the victim or his family. The pattern of witchcraft accusation, therefore, follows the pattern of tension and conflict in society, and this tends to influence witchcraft beliefs themselves. For example, male bias may influence accusations and beliefs. In most societies it is the men who are the diviners, and men who take the initiative in accusation. They tend to accuse women of witchcraft. Where poisoning is linked in people's minds with witchcraft, women are naturally suspected because they cook the food and often brew the beer. Witchcraft is therefore more often associated with women than with men.

Since witchcraft accusation follows the pattern of tension and conflict in society, someone who believes that he is the victim of witchcraft will suspect as the witch someone else who is in a state of enmity with him, or who is a possible rival. It follows that accusation only takes place between certain categories of people, those with whom it is likely or possible to be at enmity. Enmity is less likely to occur between people of differing social status or of considerable social distance.

It is more likely to occur between equals—for instance, between co-wives in a polygamous family, between neighbours who are not kinsfolk, between rival suitors, between members of a lineage when there is no recognized form of arbitration or working out tensions, between paternal half-brothers, between a barren woman and women who have children of whom she is jealous, and so on. It can be seen, therefore, that behind the imaginary witch-victim link is a real accuser-suspect link. A distinction must be made between them, although both may present a fundamentally similar picture of society and of tensions within society.

With increased urbanization and the development of new types of social relationship it is natural that there should be an increase in insecurity, anxiety and tension. Such tensions are expressed in the traditional way through accusations of witchcraft. Accusations occur between workers competing for the regard of their employers, between rivals for the inheritance of money earned at work, even between political opponents. Modern changes bring about situations for which there are no traditional precedents; tensions arise and witchcraft accusations are likely to occur. There is also an obvious tension between those who adopt new attitudes and those who remain faithful to traditional practices and ways of life. The returning migrant labourer with pockets full of money easily arouses envy. With increased social change, witchcraft belief is strengthened, and finds new and wider areas of application.

African countries often possess a 'witchcraft ordinance' which by law forbids anyone to claim to be a witch, to threaten witchcraft, to accuse anyone of being a witch, or to employ or solicit any person to resort to witchcraft. Such laws have prevented the killing of suspect witches, but they have tended to increase the fear of witchcraft. In traditional African societies witches were cruelly treated, but people felt more secure. Governments now rob people of the power to identify and retaliate against the witch. Witchcraft is more insidious, and public accusations are rare. People who imagine themselves to be the victims of a witch will move house rather than risk a public show-down with the suspect; or they will use secret, retaliatory magic. People say very often that witchcraft has got worse since the laws were passed. The laws are certainly a factor in causing insecurity, and they demonstrate that a direct attack on witchcraft is not likely to be successful.

Why should anyone want to confess to being a witch? A witch is a hated, antisocial person whom people would like to kill. However, it is a fact that people accused of witchcraft do sometimes openly boast of being witches, and take pleasure in uttering threats which inspire terror in those at whom they are directed. Such people belong to social categories which are subordinate and depressed, deviants from the common social pattern, more often women than men, and claiming to be a witch is a peculiar way of enhancing one's status in society, of wielding power over others. In particular, when a person is accused of witchcraft and threatened by social displeasure and ostracism, the most effective way of retaliation may be to claim to be a witch and make people afraid to take any steps against him.

As we have seen, witchcraft belief is of such a nature that it is impossible to establish whether witches exist or not. It remains a belief which reflects ascertainable social situations. This belief may be efficacious in causing illness or even death, in the same way that belief in sorcery can cause these things. It is not important whether witches exist or not. What is important is the sociological reason for belief in witches and the consequences of such belief. Missionaries and expatriates often waste time speculating whether witches exist or not, or reasoning with Africans about their existence or non-existence. Some missionaries, finding it impossible to remove the African's belief in witches, come to believe in them themselves.

Witch-finding is the term used to refer to the process by which an individual resorts to a diviner or to an oracle to discover the identity of a particular witch believed to be afflicting him or his family. We have already dealt with oracles. It need only be repeated here that divination by means of oracles is one of the chief props of witchcraft belief. Witch-eradication, on the other hand, is a community or mass movement which seeks to expose and eradicate all witches in a given area. It operates through public sessions. Absentees from such sessions are branded as witches, a fact which ensures a large attendance. At these sessions people are identified as witches either through a magical technique, or they are denounced for secret faults. Often the accused willingly confess to such faults, and it may be that the leader or diviner has received confidences from people on the subject before the public session. The accused are purified in a rite of purification. Sometimes eradication takes the form of everyone present renouncing witchcraft and sorcery and throwing down their charms and medicines.

Witch eradication is a form of millennarian movement which promises a future golden age when all witches will cease to be. It arises from the fact of social mobility and confusion, and far-reaching social change. People feel that witchcraft is more powerful, and that more efficacious means must be used against it. In fact witch-eradication is self-defeating, since it depends for its effect on a belief in the power of the witches which it sets out to destroy. Sooner or later witchcraft accusations recur. This means that there are waves of eradication started by different leaders succeeding one another.

Witch-eradication rejoins religious millennarian movements which often contain a large element of witch-eradication. The Lumpa Church of Alice Lenshina in Zambia is an example. Religious millennarian movements have the same social background of far-reaching structural change. People experience the new techniques and luxuries of Europe without being able to enjoy them. They envy the domination, self-assurance and effectiveness of those who have these techniques, and they are searching for the moral dignity which they have lost as a result of cultural and social change. The first instinct is to proclaim a return to the old ways. The next phase is to attempt to win the coveted dignity and efficacity by an appeal to traditional ideas. The ghost-dance religions of the Red Indians, the cargo cults of New Guinea, and the prophetic sects and independent Churches of Africa are examples of such movements.

Very often spirit possession plays an important part in these movements. The prophet or charismatic leader who starts the movement often receives a revelation in a trance, or goes into trances. Spirit possession is associated with healing and coming to terms with misfortunes. It is also a therapy rendering the subject relaxed, peaceful, happy and hopeful for a time. Spirit possession is in many ways complementary to witchcraft confession, for by inducing a state of dissociation depressed categories of people enhance their status in society.

It is obviously gravely wrong to accuse someone of witchcraft, to confess to witchcraft, or to encourage anyone to believe he is a witch. But witchcraft beliefs will not be destroyed by a direct attack on them. The only remedy is to deal with the sociological causes, remove tensions, and inculcate a positive approach to misfortune and the problems of evil in the world. Fear of witches must give place to confidence in God and especially in Christ who shared men's sufferings and misfortunes.

Unfortunately, it is not so obvious that witchcraft beliefs are opposed to the fundamental tenets of Christianity. The experience of European Church history shows that it is not enough merely to condemn witchcraft as evil. People's interest must be diverted from the morbid preoccupation with witches. In Europe, traditional witchcraft beliefs received a new lease of life in the later Middle Ages when they were harnessed to ideas of Christian demonology. Witches were alleged to be human servants of the Devil, and even the offspring of devils who had intercourse with human beings (*incubi* and *succubi*). They were even thought to work harm through the sacraments of the Church. Witchcraft was offered as an explanation for misfortunes such as sexual impotence and sterility, and it was closely allied to the notion of heresy as something endangering the constitution of Christian society. Estimates of the number of people burned as witches vary from 200,000 to one million. Most of these people were subjects of psychological disorders, practitioners of sorcery, people who incurred social unpopularity or who were known as evil speakers. It was considered dangerously foolish not to believe in witches, and Pope Innocent VIII actually wrote a bull against witchcraft (*Summis desiderentes affectibus*) in 1484. We should not underestimate the power of witchcraft beliefs, even in modern social conditions.

We shall now consider religious instrumental rituals. Earlier in this chapter it was pointed out that religious rituals are always instrumental in so far as they presuppose that spiritual beings influence events as a result of the action. However, religious rituals are prayers in the form of symbolic action. This means that they share in the nature of prayer by having a spirit of readiness, self-offering and dependence on spiritual beings. Just as outside agents may be thought to obstruct the instrumentality of secular rituals, so the spiritual beings themselves may be thought of as refusing to answer or co-operate or even agree among themselves. Moreover, as in the case of secular rituals, instrumentality may be diminished or destroyed by defects in the performance of the ritual, the spirits being thought to reject an imperfect rite. In any case, we must distinguish genuine religious rituals from transactions made with neutral beings—personified experiences alleged to have an existence of their own, but which are not the objects of a religious attitude.

As we have seen, a distinction is made in Africa between faults which invite retribution by God and the spirits and faults which are thought to bring about physical disorder by themselves. Both classes of fault may be deemed to need a rite of purification to put them right. In the second case the rite is usually magical, in the first it implies an appeal for salvation from the spirit world. However, the form of the rite may be similar. Since the sinner often becomes conscious of his faults in a situation of misfortune or danger of which, he believes, the faults are the cause, the salvation asked for is both salvation from misfortune and salvation from its cause, sin. Moreover, since sin is antisocial as well as offensive to the spirit world, a social reconciliation may be required. The rite may further take on the characteristics of a ritual of redress, and the purification of one man may be the occasion of the purification of the whole group threatened by a collective misfortune. Bishop Raphael Ndingi of Nakuru, Kenya, has made this fact of collective purification in Africa the basis of a plea for the introduction of general confession and absolution into Christian communities. '. . . In some areas, confession of guilt is not only a matter for the individual, but for the whole community. General confession and absolution should be introduced in Africa now.' [11]

Most rituals of purification are obvious symbols of the penitent's desire to be rid of an unclean state and they may consist in washing, sprinkling, or other forms of lustration. They may also take the form of the penitent getting rid of something, letting blood, spitting or blowing out water, throwing away a piece of firewood. The direction in which this is done may be significant.

Towards the sky signifies that salvation comes from God, towards the west signifies getting rid of evil for ever by consigning it to the evil place. Other people may associate themselves with the act by blowing out water together, or throwing another piece of wood on the pile when they pass the spot, and so on. The most explicit way of getting rid of sin is to verbalize it and confess it —'get it off one's chest'. Thus women in childbirth and sick people confess their faults in order to be saved from misfortune. Others may associate themselves with them by confessing in their turn. Anger and ill-will and hidden sins must especially be brought out in this way.

Blessing in Africa is usually an invocation to God or the spirits to grant protection to the person or persons so blessed. It may be symbolized in various ways—for example, by a rite in which water or white flour is blown out of the mouth before the person, or in which the person is anointed or invested with a religious object which he must wear or keep about him.

By analogy, rites of blessing may be applied to God, and the spirits. They, however, are not thought to be in need of protection, but it is a way of offering them praise, reverence and thanksgiving. When material objects are employed in rites applied to God and the spirits, we are really on the threshold of sacrifice, which we shall discuss now. Cursing, the opposite of blessing, has been dealt with in the last chapter in the section on oaths, religious and secular.

The giving and receiving of gifts is a very important symbol of human, inter-personal relationships. The gift represents the giver who puts himself into the hands of the receiver but the receiver, in his turn, is also bound by the gift to repay the giver. This mutuality is even more strongly expressed when the gift is one of food or drink taken together at a feast. Food and drink are bound up with the processes of life itself, and sharing food and drink is one of the most basic and powerful symbols of social life.

It is when these ideas are applied to God and the spirit world that we enter upon the notion of sacrifice and particularly of communion-sacrifice. The essence of sacrifice is that it is a sharing with God and the spirits, as well as with other men. This sharing demands a transformation or spiritualization of the gift shared, a dedication or setting apart, or else a destruction that removes the object once and for all from human use. Forms of transformation are immolation, the killing of animals; libation, the pouring out of drink upon the ground; burning; the rending of cloth; the breaking of utensils; and so on. Judaeo-Christian tradition has always imparted a special significance to immolation or 'bloody sacrifice', but even there, immolation is secondary to oblation.

There has been very great confusion in Christian minds about the nature of idolatry, let alone about the identification of traditional African religious rituals as idolatrous. Theology manuals used to define idolatry as 'giving divine worship to a creature' (*cultum divinum exhibere creaturae*), and this definition depends upon the assumption that there is a rite which can be objectively identified as 'divine worship'. The definition clearly does not envisage a worship which is divine because of the intention of the worshipper to worship the supreme being. If it did, then idolatry would, according to the definition, be psychologically impossible. If a man intends to worship the Creator, he cannot intend also to be worshipping a creature. He must erroneously believe that the creature is God, or a vehicle of God's presence. In fact, as anthropologists have shown, nobody is stupid enough to worship wood as wood, stone as stone, or the sun as a ball of fire. Such things are worshipped as God, or spirits, or else as 'natural sacraments' through which God or the spirits may be approached. Even in the ancient Roman empire emperor-worship was the logical outcome of a belief that a genius or divine creative power dwelt in the head of the Roman state.

The definition therefore implies that a ritual exists which, of its nature, demands that it be directed to the supreme being and not to a creature, and theology manuals establish categories of idolatry, according to the nature of the idolator's intention and belief : true, simulated, perfect and imperfect. The manuals identify this 'divine worship' with sacrifice. Whereas, they say, other ritual actions such as bowing, genuflecting, prostrating, derive their character from the worshipper's intention, this is not true of sacrifice, the character of which is objectively determined. Sacrifice, however, is often given such a general definition in the manuals that the notion of idolatry as defined becomes again impossible. The definition given is 'the offering of a material thing that undergoes some transformation' (*oblatio rei sensibilis cum aliqua ejus immutatione*). This definition can apply to the burning of candles, or the cutting and placing of flowers in a vase, and many other actions which Christians perform out of respect to creatures, saints and holy souls—actions which clearly derive their character from the worshipper's intention. More logically, some authors identify 'divine worship' as 'bloody-sacrifice' because, according to the Jewish tradition, the taking of life in God's name symbolizes the absolute sovereignty of the Creator over living things. However, it is quite incorrect to interpret all forms of immolation in every part of the world in this restricted Jewish sense. Other worshippers give different meanings to immolation and have different intentions when immolating a sacrificial victim.

It is clear, therefore, that the reality of 'idolatry' disappears, if we adhere to the traditional textbook definitions. Clearly also, sacrifice is a broader concept than 'divine worship' and can be applied to creature-spirits without the charge of idolatry.

Finally, it is clear that sacrifice only becomes 'divine worship' when the intention is present to acknowledge the sovereignty of the supreme being.

It is to scripture that we must turn for an understanding of idolatry. In the Bible we find two kinds of texts on the subject : texts which satirize idolators and which actually give the impression that they are stupid enough to bow down before wood and stone, and texts which suggest that idolatry is an attack on the spirituality and autonomy of God. It is to these latter texts that we must look for a true understanding of idolatry. There it transpires that idolatry is not 'giving divine worship to a creature' but 'giving the quality of a creature to the supreme being'. Idolatry is wanting to have 'a God one can carry around' (*deus portatilis*), a God who is tangible, who can be carried into one's battles, in short, a God who can be made to do what one wants. The golden calf is the perfect example of such a god. The real God, however, is a hidden, inscrutable God to whom the worshipper must submit himself in humble dependence. This is true worship of which idolatry is a perversion. The fashioning of a statue or a fetish, or the performance of any ritual, can, on the one hand, be an instrument for real religious worship, or it can, on the other hand, be a magical technique of auto-salvation by which spiritual beings are placed in one's power. Idolatry would make God serve man and not man God. When religious acts become simply a technique for getting what one wants, they are idolatrous. Needless to say, Christians are not immune to the temptation of idolatry understood in this sense. 'You cannot put God in your pocket.'

We shall now deal with the types of sacrifice.[12] We have firstly the sacrifice of first-fruits, sometimes called the sacrifice of purchase. This type of sacrifice is especially common among hunters and people with a more theistic kind of belief. The supreme being, the master of the animals and the other spirits are regarded as the real owners of material things. They are especially regarded as the ultimate controllers of life. One needs their permission to partake of what nature has to offer, especially to take life, to hunt and kill animals. It is therefore necessary to set aside a portion of the hunt, or of the food collected, for the spirit powers. Often this portion is taken from the most vital organs, or consists of the victim's blood which symbolizes the life of the victim. There may be no verbal formula accompanying this rite at all. Much of African ancestor-veneration is a form of first-fruits. Some peoples set aside part of their daily meal before eating as an offering for the ancestors. Other peoples who make the offering less regularly see it nevertheless as 'feeding the ancestors'. This type of oblation is a kind of purchase of the right to make use of material things. It is therefore sometimes called a 'sacrifice of purchase'.

The interested gift oblation, or sacrifice of sacralization, is based more explicitly on the gift and assumes man's right to ownership of property. Gift-giving is an exchange of courtesies and goods between people linked by some inter-personal, social relationship. The giving and receiving of gifts are an external symbol of this relationship, but they also in some way effect or bring about the relationship. In gift-giving there are the three obligations: the obligation to give, the obligation to receive, and the obligation to repay. To refuse to give and to refuse to receive are like a declaration of war, a refusal of friendship and social intercourse. People have some kind of proprietary right over one's possessions so that one is bound to share them. A gift represents the giver; it is a part of him, and even after the gift has been given it is still somehow his. Through the gift, the giver has a hold on the receiver, until he repays it. There is a *do ut des* motivation, but this is not necessarily a contract which must be immediately or equivalently honoured. It sets up a relationship between the giver and receiver, a reciprocity. In Africa you do not buy a man's goods or his services—you buy the man. As a result, gift-giving very easily takes on a magical interpretation : by giving someone a gift, you are putting him in your power. He is powerless to refuse to help you in need.

The idea of an exchange of gifts with the supreme being or with the lineage spirits is an obvious development of human gift-giving. The spirits, after all, are the real owners of the world's wealth and exchange is particularly important with them. However, the gift must be transformed in some way, and rendered spiritual, so that the spirits can receive it. Hence the immolation or transformation of the victim. In the first-fruits offering, the animal was killed for food and shared with the spirits. In the gift-oblation, the animal is made over to the spirits by killing it, or destroying it. It then belongs to the spirits. The victim may be burnt. If the offering is a liquid, it is poured out in libation. If it is something not edible, but nevertheless precious, it may be broken, smashed or torn up. This transformation prevents the victim from being used by the giver or indeed by other human beings. Sometimes, instead of transformation, the victim is simply set apart and not used, but surrounded with taboos. A cow in the herd, or a chicken, may be dedicated to a spirit and carefully preserved in his honour. In this way it is removed from human usage.

Exchange with the supreme being or with spirits means entering into contact with the sacred. The rites resemble a rite of passage. There is an entry into the sacred situation, often a purification. This is followed by the transition, the transformation of both victim and sacrificer. Finally, there is the rite of exit or incorporation, sometimes an ablution or separation from immediate contact with the sacred. In a sacrifice, the place, time and instruments used are all sacred. They are specially chosen and reserved for this exchange with ultimate reality. Above all, the victim and the sacrificer are sacred. The victim is consecrated or sacralized, especially chosen as being pure and unblemished, whole and integral. When the victim is made over to the spirits, it is rendered even more sacred. The sacrificer must observe many taboos since the victim is his gift and represents himself, and he desires to share in the sacred character of the victim. When his gift is sacralized, he, too, is sacralized. The sacred qualities of cleanness, integrity and power pass from the victim to the sacrificer. Sometimes this is made even more explicit by a rite of communion. Communion is not simply sharing a meal with the spirits, as in the first-fruits, but it is receiving spirit-power from something consecrated to them. Usually, the sacrificer cannot consume the best part of his offering, certainly not all of it; this belongs to the spirits. Or it may belong to a sacred class of people—priests, if they exist, or the poor. Alms-giving always partakes of the notion of sacrifice. The poor and the stranger are sacred, and gifts to them are gifts to the spirits.

It is easy to see that sacrifices and offerings of this kind are open to magical abuse. If the gift becomes a mere technique for making the spirits do what the sacrificer wants, and if there is no reverence or submission to them, then the authentic religious character of the act is perverted. But if the supreme being or spirits are the real agents in the process, then there is a true cultic act. African gift-oblations often tend to be magical; for example, they are claimed to be infallible. If the offering is rightly performed then the spirits must do what one has asked.

The piacular sacrifice, or sacrifice of desacralization, is a gift made to the supreme being or to spirits in order to win salvation from sin, the consequences of sin, suffering, or any moral or physical calamity. In this case, the victim is not sacralized but desacralized, the sin or the calamity being imputed to the victim. The evil state of the sacrificer thus passes into the victim —not the sacred state of the victim into the sacrificer. This is symbolized in some way, for example by spreading ashes on the victim's back, or by laying hands on the victim. The victim, usually an animal, is then immolated or driven out into the wilderness with the sins of the sacrificer upon it. In the case of immolation, the evil may be thought to come out of the victim with the blood and soak into the earth. Unless this or a similar distinction is made, it is clear that there can be no rite of communion. When such distinctions are made, several types of sacrifice may be found to overlap in a single rite.

For the sake of completeness, it should be mentioned that the immolation of victims may accompany secular rituals of fertility or the seasons. These are 'mystic celebrations' which should not be confused with sacrifices. Since the rites concern the life, death and rebirth of nature, the killing of an animal may be one of them. The hero or archetype of the myth charter for the rites may actually be worshipped as a god or spirit and this spirit may be deemed to have entered into the animal. The killing and eating of the god-animal is a theurgy, or magical science, by which the life of the god passes into the initiates. Such ritual characterized the mystery-cults of the ancient Mediterranean area.

Religious action		Religious object of action	
A *Yes*	B *No*	C *Yes*	D *No*
Attitude of worship or dependence	Magic Commerce Medicine Communication	God Ancestors Some nature spirits	Personalized extrapolations Personalized illnesses, etc. Spiritual beings who are not normally worshipped.

Fig. 4

As we have seen, we do not have to condemn sacrifices simply because they are sacrifices; indeed these and other religious rituals of African tradition may be perfectly compatible with Christian faith and practice. In order to judge the morality of a religious ritual it is necessary, first of all, to see whether it is religious. Two facts must be verified : that the action is religious, and that the object of the action is religious—namely a spiritual being having religious reality.

In the above table AC would be true worship, BD would be a secular activity, BC would probably be idolatry, AD would probably be psychologically impossible.

A religious act must, then, be judged as being in harmony with Christian belief and practice, contrary to it, or else superfluous (Fig. 5).

Christians have sometimes condemned ancestor veneration for a number of reasons. As we have seen, to pray to and make offering to ancestors, knowing them to be creatures of God and mediators, cannot be idolatry. In so far as they are thought to act independently of the Creator, this is contrary to faith. In fact, African traditional religions do not teach this. It is, nevertheless, superstitious to believe that the souls of the dead possess the living and give them powers of divination.

We know that we can intercede on behalf of the departed, but opinion differs as to whether they can hear our prayers and pray for us. St Thomas Aquinas thought the state of purification

Contrary = sin against faith ('heresy')	**Superfluous** = sin against religion ('superstition')
Directly denies or opposes something the Church believes or does	Believes or does something which the Church does not believe or do. (Gravity depends on how far it puts you outside current Church belief or practice.)

Fig. 5

precluded any possibility of their helping others. There is another opinion, however, that it is extremely probable that they can do so. After all, souls undergoing purification are impeccable. Moreover, the purification that takes place in death is not measurable in terms of human time. The departed may also be regarded as having received their glorification. In any case, God is perfectly able to give them the ability to communicate with, and intercede for, us. It is notable that scriptural texts from 2 Maccabees in support of prayer for the departed are balanced by texts in the same book which show the departed praying for the living.

It may be true that ancestor veneration undermines the sense of good and evil if all ancestors, even those who gave a bad public example, are regarded as 'good' after death. This tendency, however, may be counterbalanced by the doctrine of purification in death. Secondly, if immortality is bound up with physical fecundity this may also undermine the idea of moral retribution. This could be counterbalanced with the idea of 'spiritual fecundity'. The imputation of human failings—jealousy, revenge, and so on—to the departed is also incompatible with the idea of 'dying in Christ'.

It is alleged that ancestor veneration tends to make men judge the departed in the worldly terms of their usefulness or harmfulness to the living. But even in Christianity the fate of those who die is believed to be bound up with the deeds by which they are remembered on earth, and fantasies about 'another world' are not helpful. The kingdom of heaven is already amongst us and our world is on the point of being re-created.

Practically speaking, interest in the causes of new saints and the cult of local patron saints is confined to Europe and North America, particularly the Mediterranean area of Europe. Moreover, canonization is a long and expensive process, requiring considerable outlay for making the cause known to a wide number of people, and depending on the faithful for reports of cures and favours. In this situation, it is not surprising if Africans should get the impression that Europeans become saints while Africans do not. Even the canonization of the African Martyrs of Uganda took 70 years and the cause was promoted from and within Europe and North America to a great extent. In view of this, the suggestion is made that a purified version of African ancestor veneration might be a better vehicle for African devotion and moral example than the attempt to find and promote the causes of a few individuals of heroic sanctity.

In the next chapter we shall deal with African social institutions, especially with the family and its supporting institutions.

Notes

1 cf. Lévi-Strauss, C, *The Savage Mind*, London 1966.
2 Much of this chapter, particularly the analysis of ritual, is taken from the works of V W Turner, *Schism and Continuity in an African Society*, Manchester 1957; *The Drums of Affliction*, Oxford 1968; and *The Ritual Process*, London 1969.
3 Wilson, M, 'Nyakayusa Ritual and Symbolism', *American Anthropologist*, Vol 56, no 2, 1954, p. 241.
4 The term 'rites of passage' was coined by A van Gennep in his classic work on ritual, *The Rites of Passage*, London 1969.
5 Goetz, J and Bergounioux, F M, *Prehistoric and Primitive Religions*, London 1965, p. 117.

[6] These twinning rates were quoted by Dr J Owen in physical anthropology lectures at Oxford University in 1964.

[7] Lévi-Strauss, C, 'The Sorcerer and his Magic', in *Structural Anthropology*, London 1968, p. 168.

[8] The idea of this graph comes from a lecture by F B Welbourn on 'The Christian Impact on East Africa', given at Rhodes House, Oxford, 2 June 1967. It has been slightly adapted here.

[9] cf. Goodman, F, 'Phonetic Analysis of Glossolalia in Four Cultural Settings', *Journal for the Scientific Study of Religion*, Vol VIII, no 2, 1969, pp. 227–39.

[10] Evans-Pritchard, E E Y, *Witchcraft, Oracles and Magic among the Azande*, Oxford 1937, pp. 300 ff.

[11] Ndingi, Bishop Raphael S, 'To Take Deep Roots: Thoughts on Making the Church truly African', *Worldmission*, Vol 22, no 4, Winter 1971–2, p. 19.

[12] The section on sacrifice owes much to Mauss, M, *The Gift*, London 1950; and Hubert, H and Mauss, M, *Sacrifice: its Nature and Function*, London 1964.

Suggested further reading

Beattie, J H M and Middleton, J (eds), *Spirit Mediumship and Society in Africa*, London 1969.

Bergounioux, F M and Goetz, J, *Prehistoric and Primitive Religions*, London 1965.

Crawford, J R, *Witchcraft and Sorcery in Rhodesia*, London 1967.

Evans-Pritchard, E E Y, *Witchcraft, Oracles and Magic among the Azande*, Oxford 1937.

Field, M J, *The Search for Security*, London 1960.

Hertz, R, *Death and the Right Hand*, London 1960.

Hubert, H and Mauss, M, *Sacrifice: its Nature and Function*, London 1964.

Lévi-Strauss, C, *The Savage Mind*, London 1966; *Structural Anthropology*, London 1968.

Marwick, M G, *Sorcery in its Social Setting*, London 1965.

Mauss, M, *The Gift*, London 1950.

Turner, V W, *Schism and Continuity in an African Society*, Manchester 1957; *The Drums of Affliction*, Oxford 1968; *The Ritual Process*, London 1969.

6 Christianizing African Marriage and Family Life

EARLY evolutionists used to imagine that there was a time when there were no such things as marriage and family life, but a 'state of general promiscuity'. Such an idea is nonsense. Every human society in the world has always had some form of marriage and some method of classifying people socially on the basis of blood relationship and relationship through marriage. However, there were and are local differences. 'Family' is not a single, fixed concept the whole world over. The English word derives from the Latin word for 'household' (*familia*), and the principles according to which relatives group themselves into households vary from one culture to another. One thing, however, is certain : social organization according to kinship and marriage is basic to every human society.

As Christians we often say we believe that 'the family is the cell of society'. There is a serious danger of confusion here. The biological analogy might make us think that all societies are composed of distinct, interacting cells which are continually producing new cells. This may be the picture of the family in Europe and the Western world but it is not the concept of the family in Africa. The question is : How far is the ideal of Christian marriage as revealed by God separable from its Western form, and how far can it be expressed in and through the African form?

This question is important because there is a general impression in Church circles that Christian marriage and the Christian family are failures in Africa. Marriages in church are not keeping pace proportionately with baptisms, and even customary and civil marriage is neglected. The family does not exert the desired Christian influence, and Christian allegiance is still very much of an individual affair. There is an increasing feeling that Christian marriage has not been effectively proclaimed in Africa, and that marriage preparation has not hitherto taken African social facts and institutions sufficiently into account.

Kinship is a relationship founded, or presumed to be founded, on a biological or blood relationship, known as consanguinity, and which implies descent from a common ancestor. It is not the same thing as the biological relationship itself. After all, at the biological level, animals have mothers, fathers, brothers, sisters, uncles, aunts and cousins, but they do not have kinship. Biological relationship does not generate true social relationship among animals. Affinity is a social relationship generated by marriage, between one partner and the other partner's consanguines, and even—in Africa—between the consanguines of both partners. Those who marry a man's consanguines are called affines.

In the Western world it is assumed that biological relationships are identical with kinship and affinity as social phenomena. Careful distinctions are made about foster-children, step-parenthood and so on. The legal fiction must be known as such. In Africa legal fictions abound, but they receive scant attention because, ultimately, what matters are the social relationships and not the blood or affinal relationships on which they are based. Some examples of legal fictions in African kinship are the levirate, ghost marriage, and woman marriage.

When a man dies without children, his brother may take his widow and raise up children to the dead man, who are reckoned as his legal children and who inherit from him and not from their biological father. This is known as the levirate, and is to be distinguished from widow inheritance which is not a legal fiction. In widow inheritance, a man inherits and marries his brother's widow or widows. The children inherit from their biological father in this case and not from the deceased.

When a man dies without children, his ghost may be married to a woman who becomes his legal wife but who is made pregnant by another man. The latter is not the legal father of his biological children who inherit from the deceased. This custom of ghost marriage is practised by the Nuer of Sudan and is a device for ensuring the continuance of the family group.

Another such device is that of woman marriage. When there are no males to inherit, a woman may be treated fictitiously as a man and is married to another woman. The 'wife' is made pregnant by a man who is not regarded as the legal father of the children born to the 'wife'. The legal 'father' is the first woman. She may, nevertheless, have liaisons with other men and be a biological mother. This custom is practised, for example, among the Simbiti people of Tanzania and is reported as occurring in the Yagba district of Kware State, Nigeria. For the sake of completeness and to avoid confusion, we should also mention the sororate, although it is not a fiction. This is the practice that, when a woman fails to bear children to her husband, the latter has the right to demand one of her sisters as a replacement or as a secondary wife under the terms of the bridewealth.

Every language in the world has its own kinship terminology, but there are big differences between them because they refer to different systems. There is, therefore, always a danger when translating terms from one language into another language. However, in order to make a comparison of systems some terminology must be used. Anthropologists customarily employ combinations of eight terms:

(1)   F = Father
(2)   M = Mother
(3)   B = Brother
(4)   Z = Sister (C = Child is also sometimes used for S and Z)
(5)   S = Son
(6)   D = Daughter
(7)   H = Husband
(8)   W = Wife

Thus the man called in English 'grandfather' can be FF or MF, and the woman called in English 'aunt' can be FZ or MZ. Terminologies vary for the same relationships in different systems. Thus in Dutch, the word *neef* refers to all the following relationships: BS, ZS, FBS, MZS, FZS, MBS. In French, two terms are used: *neveu* for BS and ZS, and *cousin* for all the rest. The Nyamwezi and Tanzania, however, employ four terms: *mwana* for BS, *mwipa* for ZS, *nkulu* for FBS and MZS and *myala* for FZS and MBS. Finally, the Zulu of South Africa use a different combination of four terms for the same relationships : *mtana* for BS and ZS, *mfo* for FBS, *ukanina* for MZS, and *Mzala* for FZS and MBS.

There are four main constitutive principles of the family : prohibition of incest, descent, residence and domination.[1] Incest prohibition means, at least, that primary kin do not mate with one another. Primary kin are parents, children, brothers, sisters, uncles, nieces, aunts, nephews. In every society in the world there are prohibitions against sexual intercourse between such categories. The prohibition usually also extends to other categories as well, especially in Africa where a very large kin-group is affected. It is only in very special ritual, and often royal, situations that the rule may be broken, and then the breaking of the rule serves to underline it even more. For example, the Mukama of Bunyoro in Uganda was allowed to have sexual relations with his half-sisters to show that he was exceptional and above ordinary prohibitions. Various reasons for incest prohibition have been put forward.

Firstly, there is the biological reason. It is alleged that inbreeding is harmful and will either result in madness or in the extinction of the family. Doctors and physical anthropologists are not in agreement on this point.[2] The majority probably thinks that inbreeding is harmful in the long run. However, the rate of producing homozygosis (identical genes in each member of the chromosome pair) is slow. Parent/offspring and brother/sister mating would have to be continued in each generation for seventeen generations before the same amount of homozygosis occurred as is produced by six generations in plants that fertilize themselves. The chances of a recessive condition being intensified and becoming dominant are also not as great as are imagined. For parent/offspring and brother/sister mating the chances are 50/50. For grandparent/grandchild mating and aunt-uncle/nephew-niece mating, the chances are 1 in 4; and for first cousin mating 1 in 8. It should be remembered that good characteristics can also be intensified by inbreeding. The biological reason is probably not the most important one because in many African family systems, although one is forbidden to marry first cousins on one side of the family, one may—or even must—marry a first cousin on the other side of the family.

Some psychologists maintain that human beings have a

universal instinctive horror of incest. If this were the case, one might ask : Why then are laws necessary to prohibit incest, and why are these laws sometimes broken? Another group of psychologists (Freudians) maintain that human beings have an innate, unconscious desire to commit incest. This desire is repressed in response to inherited guilt-feelings. However, the theory does not explain why the categories of forbidden relatives vary so much from one society to another.

Some social anthropologists assert that incest prohibitions are prompted by the fear of confusing social relationships. Certain relationships—for example, mother-son, father-daughter are incompatible, it is said, with sexual relations, because the latter would confuse the status of the partners and their children. However, we are not only speaking of marriage here, so presumably the partners would retain their status after the incestuous act. But even if we were considering the marrying of relatives, the partners would exchange one status for another— for instance, father or daughter for husband or wife—and the relationships would not be confused. The children would still belong to the father or mother according to the principle of descent.

The sanctions and motivations which uphold the prohibition do not, on the whole, explain why the prohibitions exist. The reasons are often mystical—vengeance of God or spirits, sign of witchcraft, and so on—and they are also often contradictory. Sometimes they are the biological reasons cited above.

Demographic factors suggest that in early societies of hunter-gatherers and shifting cultivators surviving children were so widely spaced in the family as to render parent-offspring and brother-sister mating practically impossible. When a boy came of age, his mother might be beyond the age for childbearing and his sister might already be taken in marriage. Father-daughter incest would remain the most likely form. And it is probably the most common form today as the experience of social workers testifies.

On the other hand, incest prohibition would reinforce the law of exogamy (marrying non-relatives). Exogamy has the distinct social advantage of making people forge wide networks of alliance between different family and clan groups. The chief means of treaty-making is the marriage alliance, and marriage is the cement of society. Exogamy applies to a wider grouping (the clan) than incest prohibition (which applies to the lineage or extended family). Incest prohibition stands, therefore, at the very heart of social relationships and is the foundation of the social structure. For this reason it is surrounded by the highest sanctions.

Marriage is forbidden by the Church between all lineal ascendants and descendants (father, mother, grandfather, grandmother, son, daughter, grandson, granddaughter and so on), between collateral relatives to the third degree inclusive (brother, sister, first cousin, second cousin, aunt and uncle and all descendants of a common ancestor to the third generation), and between a man and his wife's consanguines and a woman and her husband's consanguines—that is to say, all lineal ascendants and descendants of the spouse, and collateral relatives to the second degree (brother, sister, first cousin, aunt, uncle).

The Church is conscious of being able to dispense from the prohibition in all cases save that of lineal consanguine ascendants and descendants in contiguous generations, and brothers and sisters. She regards this as a divine law which cannot be dispensed from. The prohibition of marriage between grandparents and grandchildren and other lineal ascendants and descendants is thought to be probably a divine prohibition. All other prohibitions are regarded as ecclesiastical laws which can be dispensed from. Ecclesiastical prohibitions have been inherited by the Church from the Jewish, Roman and Teutonic societies, and have been constantly modified.

Moral theology textbooks base the prohibitions on three reasons: the biological reason (already discussed), the need to restrain carnal desire within family groups, and the need to foster mutual love and friendship between human groups. The last reason rejoins the anthropological conclusion drawn above.

One hopes that the Church's law on incest prohibition could incorporate the social norms of African societies, instead of applying a foreign set of forbidden categories to the African family and then dispensing from this foreign prohibition gratuitously imposed. The prohibitions founded on divine law are always part of the African prohibitions. Ecclesiastical prohibitions could surely be decided on a regional basis in accordance with local African custom?

161

The second constitutive principle of the family is residence. Residence is either virilocal (the wife resides with her husband and his family), or uxorilocal (the husband resides with his wife and her family). Sometimes it is neo-local : the husband and wife found a home in a new place, away from the families of either.

The third constitutive principle is descent. Children may inherit property and status (for example, clan affiliation) from the family of one parent (lineal). It may be the father's family (patrilineal), the mother's family (matrilineal) or it may be from both families (bi-lineal; this is usually a situation in which a matrilineal system is being converted into a patrilineal one).

Finally, there is the principle of domination which means, in practice, male domination. The fact that men impregnate women and women bear the children means that the male enjoys more freedom than the female. After mating he can go his own way, hunt, fight, engage in politics and so forth, while the woman has a long period of childbearing and child-raising in front of her. For dietary reasons there are long periods of lactation in Africa. This means that a woman becomes pregnant again soon after the weaning of her last child. She therefore has to specialize in child-raising, and this activity absorbs most, if not all, of her energy and time. This fact, perhaps more than any other, underlies the social separation of the sexes and the sex-division of labour in Africa. In Africa there is traditionally no place for the single woman, or even the single man. The woman cannot ultimately refuse marriage, and there is no tendency for men to flee from women and create their own bachelor society. In Europe, bachelordom is associated with the phenomenon of the domineering mother; in Africa, children receive specialized training in the life and duties of their sex from the parent of their sex. The result is the formation of two complementary, but separate, social worlds. The male world, as is perhaps the case in every culture, dominates, and there is no possibility for the woman to enter it. In the Western world, the social division of the sexes has broken down. Technological progress has created jobs which can be equally well filled by men and women. Voluntary abstention, contraceptives, greater longevity of women, the ability to lead a single life, educational and economic opportunity, mean that the woman is freer of the traditional task of child-raising and can challenge the man on his own terrain. In Africa, such forces are beginning to affect the urban élite, but male domination is not yet effectively challenged.

Domination by women in the family system is practically non-existent in Africa, except possibly in the few cases where women may become political rulers. In these cases the exception applies only to the Queen's own immediate family. Even in matrilineal systems it is the males of the group who dominate and not the females. Children inherit, not from their mother, but from their mother's brother, via the mother. True matriarchy therefore does not exist, and one should avoid using the term when one really means matriliny. Patriarchy comprises patriliny, ownership of property by the patrilineage, virilocality and the rule of men. True matriarchy would consist of matriliny, ownership of property by the matrilineage, uroxilocality and the rule of women.

There are basically two main types of family, the nuclear (or cognatic) and the extended (or lineal). In the nuclear family, the family unit is reduced basically to the husband, wife and their children. Marriage symbolism centres on the 'going away' of the bridal pair, and on the wedding gifts to furnish the new home. Marriage is essentially neolocal and families are seen as a network of interconnected, but autonomous, nuclei. There is no rule of descent; inheritance may pass through either or both the paternal and maternal lines. There is no theoretical limit to kinship; it is simply identified with unlimited biological relationships. This is known as the 'cognatic situation'. The cognatic situation is easily recognized from the terminology. There is no distinction between descendants of one's father's or mother's group in one's own generation. Parallel cousins (FBC and MZC) go by the same terms as cross cousins (FZC and MBC). There is also often one term for MB and FB, and for FZ and MZ; and also for BC and ZC.

Cognatic situations are not unknown in Africa but, although there is no fixed rule of descent, family groupings are larger than the nuclear family. An example are the Lozi of the Upper Zambezi. In general, the nuclear family is a Western phenomenon.

In the extended (lineal) family, the family unit (or lineage group) consists of a fairly large number of people related by descent in one line from a living, or recently dead, common ancestor. When the group is separated by more than one generation from a deceased common ancestor, the family or lineage group tends to split into two or more groups. The extended family is seen as extending both in space and time. Ideally it continues forever. Even though the numerous lineage groups that come into existence over the years do not know the precise biological relationship of one to the other, they are conscious of being one clan. Clan names, clan totems and clan food avoidances are inherited lineally within the extended family. Rules of exogamy also apply to the clan. However, in most African societies the clan is too large and too dispersed to operate as a corporate entity. It is the extended family or lineage group within the clan that operates in this way. Commonly the extended family is composed of numerous nuclear households but, unlike the nuclear families of the West, they do not operate independently of each other. There is a spirit and a practice of co-responsibility and corporate action among them, even when they are not resident in one place. There are two main types of lineal or extended family; patrilineal and matrilineal.

Patriliny is the family situation in which status and property are inherited through the paternal line. It is almost always associated with virilocality. Women leave their paternal group and reside with the paternal group of their husbands. The terminology, consequently, reflects a distinction between family ('patrikin') and relatives who are not 'family' ('matrikin' and others). There is therefore always a distinction between parallel cousins and cross-cousins : FBC, MZC and FZC, MBC. There may also be a phenomenon known as the Omaha terminology, by which a man may refer to all the members of his mother's family collectively as 'mothers', and to all the children of the family into which his FZ has married as 'children'. This is called 'group-reference'. Patriliny is sometimes called 'agnatic descent', and is the most common type of extended family in Africa. Examples are the Ganda of Uganda, the Nuer of Sudan, the Nyamwezi of Tanzania and the Ibo of Nigera.

Matriliny is the situation in which status and property are inherited through the maternal line. It is associated with uxori-locality, but there is always tension between the husband and males of his own maternal group on the one hand and the males of his wife's maternal group on the other. This often means that uxorilocality is temporary and may be converted into virilocality. If this does not happen, the marriage may become unstable. It is impossible from the terminology alone to discover whether one is dealing with a patrilineal or a matrilineal system. Matriliny makes the same distinction between parallel cousins and cross-cousins. However, there is also sometimes the presence of the so-called 'Crow' terminology which is the reverse of Omaha. According to this terminology, a man may refer to all the members of his father's family collectively as 'fathers', and to all the children of the families into which males of his own group have married as 'children'.

Matriliny is associated with a weak authority structure, with strong intergroup relations, and with open recruitment of talent for leadership.[3] Matriliny is flexible and able to adapt to economic expansion, as for example among the Ashanti of Ghana. In the subsistence farming situation, matriliny may well be at a disadvantage because it does not need, and does not produce, sophisticated forms of collaboration. Matriliny is not necessarily doomed to disappear. Examples of matrilineal systems are the Sagara of Tanzania, the Congo of Zaire, the Ashanti of Ghana, the Bemba of Zambia, and the Chewa of Malawi. All other systems, including the bi-lineal and the various forms of wife-exchange and cross-cousin marriage, are based on either a patrilineal or matrilineal foundation.

Let us now examine the supporting institutions of the extended family. We have already noticed the phenomenon of 'group reference' by which members of one extended family may refer to members of another extended family by a single term. Within the family itself classificatory terms help to express the cohesion of the group. Thus F and FB go by the same term; so do M and MZ; also B and FBS (and MZS). Distinctions between parallel and cross-cousins, between BS and ZS, and between siblings of the same sex and siblings of the opposite sex (sibling=brother/sister, not specified) point the difference between members, or potential members, of different families. The terminological merging of alternate generations, which may be accompanied by a belief in some form of nominal reincarnation, is another means of expressing the solidarity of the extended family.

Marriage, more than any other institution, helps to bring out the solidarity of the family groups involved. Marriage in Africa is communitarian, the alliance between groups. In bride-service, one family makes the sacrifice of an able-bodied man; the other enjoys his services. In bridewealth, one group co-operates to help one of its members obtain a wife to bear children to the group; while the other group shares out the profits of the payment received for the bride. These institutions, rightly practised, strengthen the extended family.

As culture advances in a pre-technical society, women cease to be the only 'scarce goods' exchanged between family groups. When agriculture replaces hunting and gathering as the economy, then services and goods are exchanged instead of women. Women can be evaluated and their value in goods and services demanded. Where small-scale, shifting agriculture is practised and where stock-rearing is virtually unknown, services are in demand more than goods. The group taking the bride is obliged to loan an able-bodied man to the bride's family for a specified period and to perform specific tasks for them. This is called bride-service. Since, in most cases, it is the bridegroom himself who has to work for his bride, it is sometimes known as groom-service. The bridegroom may have to reside from between three to four years at the homestead of his parents-in-law, building his own house and carrying loads for his father-in-law, cultivating, building, and carrying his axe and gourd when out hunting, or when travelling. The marriage is not regarded as fully stable until the period of service is complete and the man and his wife have moved back to the village of the husband's lineage.

Marriage is primarily the alliance between two potentially hostile kin-groups. This alliance is symbolized by an exchange of goods, but the exchange is not necessarily part of the marriage contract. Furthermore, the goods exchanged are not exclusively real wealth or personal property. They are courtesies, ritual, entertainments, dances, feasts, sometimes even the loan of one or more children to help in the homestead or on the farm. The bride brings with her her own dowry or endowment of personal possessions, her pots and pans, and utensils for preparing food and looking after the house. These possessions, together with the cost of the feast provided by the bride's family, may be the equivalent of the gifts brought by the groom. In 'town' or 'church' marriages, the extended family co-operates to meet the expenses of the reception, wedding-dress, photographers, band, and so on.

The bridewealth system is so widespread in Africa as to be regarded a typical feature of African marriage.

It is best to keep to the term *bridewealth*. This was decided as the result of a long controversy between anthropologists over the years from 1929 to 1931, during which other terms like *dowry, dower, bride-price, earnest, settlement, indemnity* were rejected as misleading or unsuitable. Evans-Pritchard settled the matter once for all by coining the word *bridewealth*.[4] The advantage of this term is that it admits of many interpretations and corresponds to the established term *bloodwealth*, the compensation paid for injury or death.

Is bridewealth a bride-price? Some people have thought so. According to them it is real buying and selling. The woman is regarded as a chattel, and the ownership of the woman is bought from one kin-group by the other for goods or money. The object would be to sell the women members of one's family. A high price would be demanded, so that an individual would be forced to borrow from his relatives on mortgage terms. The result would be marriage by co-emption or collective buying. The bride would be jointly owned by all the members of the family who contributed. Needless to say such an explanation is not true. If it were, then cupidity would rule the marriage contract, the rich would be favoured by the system, and women would be held in a state of slavery.

There is not necessarily any economic *quid pro quo*. Sometimes the bridewealth is so small that it could not represent the real value of a woman. The Zulu of South Africa, for instance, give only a hoe or a basket of maize, a purely symbolic payment. Moreover, some tribes distinguish between marriage proper and simply exchanging a girl for cattle in order to have a concubine. This is the case among the Nuer of Sudan. Above all, there is no question of the woman's ownership being transferred. She remains almost always a member of her own lineage or clan after the marriage. She returns to her own people often at the slightest provocation and rules exist for dissolving the marriage on various pretexts, at which time the bridewealth is returned either in whole or in part. The woman's status may be inferior, but she is not a chattel, she is definitely a person with rights. This is especially true in matrilineal societies, where there is no question of her leaving her matriclan or lineage, and often no question of leaving her family homestead or village for that of her husband.

It would be truer to say that a price is paid for the right of exclusive sexual access to the woman by the husband and for the power to bequeath status and property to the children of the union as to the descendants of the husband's group. However, an economic aspect does enter into bridewealth payments. They are often assessed taking into account the beauty and capabilities of the woman, and the status, wealth and material prospects of the husband. Bridewealth payment also depends on the availability of movable goods, stock, valuables, money. As long as stock (cattle, goats, etc.) is the currency used, and as long as bridewealth is distributed widely in the family of the bride, then the amount demanded will be limited. When a money economy is introduced, and where domestic animals are bred for sale, then cupidity is aroused, and fathers of girls are induced to traffic in them as a source of income to themselves. This is the degeneration of the institution.

It also remains true that the bride is regarded as a source of wealth. She will bear children to the group into which she marries, and some of these will be girls who will also receive bridewealth. We can say, therefore, that brides have an economic value, but that bridewealth does not have the function of a price, except in societies where the institution has degenerated.

One of the important effects of the payment of bridewealth is that the children born of the union belong not to their mother's lineage but to the lineage of their father in a patrilineal society. The payment of bridewealth legitimates the children within the father's lineage, even if it does not transfer their mother to that lineage. In the case of adultery, or even institutionalized concubinage, the children would not pass over to the husband by a later payment. When a marriage breaks up, in many African societies the bridewealth is returned if the woman is still marriageable but, depending on the number of children born to her husband's lineage, the amount returned will be diminished. Thus among the Nuer, if there is one child of the marriage, the more distant kinsmen have to return their share of the bridewealth but not the parents, but nothing is returned if there is more than one child. If the bridewealth were not returned according to custom in the case of one or no children, then the husband would claim as his own any children born subsequently to his former wife.

In view of this, some anthropologists have talked about 'child-wealth' rather than 'bridewealth', but this is not an adequate description of the institution. As we shall see, there are other effects of bridewealth besides the legitimation of children, important though the latter may be.

The word 'dowry' is frequently used by uninformed people to refer to the institution of bridewealth. It means the same thing as dower, endowment or settlement. It is a highly misleading word, since dowry refers primarily to the endowment of goods or money which either or both of the partners bring with them to the marriage from their own family. As we have seen, even when the bridewealth is paid for a bride she will still be endowed with a *trousseau* of personal clothes and her own cooking and house utensils. In Europe, the dowry has often amounted to considerable possessions or payments made over to the family of the bridegroom by the bride's family, even though the bride leaves her own family group more completely than in Africa. Besides being the reverse of bridewealth, this dowry serves a totally different purpose. The motive behind it is to maintain the prestige of the bride's family. The young husband will not at first be able to maintain his bride according to her accustomed level of living in their new home. The dowry is there to help him keep her at the proper level, so that the prestige of her family will not suffer. It serves a neolocal type of marriage. Bridewealth is definitely not dowry.

The anthropologist, Emile Torday, suggested the term 'earnest' because he saw bridewealth chiefly as a method of sealing the contract of marriage. It also has the character of a public thank-offering by the bridegroom's family for the benefit received, namely the bride in her role as mother of her husband's children. Bridewealth is concrete evidence of the legal bond of marriage—a kind of marriage certificate. Because of it, the husband's rights can be publicly acknowledged in, say, a paternity or adultery case. Once again, this is a perfectly true, but inadequate, aspect of bridewealth.

Bridewealth is widely distributed among the members of the bride's family. It does not remain only in the hands of the parents of the bride. Among the Nuer of Sudan, Evans-Pritchard recorded that usually forty head of cattle were paid in bride-wealth. Of these, twenty went to the family of the bride's father, and twenty to the family of the bride's mother. Again, to take another principle of division, twenty cows went to the father, mother and immediate lineage of the bride, and ten cows to the more distant relatives on either side. Many persons are involved therefore in the benefit of bridewealth. Brothers are able to obtain wives with the bridewealth paid for their own sisters, and the bride's mother's family receive their portion as a kind of delayed instalment of the bridewealth paid for the bride's mother when she was herself a bride. In itself it is not easy to get back all this wealth if the marriage is dissolved. However, one should not exaggerate the stabilizing influence of bridewealth. In all societies which practise the payment of bridewealth, there are rules for the return of bridewealth in the event of divorce. What stabilizes the marriage is the climate of society about the propriety of divorce, or about the loyalty due between husbands and wives.

Radcliffe-Brown built up his notion of bridewealth on the idea of indemnity. Bridewealth, according to this theory, is compensation paid to a lineage for the loss of a member, or at least for the loss of rights over the children she bears. In this it is comparable to bloodwealth paid by one lineage when one of its members had purposely or accidentally killed a member of another lineage. If the woman had stayed in her own lineage and had had children out of wedlock these children would belong to her own lineage. The notion of compensation is definitely present in bridewealth, even though one must not exaggerate the 'loss of a woman' idea too much. After all, the woman does not leave her lineage completely. Compensation, however, is explicit when bridewealth includes, for example, payment to the parents of the bride for her up-bringing, or even, as among the Nyamwezi of Tanzania, the replacement of the cloth in which the bride was carried as a baby. In societies where bloodwealth is paid, the reason behind it is to acquire wealth by means of which a woman can be obtained as wife for a member of the family and so raise up a child to replace the one killed. So bridewealth and bloodwealth are connected.

If bridewealth is compensation to the living, it is also often compensation to the spirits of dead members of the lineage. Sometimes a cow or animal paid in bridewealth is earmarked for, or consecrated to, one of the ancestors. In this way the spirits of the family are also witnesses to the marriage and to the continuance of their line. Part of the bridewealth is therefore used for an offering of this kind.

We have already seen that when the economic aspect of bridewealth is emphasized, it becomes an intolerable burden. This is especially true where a money economy is being introduced. In, say, a cattle-herding economy, cattle do not have a conventional or even a merely nutritive value. They are looked upon as especially a 'bridewealth currency'. Cattle are the means by which adjustments are made between conjugal and affinal relationship, the means by which links are formed through exogamy. Cattle are the means through which the great blessing of children is brought into a lineage. They are therefore very much cherished and desired, but not for ordinary economic exchange. The same was true of ceremonial goods in the past, such as shells, beads, ornamental hoes, and other valuables. When ordinary money is introduced, then it has a value outside the institution of marriage, and high bridewealth is demanded out of the cupidity of an individual and not primarily for the reasons given above. Marriage is delayed because of prohibitive bridewealth, and marriages are even broken as a result of the cupidity of parents wishing to sell their daughters more profitably. It is also possible for a man to play the marriage market and to leave his home area where bridewealth is high in order to look for a girl in another area where bridewealth is low. Bridewealth may be a typical institution in African marriage but its spread in areas where it was previously unknown is undoubtedly due to the introduction of a money economy. High bridewealth, although flattering to the bride, may also lead to the husband treating her as a chattel.

Bridewealth at the present time is certainly subject to abuse, and the cause of a great many evils. Its original character was as a process of real or symbolic gift exchange, legalizing a marriage, legitimizing the children of the union, indemnifying the bride's family, stabilizing the marriage to a limited extent, and propitiating the lineage spirits. Above all, it had the function of giving cohesion to the extended family. Today the abuse of bridewealth actually operates against the extended family, disrupting it, and serving the profit of individuals within the family at the expense of others.

What alternatives are there?

Abolition seems impossible. Bridewealth cannot be abolished by legislation when economic and social pressures are keeping it alive. Attempts, both by Church and government, to abolish bridewealth have met with no success.

Reduction is not likely to be more successful than abolition. Church and government in many countries have tried to impose a ceiling limit on bridewealth, but people continue to demand and to pay unofficially more than the legal limit.

Toleration is really the policy of drift, in the hope that bridewealth will disappear of its own accord, as economic changes take place. Although it is true that in some areas which enjoy a relatively high standard of living bridewealth has diminished in importance, in many of these areas bridewealth has escalated. It does not look as if the custom is simply going to die out. Some people hope to remedy the situation by revaluing the institution of bridewealth and restoring it to its original purpose through public re-education. If this is a realistic attempt to deal with the problem and not an attempt to put the clock back, then there may be something to be said for it. In general, one might recommend a public re-education for restoration and reduction through the joint action of Church and State, and the abandonment of legal measures of control.

Another practice which operates in support of the extended family is polygamy. We shall use the term 'polygamy' to refer to the union of a man with two or more wives (technically called 'polygyny') and not to refer to the union of a woman with several husbands (technically called 'polyandry')—a situation which is almost non-existent in Africa. Polygamy is widespread in Africa and takes two main forms: simultaneous polygamy and successive polygamy. We speak of simultaneous polygamy where the polygamist is living with (or visiting by rotation) and supporting two or more wives and their children. Simultaneous polygamy is really only possible in patrilineal families where the woman passes more completely under the authority of the husband and the members of his patrilineage. Successive polygamy is the case where the polygamist takes another wife without specifically

repudiating his previous wife or wives. He nevertheless, for all
practical purposes, deserts her/them, and he is not living with or
supporting her/them.

It is completely wrong to imagine that male lust or male
selfishness is the principal motive behind polygamy. Men could
satisfy their lust through adulterous unions and concubinage.
Polygamy serves the prosperity and growth of the extended
family and provides status and support for women in societies
where they have no vocation other than marriage and the bearing of children to their husband's lineage.

Polygamy ensures the bearing of many children so that status
and property may be passed on and the family may become
more extended in space and time. It follows that men in matrilineal societies have no incentive to practise polygamy, since the
children do not belong to them and do not inherit their status
and property.

Polygamy is the kindest solution in the case of the first wife's
infertility. She would prefer to remain a first wife, rather than
be divorced and be faced with the impossible task of finding
another husband.

Polygamy ensures wealth and prestige in agricultural communities. Having many wives is a sign of the wealth needed to
pay bridewealth for them, but it is also a source of wealth, since
the wives work in raising food, and the daughters they bear will
bring in bridewealth in their turn. Because of the prestige of
polygamy it was often forbidden for a commoner to have more
wives than the chief or king.

Polygamy, in its forms of the levirate and widow inheritance,
is a way of catering for unsupported women in a society which
does not tolerate the independent woman, and for ensuring the
continuance of the line. It is sometimes said that polygamy caters
for the surplus women in society, ensuring that all are married.
It is true that there is a surplus of women in most societies. This
is because, although more male babies are born than female,
more females survive into adulthood and old age. However, at
maturity the sex ratio is held by physical anthropologists to be
equal. This means that polygamy works disadvantageously
against young men, because the older men take the young
women as junior wives before the young men can afford
to marry. One effect may be to force down the age for

marriage and another may be to delay marriage for many young men.

In societies where sexual intercourse is forbidden during the period of lactation, polygamy helps to satisfy the needs of the husband. Children are often not weaned until their second year, and another pregnancy would mean that the mother has to breast-feed two babies at once. There is often also an unfounded fear that a pregnancy will cause the milk to fail.

Africans have long recognized the disruptive potentialities of the polygamous family. Tension between co-wives is catered for by custom and the attempt is made to minimize them by careful grading of the wives, careful delimiting of their rights and duties, separating their huts and even their homesteads. Generally speaking, it is impossible to avoid partiality on the part of the husband and jealousy on the part of the wives.

Simultaneous polygamy is increasingly difficult to maintain as the cost of living and the cost of bridewealth rise. In urban and industrial communities it is difficult to provide housing for polygamous households, and the increased mobility of families also militates against polygamy. However, it still has its uses when an urban worker depends for his food on a farm or farms cultivated on the outskirts of the town by a secondary wife or wives. In general, however, simultaneous polygamy gives place to successive polygamy and the transient character of many town populations favours the casual union rather than marriage. It has been estimated that in Eastern Africa polygamists are not more than 35% of the total of married men and not less than 25%.[5]

Polygamy creates a family of considerable legal complexity, lessens the educative influence of the father over his children, and is irreconcilable with the educational and economic emancipation of women and the desire of women to play independent roles in society. In addition, polygamy is well known to be one of the most fruitful causes of desertion and divorce. The taking of a second wife may, in many instances, alienate the first wife to this extent, Polygamy, therefore, was recognized in traditional societies to have as many social disadvantages as advantages.

There is no doubt that monogamy, and not polygamy, is the Christian ideal. The Yahwist creation account presents us with the picture of a 'paradise lost' in which '. . . a man leaves his father and mother and joins himself to his wife and they become one body' (Gen 2:24). This sentence suggests that the ideal is one of a profoundly personal union with some degree of autonomy. The dominating ideals of the rest of the Old Testament, however, resemble those of traditional Africa : polygamy serving the needs of fertility. It is only with the prophets that the ideal of the couple and the personalization of marriage reappears in the images of God the bridegroom, faithful to Jerusalem the 'wife of his youth'. In this image of God's redemptive love, Samaria and the other cities are no longer rival suitors or co-wives, but 'daughters' of Jerusalem, the unique bride of Yahweh. In the books of Judith, Job and Tobit we also find that fidelity to one partner is the ideal. This is especially clear in the Book of Tobit, in the prayer of Tobit and Sarah on their wedding night, which makes explicit reference to the marriage of paradise. In spite of this developing ideal of monogamy in the Old Testament, Jewish social practice and legislation lagged far behind.

The New Testament nowhere deals explicitly with the question of polygamy, but the principle of indissolubility is very strongly affirmed both by Christ himself and by St Paul. In Mt 19:9 and the parallel synoptic texts, Christ appears to place himself above both the schools of Hillel and Shammai. The first taught that one could divorce a wife for any reason; the second, only for the infidelity of the wife. Christ appeals once more to the paradise ideal of 'one body' and in the Marcan text stresses the absolute equality of husband and wife. The husband must not divorce the wife, nor the wife the husband. Clearly, equality is bound up with indissolubility, and monogamy is necessarily implied by equality. St Paul (Eph 5:21–33) also appeals to the 'one body' text when he makes human marriage the symbol and instrument of God's love for his bride, the Church. This symbolism is analagous to the passages of the Old Testament prophets, already cited, a fact which seems to undermine the argument (of Fr Hillman) that it is compatible with the idea of polygamous marriage.[6] It is clearly going too far to ascribe the Church's teaching on monogamy merely to the monogamous tradition of ancient Greece and Rome and pre-Christian Europe.

The Catholic Church has always strongly affirmed the practice of monogamy and has never considered modifying her teaching on the point. Nevertheless, it was only when missions were begun in Asia and Africa that the Church was effectively confronted with polygamy as a pastoral problem.

Promoting the ideal of Christian monogamy is one thing, admitting to baptism those who have contracted polygamous unions in good faith is another. The Christian Churches have debated this question on a number of occasions; in general, and especially in the case of the Catholic Church, they have maintained a strict policy. The Pauline Privilege and its various canonical extensions have made it easy for a polygamist, desirous of being converted, to repudiate all but one of the partners, but this causes great hardship to those repudiated and it does not cater for all the possible situations, especially where one or more of the wives desire baptism.

The possibilities are :

husband alone desires baptism;
husband and all wives desire baptism;
husband and one wife desire baptism;
husband and some wives desire baptism;
one wife alone desires baptism;
some wives desire baptism but not the husband;
all wives desire baptism but not the husband.

Unless polygamists are admitted to baptism they are faced with the cruel choice of either breaking up the family or waiting as catechumens for a death-bed baptism. Sometimes a special category is created by the Church for polygamists who cannot be baptized. They may be called 'hearers', for example, and their names entered as such in the parish registers. What justification, it may be asked, is there for keeping such people on the fringe of the Church when they are the victims of circumstances not of their own making?

Some theologians today are proposing, as an unofficial opinion, that people who have divorced and remarried in defiance of the Church's teaching, and who are now confronted with the fact and the obligations of the second marriage, should be allowed to have access to the sacraments. *A fortiori*, therefore, polygamists who have broken no law and who have obligations towards their wives and their families should also be allowed to have access to the sacraments. Such an opinion is reinforced by the argument of modern theologians that natural marriage is not inherently indissoluble or monogamous. There would be no question of the polygamist receiving the sacrament of marriage in this case, but his polygamous, natural marriage would be tolerated by force of circumstances.

It can be argued against the baptism of polygamists that it would be a scandal to Christians who have already accepted the stricter ruling. That a disparity of practice would result in the Church between areas where polygamy is a problem and areas where it is not a problem. That the Christian community would not be united, or even viable, if it contained both polygamist Christians and Christians for whom polygamy was prohibited because of their prior baptism. That it would seriously prejudice the inculcation of the monogamous ideal among African Christians, and that it places too much stress on baptism as an attribute of individuals. Baptism is the sign of incorporation of the individual into a community. The good of the community and the climate of opinion in the community must therefore be taken into consideration. If the baptism of polygamists is to take place, all these objections must be taken into account.

Avoidance is another supporting institution of the extended family. The relationship between families linked by marriage is one of potential rivalry and hostility. Even after marriage has taken place there may be an undercurrent of mistrust between affines. This wears off as children are born to the union and the affines of one generation become the consanguines of the next. This developing relationship is expressed in Africa by customs of avoidance and these customs reinforce the solidarity of the groups involved in the relationship. Sometimes rules of avoidance apply only to the immediate categories of parents-in-law and children-in-law, but quite often it extends to all classificatory affines. The rules apply particularly to the cross-sexual relationships of mother-in-law/son-in-law and father-in-law/daughter-in-law. The relationship is mutual, but not equal; the younger generation must 'fear', respect and obey the older generation of in-laws. At the beginning of marriage the relationship is strict and formal; later it is relaxed. When a family receives a visit from its affines, it has special obligations of hospitality and service towards them—for example, the cooking of special food. The relationship is called 'avoidance' because it frequently entails avoiding something connected with the persons one respects, avoiding using their name, avoiding coming face to face with them on a path, avoiding their village, their homestead and especially their sleeping quarters. In both virilocal and uxorilocal marriage the onus of respect lies on the partner who is a stranger to the locality. Avoidance rules are some of the strictest in traditional Africa and often carry severe social sanctions if they are broken.

Joking relationships express the ambivalent position of cross-cousins. They are affines to each other, but they belong to the first generation of blood descendants from a common ancestor. The relationship is therefore one of part-familiarity, part-antagonism. It is an attitude of mutual disrespect in which each is entitled to invade the privacy of the other and make bawdy jokes at his or her expense, often involving obscenity and buffoonery. The person jibed at has to take it all in good part and cannot show anger or retaliate with blows. The joking relationship is often the model for the pairing of tribes which have enjoyed sustained social or economic contact, and for the amalgamation of the smaller ethnic groups in towns.

We must now ask the very vital question: Is the Christian 'personalist' view of marriage and family life compatible with the African extended family? It has often, until now, been assumed that it is not—that it was necessary to substitute the European nuclear type of family for the lineal or extended type. The Church gave the impression that it wanted to pit the 'nuclear' couple against the extended family as a whole, and that couples must be prepared for marriage in isolation from it. Against this it can be said that the extended family embodies an ideal of co-operation and mutual service which goes beyond the limits of the nuclear family and involves a relatively large community of kinsfolk. This is a step in the direction of Christ's teaching that the Christian's love must transcend his family circle and be all-embracing. Parental roles are shared among different members of the family. For example, in a patrilineal family the father has jural authority while the mother's brother shows manly or parental affection. The grandparents on the other hand show indulgence to children when young. This sharing of roles reduces psychological tension in the family. There is also co-responsibility for the upbringing of the child and several members of the family contribute to it. The child is thus educated by a community for membership of a community; and the different facets of social life are catered for in the education.

On the other hand, there is a danger that the rights and duties of parents and spouses may be usurped by other members of the family and that pressure may be put on them. Co-responsibility in the extended family should not go so far as to rob the actual parents and spouses of their ultimate responsibility towards each other and towards their children. If other members of the extended family (for example grandparents) play a greater role in the upbringing of the children than their own parents, this may have a bad effect on the children themselves.

Marriage is a covenant between persons for the bringing into existence of other persons. This is the foundation of its seriousness and, ultimately, of its indissolubility. Personality is achieved through relationships, not through the selfishness of individualism, nor through the constraint of collectivism. The friendship between husband and wife must be open-ended—that is, it must open firstly onto their relationship with their children, then onto their relationship with their kinsfolk, and finally onto their relationships with society at large. The experience of community has an important part to play in the development of personality, and ultimately the nuclear family must function within the wider social group, the community of the extended family and the wider community. In doing this it contributes to personalization. Ultimately, however, it must be acknowledged that community has no existence apart from that of its members, that partners to a marriage are points of contact between family-communities and points of contact which are not passive instruments of the family-community. The rights that others in the family have over them derive from the partners themselves, who exercise their freedom within the community.

It is frequently asserted that priests and missionaries have felt more at home in patrilineal societies than in matrilineal ones in so far as the proclamation of Christian marriage is concerned. These authors may be correct in saying that missionaries imagine patriliny to be more compatible with Christian teaching than matriliny, but this assumption of the missionaries is a mistaken one. Indeed, Pope Paul VI in his letter to Africa (*Africae Terrrarum*, 1967, no 11) goes so far as to say :

'*Patria potestas* is profoundly respected even by the African societies which are governed by matriarchy [sic]. There, although the ownership of goods and the social status of children follow from the mother's family, the father's moral authority in the household remains undiminished.'

It is a fact that many of the pastoral marriage problems facing missionaries are associated, not with matriliny, but with patriliny, as in the cases of polygamy and bridewealth. In some way matrilineal families appear more Christian than patrilineal ones. This is particularly so where equality in marriage is concerned. In patrilineal societies it is usually accepted that a husband can beat his wife, and this practice becomes more prevalent the younger the bride. The wife is 'a child', to be treated like a child. In matrilineal societies, however, the right to chastise a wife is carefully circumscribed by law and custom, and the wife's male relatives are on hand to avenge her. The woman's position is more honourable and there is more respect for her in matrilineal societies.

It is, perhaps, the fact that the matrilineal father does not bequeath status or property to his own children that is disquieting to the Westerner, but this is not to say that he does not fulfil the role of a Christian father. We have already noted the Pope's favourable attitude to the matrilineal father. Bishop Peter K Sarpong of Kumasi goes even further. He sees the patrilineal father as domineering, masterful, inspiring reverential fear in his sons, and jealous of their service. Patrilineal sons are potential rivals of their fathers, whose status and property they inherit. In matriliny the tension between father and son is reduced, and there is a genuine and deep affection. The love that exists between a matrilineal father and his son is love for the sake of the one being loved—a love which does not ask or expect a return. The bishop concludes: '. . . It appears that the concept of fatherhood in a matrilineal society approaches the idea of the fatherhood of God more than the patrilineal fatherhood does.' [7]

We have already noticed that matriliny favours the open recruitment of talent for leadership. Given opportunities, the individual can assert himself more freely in a matrilineal society than in a patrilineal one. Although the interrelations of patrilineal and matrilineal systems in a single nation may be a source of difficulty, and although matriliny, in some areas at least, appears to be losing ground, it does not seem to be in conflict with Christian ideals—rather the reverse. The Church has the duty to help African matrilineals achieve the Christian ideal within their own family system, for as long as this system remains viable.

We shall now examine the institution of marriage itself. Whatever differences we may discern between African marriage and European or Western marriage, both institutions are called marriage and are susceptible of a single, general definition. We may define marriage, therefore, as a special and intimate union between man and woman as such, (i) of which mating is an essential expression, in some sense sacred, (ii) which establishes enforceable rights between the partners, (iii) which marks a change of status for them and their parents, (iv) which results in a special status for the children, higher than for the children of extra-marital unions, (v) which generates relationships of consanguinity and affinity, and (vi) which implies that other forms of mating or intimacy are deviant or preparatory to marriage. Notwithstanding this joint definition, we may tabulate the differences of emphasis in Western and African marriage as follows :

Western marriage	*African marriage*
orientated to nuclear family	orientated to lineal family
contractual	dynamic
synchronic	diachronic
consent of partners	consent of partners as members of a group
absolute stability from the beginning	growing stability
children not essential to survival of the union	children essential to the union, otherwise dissolution or polygamy
more equality between partners	less equality between partners
ideal (if not practice) of indissolubility	recognition of solubility
ideal of monogamy	polygamy sometimes the ideal; usually permitted

extra-marital unions create problems for children of such unions.	children of extra-marital unions catered for by customary law

The two most important differences concern (a) the manner in which marriage begins, and (b) whether or not the ability to bear children is a *sine qua non*.

Western legislation concerning marriage derives from Roman-Dutch law, which in turn derives from the Church's Canon Law. There is nothing in revelation about the manner of beginning a marriage and, while the New Testament is silent about child-lessness, the Old Testament is clearly in accord with African ideas. However, the Church's law itself derives from a mixture of ancient Roman law and Germanic law.

The ancient Romans held that the exchange of consent between the partners concerning almost every aspect of married life constituted the beginning of marriage. The ancient Germans held that the first act of marital intercourse between bride and bridegroom constituted the beginning of marriage. The canonists put the two ideas together, thereby narrowing down the object of consent. Marriage began through an exchange of consent concerning marital intercourse and became finally indissoluble after the first act of marital intercourse. Consequently, impotence (inability to perform the marital act) was an impediment, and sterility (inability to have children) was not considered an impediment. Although for a long time the Church taught that the procreation of children was the 'primary' end of marriage, marriage was still held to exist if this end was frustrated by sterility. Today, the terms 'primary' and 'secondary' are no longer used, but the Second Vatican Council still teaches that '. . . marriage persists as a whole manner and communion of life, and maintains its value and indissolubility, even when off-spring are lacking—despite, rather often, the very intense desire of the couple' (*Gaudium et Spes*, no 50). It is implied that children are a gift from God, and that the Christian marriage ideal includes a readiness to accept barrenness as well as fruit-fulness from his hands.

In Church Law marriage begins with an exchange of consent (ratification). This exchange constitutes the beginning of a marriage and the beginning of the mutual administration of the sacrament of matrimony. However, it can be annulled in certain cases when it is not followed by marital intercourse (consummation).

In theory, the Christian sacrament of matrimony operates in and through the ordinary human institution of marriage in whatever form society celebrates it and lives it. In practice, Church law represents the human traditions of ancient Rome and Germany and joins forces with the legal forms of the Western world which derive from the same traditions. Church marriage in Africa has not made use of the existing African institution of marriage and the two forms continue to exist alongside each other. This is very largely due to the fact that Africans see marriage as beginning in a totally different way. For them, the beginning of marriage is a growing process, comparable to the liminal phase in a rite of passage (diachronic). This process may be interrupted if the partners prove incompatible, or if essential conditions, such as fertility, appear not to be present. This interruption is not regarded as divorce or dissolution, but simply as the recognition that a marriage has been attempted but has not come into existence.

In general, priests in Africa have to deal with marriage on three levels: the preparation of a young Christian couple for marriage; the settling of a marriage case before the baptism of one or both partners; and the regularizing of the irregular marriage situation of a baptized couple. The first case is comparatively rare; the second case presents few inherent problems in view of the extensive concessions made in favour of the faith; the third case is, perhaps, becoming more and more frequent and constitutes a serious pastoral problem. The 'irregular' situation may be a customary marriage or it may be extra-marital union altogether. In either case, the reasons for not being married in Church may include the following: fear of an indissoluble marriage when compatibility (due to deficiencies in marriage preparation) is uncertain; inability to meet the expenses of a lavish church wedding; or ignorance/difficulty of complying with civil and Church legislation.

The solution of the second case depends on a thorough marriage catechesis which emphasizes marriage and married life and plays down the wedding aspect. The solution of the third

183

case depends on the legislators. Marriage is made for man, not man for marriage. The 'extraordinary form' of Christian marriage remains a dead letter—that is, the right of two Christians to marry when there is a danger of death or when a competent pastor cannot be summoned without great inconvenience and this state of affairs lasts for more than a month (Canon 1098). It is the first case which is the main concern of pastors.

The reasons why a couple may even evade customary marriage are additional to the above. They may include inability to pay bridewealth, evasion of bride-service, or the choice of a partner not acceptable to the extended family—particularly in the case of inter-tribal unions.

What solutions are there for the problem of the trial marriage? A medical check-up before marriage is an antecedent precaution to ensure that the partners to the marriage are not sterile. At the moment in Africa it is hardly practicable as part of the normal preparation for every marriage. Also, it is not foolproof; apart from the sterility of the partners as individuals, sterility may be a mutual phenomenon.

The unofficial opinion has already been cited that persons in irregular marriage situations might, under certain circumstances, be admitted to the sacraments. A trial marriage might be comparable to the remarriage of divorced persons, but the admission of such persons to the sacraments would not, of course, affect their marriage situation.

An interesting proposal is the suggestion that the Church might accept the idea of growing stability in African marriage.[8] Becoming 'one body', according to this view, is not the mere biological fact of consummation, but the growth in a union of lives and in inter-personal communication and maturity. 'One body' refers to the marriage covenant of persons, not to the marital act only. Indissolubility is linked to sacramentality, and the sacrament is the marriage ideal. According to this view, it might be possible to lay down the conditions under which a natural, valid marriage could 'grow up' into a sacramental, indissoluble marriage, it being understood that the process could be interrupted.

The Church already accepts marriage under condition in the case of doubtful potency. It is lawful to contract, and to attempt to consummate, such a marriage. The partners act on the assumption that potency is present and that the marriage will be declared null if it is not. This is nothing more nor less than marriage under condition. A suggestion has been made that fertility be made a condition of marriage; the marriage would then be contracted under the condition that the partners had everything necessary for the procreation of children.[9] A reasonable limit would then be set to test their fertility. If, when this limit was reached, they were still sterile, the marriage would be discovered to be null beyond any doubt and they could still contract a new marriage, if they wished, knowing themselves to be sterile. On the other hand, they could separate and remarry. The disadvantage of this (and the previous suggestion) is that it is unfair to the woman. Although male sterility is as common as, if not more common than, female sterility, the reproach of sterility rests mainly on the woman in Africa and it would be difficult for her to remarry.

Another suggestion argues that Christians can live in natural marriage with the blessing of the Church—for example, in the case of the Christian convert living happily in a natural marriage with his/her non-Christian partner. Would it not be possible for Christians to contract a valid, natural marriage, without envisaging the sacrament immediately?[10] Indissolubility being a special disposition from God, natural marriage would not appear to be necessarily indissoluble. The natural marriage of Christians could, therefore, be dissolved or converted into sacramental marriage.

The Church has the power to constitute diriment impediments. A further suggestion would be that the Church should declare sterility a diriment impediment, rendering a marriage null when infertility was ascertained beyond reasonable doubt.[11] The disadvantage here would be that sterile people who wanted to marry would presumably not be allowed to do so.

Up until now we have been dealing with trial marriages. What solutions are proposed for Christian marriages which have broken down because of childlessness? There are two principal solutions. After the marriage has broken up, it could be established that, because of the prevailing African mentality that a childless marriage is either null or soluble, a Christian marriage had never been ratified. The actual break-up of the union would

185

constitute evidence of this. Some canonists recommend this course. Secondly, some theologians are proposing that the Church could recognize that a validly contracted and consummated marriage had ceased to exist, and was *de facto* impossible to reconstitute. The subsequent union, they urge, should be recognized as a genuine, marital situation, which could be converted into Christian marriage.

The first solution is already acted upon by some canonists; the second solution is still in the realm of speculation. Neither solution deals with the problem at its roots. The question remains whether pastors have the right to force people to contract an indissoluble marriage, with the possible prospect of childlessness, when they are not ready for it. Those who are aware of the absolute character of Christian marriage prefer not to be married in Church; this goes to show that those who do agree to be married in Church may not be fully aware of the character of Church marriage. Moreover, what right have we to condemn the customary marriage of Christians who are in good faith when we have no solution to offer?

We must now consider socialization and the preparation for marriage.[12] By socialization we mean the inculcation of attitudes and skills that are necessary for individuals, especially children, to play roles in society. Socialization can consist of deliberate initiatory processes and pressures, or it can consist of more or less voluntary practices undertaken by the initiates themselves. These practices are known as peer-group activities, although they may be adult-inspired or adult-led. Formal education in school is part of the socialization process; so also is the preparation of youth for marriage.

We have already noted that the co-responsibility of the extended family introduces the child to a wider community, and this education by relatives who are not immediate parents has many of the advantages that are claimed for the boarding-school. Different relatives take care of different levels and emphases in the child's education. Thus the grandparents and older kinsfolk inculcate the deeper moral values, and introduce the child to basic religious beliefs and practices. The children's own parents, on the other hand, introduce them to the practical duties of their sex in the home and outside. Father's sister and mother's brother, in patrilineal societies, take an affectionate interest in the child's moral, personal and social education and may play special roles at moments of crisis.

The fact that children spend lengthy periods in the households of relatives who are not their parents holds several advantages. The frustrations which young people feel as they gradually lose the freedom of childhood are not experienced with their parents with whom they are emotionally involved. The foster-parents are less squeamish about applying discipline to these children than they are to their own children. The children receive more attention than if they remained at home, because their own parents intervene when they are badly treated, whereas at home there is no one to intervene for them. Such children appear to have more success in life, both because of the advantages in the education itself and because of the personal links established. The system caters for the care of children in crisis. It may also be related to apprenticeship for the learning of special skills. Finally, on the part of those who foster children, it helps to compensate for childlessness in cases where it occurs.

Great emphasis is placed upon obedience and submissiveness in traditional society. Traditional education is essentially group-orientated, and stress is laid on outside behaviour and on correct social relationships, courtesies, rights and duties. Responsibility is given early, in errands outside the home, in caring for flocks and herds, collecting firewood, in looking after younger brothers and sisters, and in deputizing for parents in communal projects. African children are creative, making their own toys and inventing their own games. There are usually plenty of opportunities for play-activities with other children, though boys are generally freer for these than girls.

Values pervasive to the whole society are taught. For instance, in Buganda (Uganda) it is the supreme value of the Kabaka (king), epitome of paternal authority; in Uchagga (Tanzania) the dominant value is that of Kibo (Mt Kilimanjaro), symbol of precedence within a hierarchy of relationships. In Buganda, the young huntsman is taught to kill animals 'in the name of the Kabaka'; in Uchagga, the youth is taught to allow seniors to pass on the side of the mountain. Clan values, names, places, histories, relationships are also taught.[13]

The child learns by imitation, through work. Punishment, even for light offences, is likely to be corporal punishment. Discipline is harsh and generates fear. Elder brothers have authority over younger brothers and sisters. Children are taught to obey and serve all adults in the community. Rewards are few, and there may be few strong motives for the child to give of his best.

The modern school also places emphasis on obedience, but stresses self-reliance and intellectual achievements more than traditional education. Sociability is important, but is more concerned with 'being a nice person' than readiness to serve and obey outsiders. Educated parents expect children to be more useful in the home than outside it. Punishments tend more often to be non-physical; rewards are given. Frankness, honesty, trust are inculcated. At school the child learns the value of private ownership and is taught self-control. Great importance is attached to hygiene. The school may be less obviously a preparation for membership of the society the child knows; it is in itself another world, and opens onto a larger scale of society that is hardly yet in being.

It is sometimes said that there is no such thing as adolescence, or the problem of adolescence, in Africa, and that the African child passes immediately into adulthood. This is fantasy. Adolescence is a psychological phenomenon that applies to all human beings during the period of development, and in early physical maturity all human beings tend to react in comparable ways. However, the stimuli which provoke these reactions vary considerably from one society to another; and different societies may be either more or less successful in coping institutionally with adolescent reactions. We are concerned here with the social pressures and solutions.

In some societies male adolescence is necessarily long because the practice of polygamy means that girl adolescents are being married off to elders all the time. The rate of development of the boys, therefore, has to be slowed down; also their chagrin at losing girls to whom they are attached and their general rebelliousness against adults has to be canalized for the good of society as a whole. The young men are separated from society and given a special role as warriors, the chief's pages or bodyguard, or a kind of police. Their condition is a 'liminal' one. They may have to live and eat in the bush and sleep in special communal huts. Their morality is collective, and all are rebuked for the faults of one. 'Sweethearting' is an important value, but it must be public and not private sweethearting. Private love-making would lead to pregnancies and 'spoil' the girls as brides. The peer-group is conservative, but autonomous. It is not anonymous, which is to say that it fulfils a recognized social role and corresponds to recognized social expectations. Some classic examples are 'moran-hood' among the Masai, Samburu and other pastoral peoples of Kenya; the ancient court page system of Buganda; the initiation into the palace associations of Benin Kingdom in Nigeria. These are either dead, dying or, while remaining a value, are losing their explicit social purpose.

Modern attempts are made to bring such peer-groups into existence, but these are more obviously adult-inspired and adult-led, as in the case of modern political youth associations and national service. The strength of the traditional peer-groups lay in the fact that they combined social control with autonomy.

When urban teenagers form their own voluntary peer-groups, they tend to be radical and explicitly anti-adult. The fact that in towns such associations are anonymous means that there is a strong temptation to delinquency, though it should not be imagined that members of such associations are always delinquents. A typical example is provided by the street gangs of Kinshasa in Zaire. Membership is inter-tribal and follows the patterns of residence, the streets. The gangs have an antipathy to school and schoolboys. Schoolboys rarely belong to them. Members are in and out of temporary jobs. The gang's head-quarters is in a disused building or in a bar. They subscribe to a youth culture which is an African adaptation of the values, symbols, and figures of cinema and advertising. The teenagers are known collectively as 'Indoubils', a corruption of Indian or Hindu and 'Bill' from Buffalo Bill. The names of gangs include Indians, Cowboys, Russians, Americans. There is even a secret teenage language known as 'Kindoubil'.[14]

The overriding value in the gangs is personal superiority brought about by sexual success. One must be physically attractive, have a clear skin, and wear smart clothes. Drug-taking (Indian hemp) is practised in order to increase sexual desire and dull the discomfort of hunger. Advertising is interpreted absolutely literally, and magical efficacity is attributed to cosmetics. The gang-member must have several girl-friends. Casual relationships are formed, and there is some co-habitation for short periods.

189

Marriage is alien and heterosexual relationships are based on mutual attraction and character. Girls consent to be lovers of gang-members as an insurance against molestation.

Today, when older methods of controlling adolescence socially are breaking down, and when the social order is being transformed, the youth culture tends to be detached from the social system, even anti-social. Although teenagers may not be as well organized as the street gangs of Kinshasa, they tend to subscribe to the common value of sexual success, and considerable pressure is exerted on the individual to conform.

The school being another world altogether, scholars form their own associations. Such associations are less radical and more open to adult influence, but they may subscribe to a similar youth culture and develop their own language. Sex and alcohol are major attractions. Groups tend to serve a specific purpose within the school: entertainment, hobbies, music, dancing, etc.

Many African tribes used to have puberty rituals for either or both sexes. A few tribes still preserve them, some as a formality without meaning, some as still serving a dominant social value. Puberty initiation is a rite of passage to maturity and adulthood, though this does not mean that adolescence is bypassed. It is also a school in which the initiates are taught specific group-values and specific roles such as those of husband, wife, father, mother, educator. It is a life-crisis ritual, enabling the child to accept the demands that society is about to make on him or her. It is usually collective, the sexes being segregated. Initiates are separated from normal society, normal duties and relationships.

Initiation at puberty includes sex instruction and at least the remote preparation for marriage, but this does not mean that it is wholly orientated towards sex. Even the genital mutilation which is often the high point of the ritual does not necessarily have any direct connection with marriage. Sometimes the operation is not on the sex-organs but on another part of the body (for example, the six cuts on the forehead of the Nuer of Sudan) and the importance of the operation may be in the sublimation of pain. At the very least, the cutting or marking of the body signifies a changed personality. When it refers to the sublimation of pain, accent is put on the courage of the candidate and his ability to bear pain without flinching or crying. There may be other trials, punishments and physical hardships which serve the same purpose : the support of the male adolescent culture to which youths subscribe in the years before marriage. On the other hand, crying may be permitted during the operation. In this case, genital mutilation serves the purpose of marriage. The operation may be thought to ensure greater satisfaction from sexual intercourse. For boys it is usually circumcision. For girls it is either clitoridectomy, labiadectomy, or the enlargement of the labia (which is thought to give the husband greater satisfaction).

Before initiation, children do not officially know the secrets of the ritual and they are not allowed to ask about them. However, they may not be ignorant of sex. The close living of the African homestead, the behaviour of joking-partners and the instances of formal obscenity—not to mention informal, spontaneous obscenity—may already have taught them about sex. Sex-play between children may even be condoned as being without social significance. At initiation more is taught about the physical side of sex than about the moral or psychological side. Fertility and virility are the main values that are stressed. Some physiological theories which are wholly erroneous may be taught about lactation, conception and difficult childbirths, and divorce may be recommended as the only solution for childlessness or incompatibility. Contraceptive practices, some of them magical, may also be taught as a precaution in cases of infidelity.

After initiation parents continue to answer the adolescents' questions, and to offer advice and warnings about love-making, courtship and the duties of married life. If virginity is highly prized in a society, steps will be taken to safeguard it, but with the breakdown of social control, especially the social separation of the sexes, virginity at the time of marriage is less and less common.

While courtship in Africa is perfectly adequate in a situation where the first years of marriage constitute a trial, it is not at all adequate for a marriage that is expected to be absolute and indissoluble from the beginning. Although young people increasingly esteem the value of romantic love and personal attraction, they do not tend to marry the sweethearts of their adolescence. Customs such as exogamy often demand that young men look for a bride in a neighbourhood at some distance from home.

191

Ideally, romantic love flowers within the marriage, and although parental pressure is decreasing young people do not necessarily enjoy complete freedom of choice. In general, the boy is freer than the girl. For the girl, marriage is more important than whom one marries, and the great desire of the girl is to get a husband who will be faithful to her. Custom often demands that courting be carried out by a 'go-between'. This is very necessary when exogamy requires the boy to look far afield for a bride. The go-between advises the prospective bridegroom and conducts most of the negotiations. The boy may first become interested in a girl because of hearsay, or because a relative or friend deliberately draws his attention to her. In his own acquaintance he may look for superficial qualities and skills that emphasize male superiority: obedience, skill at cooking, good reputation, a lower standard of education than himself, and so on. Courtship customs make it difficult for boys and girls to really get to know one another, but outside the village and in more educated circles it is possible to break free of custom and to choose a partner whom one really knows. It must be said that there is no real desire on the part of the boy for equality in marriage.

Financial problems, also, are likely to protract or obstruct courtship—especially the problem of bridewealth and the problem of wedding expenses.

The following is a summary of a true account by a young Tanzanian of his frustrations in his attempt to get married:

1964 *First engagement*: the boy pays 200/- of a 400/- bridewealth, but the girl's father demands that he commence bride-service. This would take him away from his job and he would be unable to pay the rest of the bridewealth. He refuses, and the money is returned to the boy's father. 30/- is paid to the go-between and the boy's father spends 70/-. 100/- are left.

1965 *Second engagement*: the boy's father recommends a girl in another village. He contrives to see her and finds out she has a good reputation and is a Catholic catechumen. He pays the 100/- he already has towards the 500/- bridewealth. Later he brings it up to 350/-. The wedding is fixed and the boy buys provisions for the wedding. The girl goes off to a funeral in a distant village and never returns. The wedding is called off and 150/- are returned. The boy loses the rest: 200/-.

1967 *Third engagement*: the boy courts another girl and agrees to pay 300/- bridewealth. After paying only 150/- he decides to co-habit with the girl, whose parents live elsewhere. The girl's aunt denounces the boy and there is a neighbourhood court hearing. The 150/- are kept by the girl's family as a fine for deflowering the girl, and the girl is taken away.

1969 *Fourth engagement*: the boy goes to a faraway village and courts a Catholic catechumen. She agrees to the engagement and 150/- is paid. However, when the catechist comes to write down the engagement it is discovered that she is a classificatory matrilateral cross-cousin, so the marriage is called off!

1970 *Fifth engagement*: with the money (150/-) returned from the last engagement, the boy begins paying the 500/- asked for another girl whom he courts in a village even further away. Later in the year he pays another 150/-.

1971 He is still unmarried but hoping to marry fiancée no 5.

With these insufficiencies, it is clear that a much more thorough preparation must be given to young people before marriage. Above all, there must be an opportunity for them to understand each other's psychology and get to know one another well. Attention must be diverted from the wedding and focused on Christian married life itself. As far as possible, preparation for marriage should involve not only the couple but also other members of the extended family. The ideal would be if it could take place in the home, with some of the elder people participating. The Christian community might, perhaps, be able to organize and carry out such a catechesis. The same would apply to post-marriage family apostolate. Courses arranged on a diocesan basis would help to educate parents and spouses in their faith and would contribute to the Christian and sacramental understanding of their marriage.

Marriage rites vary very much from one people to another; and they are full of rich and complex symbolism. The first marital intercourse may precede or follow the ceremonies. These may either be an undertaking or agreement which is later consummated, or they may be a declaration or confirmation of the physical coming together of the people. Usually one or more of the following elements are found in a traditional marriage ceremony in Africa :

public witness to the social event of the marriage, speeches, acclamations, feasting, dancing, songs

the seclusion and instruction of the bride

a mock hostility between the two lineages involved

the capture or handing-over of the bride

the symbolism of the merging of the lineages—for example, the bride sits on the laps of women of the bridegroom's family, and members of the bridegroom's family sit on the laps of women of the bride's family

initiation of the bride into her domestic duties by means of symbolic mime

the veiling and unveiling of the bride

the ceremonial bath of the bride

the anointing of the spouses

the final discussion to fix the bridewealth

consummation of the marriage in the presence of the grandmother or an old woman (she may be in the next room, or even in the room itself), or at any rate verification of the consummation by the older women

presentation of a gift to the bride or bride's family, indicating that she has been found to be a virgin

gift-exchanges.

Such ceremonies express the potential hostility between the lineages, their merging and the bearing of children to both groups, the reciprocity between the lineages, and particularly the idea that the bride herself is a precious gift. Fertility and the physical aspects of marriage are underlined. Much, if not most, of this ritual is acceptable to Christianity and should be used. The ideal would be simply to bless the customary marriage itself but as we have seen, everything depends on the understanding that society has about the institution of marriage and whether it is compatible with the Christian understanding. One cannot assume that both ideas concur. In this, both African marriage and Christian teaching must move to meet one another.

[1] A number of ideas in this chapter, notably on the constitutive principles of the family and on the question of incest, have been taken from Robin Fox, *Kinship and Marriage*, London 1967.

[2] Information about the effects of inbreeding is based on lectures given at Oxford University in 1964 by Drs Owen and Harrison.

[3] cf. Douglas, M, 'Is Matriliny Doomed in Africa?', in Douglas, M and Kaberry, P (eds), *Man in Africa*, London 1969, pp. 121–35.

[4] The controversy appeared in the pages of *Man* and was settled by Evans-Pritchard in no 42, March 1931.

[5] An estimate made by an experienced missionary from western Uganda.

[6] cf. Hillman, E, 'Polygyny Reconsidered', *African Ecclesiastical Review*, Vol X, no 3, 1968, pp. 274–87.

[7] Sarpong, P K, 'African Values and Catechetics—The Matrilineal Father', *Teaching All Nations*, Vol IV, no 1, April 1967, pp. 162–73.

[8] Ulbrich, H and Van Driessche, J, 'Some Elements for a Possible Solution of the Actual Crisis in Christian Marriage in Africa and especially Rhodesia' (mimeographed).

[9] Lufuluabo, F–M, *Mariage Coutumier et Mariage Chrétien, Indissoluble*, Kinshasa 1969, pp. 86–90.

[10] Lufuluabo, *ibid.*, pp. 91–102.

[11] Lufuluabo, *ibid.*, p. 89.

[12] Many ideas on traditional and contemporary socialization processes in Africa are taken from Mayer, P (ed), *Socialization: the Approach from Social Anthropology*, ASA8, London 1970, particularly the article by Fontaine on youth groups in Kinshasa, pp. 191–213.

[13] Ideas about the Baganda and Chagga are taken from lectures given at Gaba Pastoral Institute by Mr J Gwayambadde of Makerere University in 1970 and 1971.

[14] cf. Fontaine, J S, 1970, 'Two Types of Youth Groups in Kinshasa', Mayer (ed), *op. cit.*, pp. 191–213.

Suggested further reading

Fox, R, *Kinship and Marriage*, London 1967.

Mair, L, *African Marriage and Social Change*, London 1969.

Mayer, P (ed), *Socialization, the Approach from Social Anthropology*, ASA8, London.

Phillips, A F, *Survey of African Marriage and Family Life*, London (includes Mayer, *op. cit.*).

Robinson, J, *Family Apostolate and Africa*, Dublin 1964.

Radcliffe-Brown, A R and Forde, D (eds), *African Systems of Kinship and Marriage*, Oxford 1950.

7 Community and Ministry, Traditional and Christian

CHRISTIANITY, by its very nature, is concerned with community. Its mission is the development and fulfilment of human beings, and this can only come about through the interaction of persons in the various kinds of inter-personal relationship. Of these relationships, the most fundamental and the most fulfilling is the group or community relationship. Christians act as a community, giving a collective witness to Christ, but they are a microcosm of the total human community, acting as a transforming leaven within it. It follows that Christianity must build itself up within existing, viable, human communities.

Africans are said to have a well-developed sense of community. Pope Paul VI wrote in 1967:

> 'As regards community life—which in African tradition was family life writ large—we note that participation in the life of the community, whether in the circle of one's kinsfolk or in public life, is considered a precious duty and the right of all. But exercise of this right is conceded only after progressive preparation through a series of initiations whose aim is to form the character of the young candidates and to instruct them in the traditions, rules and customs of society' (*Africae Terrarum*, no 12).

Julius Nyerere echoes this approval of the traditional ideal of community:

> 'Our first step, therefore, must be to re-educate ourselves; to regain our former attitude of mind. In our traditional African society we were individuals within a community. We

took care of the community and the community took care of us. We neither needed nor wished to exploit our fellow men.[1]

We have to determine what contribution Africa can make to the understanding of Christian community in general and to religious community in particular, and we must decide what are the characteristic forms of community in Africa.

The first distinction that must be made is between the sense or experience of community on the one hand, and the concrete network of personal interrelationships that makes a community on the other. Both usages belong to the logical order, being models or frames of reference for speaking about certain relationships between individuals, but the first is more abstract than the second. One community, therefore, enjoys a greater or smaller measure of community experience than another. In the New Testament it is this experience of community which is referred to as *koinonia*, or fellowship.

When we use the word 'community', we imply a greater degree of sharing in common than is suggested by the word 'society'. Fr Bernard Lonergan, the philosopher and theologian, holds that there are four degrees of community, which he seees as the achievement of a common meaning.

potential community — common field of experience
formal community — common understanding
actual community — common judgements
willed community — common commitments[2]

It is in the willed aspect that community differs from society. It is in the conscious commitment to an associated activity which has as one of its objects the association itself. Community is essentially bound up with humanity because it affords a greater consciousness of what we all share as human beings. Community is also outgoing and active. It becomes dehumanizing if it adopts an attitude of collective selfishness and introspection. Fr Fergus Kerr has written that community is 'a state of honesty and trust among a group of people, or many people, if possible all the people in the world.'[3]

Having a sense of community with others and being a community with them do not necessarily coincide; but there is normally a more intense experience of community when they do. This is because in the corporate life of a concrete community there is a greater convergence of shared meanings. Thus an economic union like the East African Community means much less to its members than does the community of an African village where loyalties of kinship, clanship, language, culture, politics and religion converge. At its lowest level, the sense of community is potential community, a limited common field of experience. This can only begin to develop into formal, actual and willed community when individuals come together and interact. In the smaller community there is a greater opportunity for sharing because there is less individual anonymity, less structure, and less chance of evading personality problems. Obviously there are differing degrees of interaction between members of a community. In some communities the members may see a great deal of each other; in others, they may see each other more rarely. When there is no interaction between persons, but only potential community, we may speak of a communion. Thus, the Church is really a communion of communities. So is the typical African parish. There is the possibility of fluidity or mobility of membership between these communities.

Christianity demands some degree of intensity in community experience, because it opposes the view that individuals are fundamentally isolated from each other and in permanent conflict. It maintains that individuals are basically dependent on each other and that only the realization of this mutuality can bring about right relationships between human beings. The community of religious congregations offers an even more intense experience of Christian community.

Community is often compared to friendship, and in so far as both are a loving mutuality between equals the comparison is valid. However, friendship is ultimately something different from community. Friendship is the relationship of intimacy and confidence that exists between two individuals paired in the same role. Most relationships are formed of complementary opposites : for example, father—son, husband—wife, brother—sister, doctor—patient, employer—employee. In friendships a single role—that of friend—is shared by both members of the pair. There are relationships in which a role is shared because of the influence of a third party : for instance, two patients of the same doctor, two employees of the same employer, two wives of the same polygamist husband. But friendship is not simply prescribed by a given social situation; it must be achieved. It is not enough for two people to have something in common; they must build their own relationship as friends.[4]

In friendship there is equality but not necessarily equivalence. Friends experience a sharing in which each thinks he receives something of greater value than he gives. In other words, he gets a 'bargain'. However, he is not just interested in his own bargain, but is concerned that his friend gets a bargain too. Friendship is not just the fact of having a common interest, but it implies the interiorization of one another.

All friendship is more or less terminal—that is, terminating with the friends themselves. In so far as the friendship is carried over into other social relationships, we say that friendship is 'open-ended'. Lovers are in a terminal friendship. This is converted into an open-ended friendship when they marry, because the rights and obligations of married people are socially defined, and other categories of people are affected by the marriage. The friendship also takes on the character of complementary opposition in the relationship : husband/wife, father/mother.

Privacy is a quality designed to ensure the protection of the friendship, and to see that it is one between two persons and not a group relationship. Friendship is autonomous and achieved. It is not a product of the social structure, but the strategic disposition of two persons. The rules of friendship are not imposed by society. Friends choose each other freely, and decide freely the rule of their own relationship. It is impossible to predict the development of a friendship, since the role of friend is the same in each case; there is no super-ordination or sub-ordination in the relationship. Friends can do anything and behave in any way they agree upon.

Friends tend to be more concerned about their own evaluation by their partner than about what others think of the friend. They are more open to each other than to the rest of the world. The relationship is also useful and gives access to resources which fulfil different types of need : affective, economic, and so on. This does not necessarily imply selfishness; rather, it invokes the major value of mutual responsibility.

We have seen that friendship does not belong to the social structure. On the contrary, it forms a kind of infrastructure within society and within particular social groupings, including communities. Friendship may even be said to stand apart from, or be opposed to, social structure. In so far as kinship belongs to the social structure, friendship is opposed to kinship. Many African cultures have a saying or sayings which suggest that a friend is worth more than a kinsman or brother.

It has been suggested that Western society is friendship-orientated, and African society is kinship-orientated. Such a distinction, however, is fallacious for two reasons. Firstly, you cannot have a social structure based on friendship; and secondly, friendship is capable of co-existence with kinship. Friendship, indeed, may be a form of escapism from very strong ties of kinship. Kin-groupings may be oppressive and inward-looking. For persons embedded in such solidary groupings, friendship acts as a release. However, kinship structures and roles may be so strong as to effectively prevent an individual from choosing a friend outside the kin-group.

This limits the choice of friend, but it does not, and cannot, prevent the formation of autonomous friendships among kinsmen. Elsewhere, the kinship structure may tolerate the formation of friendships with non-kinsmen, but kinship values remain strong, and friendship is likely to be open-ended—opening on to the community of kinsmen. The contrast between Western and African friendship is therefore one between terminal, self-orientated friendship and open-ended, community-orientated friendship.

Bonding is the recognition that one's friend is one's responsibility. One has a duty to get one's friend accepted in one's own society, just as much as to defend him against society's criticisms. Friends guarantee further exchanges between each other and promise not to let each other down in any social, political or economic situation. In short, a man makes his friend a part of his social person.

Among pastoral peoples, such as the Jie of Karamoja in Uganda and the Turkana of Kenya, bond-friendship still has considerable importance. It is a genuine friendship, implying affection and mutual trust which develops into a business agreement of mutual convenience. There is an exchange of stock-rights. One bond-friend gives cattle to the other, on the explicit or tacit understanding that he can ask for a return gift. Friendship can be made with any man, irrespective of residence, age, or social status, but often friends are made in strategic areas of a country so that they can render assistance wherever the man happens to be. Often the friendship is expressed in kinship terms, thereby implying that a man's kinsmen are also committed to the friendship.

The blood-pact or covenant, commonly called blood-brother-hood, was a very common type of friendship that existed in many African societies and still survives in a few. It is based on a magical rite or oath, a pact or covenant in which blood is exchanged between the partners. After divination, incisions are made in the bodies of the two persons, usually on the belly below the navel, but occasionally also on the forehead, or on the chest, arms or calves. Food is then dipped in the blood oozing from the incisions. This may be a small ball of maize porridge, a coffee berry, or some grains of millet. Each partner then consumes the portion of food bearing the other's blood. Sometimes a drop of the other's blood is drunk in a vessel containing beer, gruel, water or some other liquid. Another method, when the incisions are made on the arms or legs, is to hold or tie them together, so that the blood mingles. The ritual is then followed by a cursing formula in which the terms of the pact are recited and the blood within each other's body is called upon to punish any infidelity. The Azande of Sudan, for example, believe that the blood 'lives on' in the belly of the blood-brother and wreaks vengeance on him by gripping his vital organs.[5] In the cursing formula, the blood is often addressed in a personalized form. The conditions that are enumerated concern the obligation to render assistance, to give gifts, weapons, food, beer, hospitality, even—if need be—a daughter in marriage. Failure to do these things incurs the magical vengeance of the blood on the guilty man and his relatives. The following is a typical blood-pact formula which comes from Kigezi in Uganda, and which refers to the blood as 'the little red one'.

'If I should kill my pact-brother, may the little red one destroy my house and kill my oldest wife and my best milk cow. If my wife refuses him food, may the blood kill her. If enemies fall upon him and he raises an alarm, if I do not come to save him, may the blood we have drunk kill me!'[6]

The rite of exchanging blood raises the bond between friends to a magical and mystical level. The sanction is thought to be automatic and the bond is one of the most sacred known in Africa. Occasionally, people believe they can find a magical remedy to help them evade the consequences of breaking the pact. The pact supposes a very strong existing tie of friendship, but, in itself, it is a formalization of the sentiment of friendship in terms of economic, commercial, political, and protective factors. It ensures safety for travellers passing through areas where they have no kin. The rite is usually only performed between males, and almost the only known case of heterosexual blood-brotherhood is between a man and a very much loved and trusted wife. For a man to make a blood pact with a woman other than a wife would be tantamount to adultery. Between spouses the rite symbolizes the perfection of marriage. After it, husband and wife may even share household tasks customarily reserved for one sex.

The rite does not create kinship, even though kinship terms may be applied to blood-pact partners. In some ways, blood-brothers have stricter obligations towards each other than kinsfolk. Yet, they are not of the same clan and do not obey each other's rules of exogamy; they can marry each other's relatives. They often joke with one another in an intimate fashion on the pattern of the joking-partnership between cross-cousins. Although the pact does not create kinship, it definitely obligates the kin of either partner who are all classificatory blood-brothers. The obligations, however, may not be as strict as those towards the blood-brother himself. The blood-pact is therefore not entirely autonomous, but is open-ended. Although the initiative lies with the friends themselves, they normally consult their kinsfolk before making the pact.

Friendship and community are evidently different. One cannot have a community which is an aggregation of unique friendships. Even if it were physically possible for each member of the community to have a unique relation of friendship with each other member of the community simultaneously, one would not be speaking of community but of a network of friendships. Friendships differ from each other, whereas community is a direct and total confrontation of human identities in which something common to all and basic to humanity is shared. It is also something conscious and willed, and lacks the effortless character of friendship. Members of a community cannot relate to each other without reference to the group.

However, friendship is perfectly compatible with community, and may support and buttress it. This only happens if it is open-ended friendship. Friendship in Africa is an example of this open-ended kind of friendship.

Even though blood-brotherhood is rare, ideals of friendship in Africa are, consciously or unconsciously, modelled on the old institution of blood-brotherhood. Even ordinary words for friend may derive from the old terms for blood-brother. The kinsfolk of friends even today may be obligated in much the same way that kinsfolk of blood-brothers were in the past, and a man adopts all the relatives of his friend as his own. Friendship, therefore, while it is basically a different phenomenon from community, can, nevertheless, be intimately related to community.

In urban industrial situations the work-team is a permanent or near-permanent grouping. However, it is questionable whether it could form the basis of community and whether it is a good image of community. The work-team exists for an end, an associated activity; but in community the association itself is an end. Religious writers who speak as if community life is a useful means to the end of apostolic activity are devaluing the idea of community. Community is primary and totalitarian; it does not just demand people's work and co-operation, it demands the people themselves! It is doubtful if true community can be developed in a work-team anywhere in the world, let alone in Africa, so long as the work takes priority. As Kayoya has written, for the African '. . . the human has no money-value, the human lives on by communicating itself.' [7]

The family is an ancient image of community which, like friendship, emphasizes the loving mutuality between its members and the community's character of 'home'. The African extended family, more than the Western nuclear family, is a community, even if it is not corporate and residential, because its ideals of collective responsibility and co-operation result in a really 'willed' community action for the sake of the community itself. The danger is that the family may become inward-looking and closed. Christ taught that men should not simply save their greetings for their kinsmen, but treat all men as kinsmen; and, while Julius Nyerere has taken the family as the basis of his community ideal (*ujamaa*), the family is not the basic community in his system; rather it is the ujamaa village in which the extended family is 'extended' to embrace fellow-villagers.

Another danger of the family as image and basis of community is the risk of infantilism under a superior father-figure or mother-figure, who takes decisions for the children and who sees the superior's task as testing the subjects' obedience and imposing a common pattern of life on them. In fact, a community should never have a 'superior'. The superior must be an equal, even if he or she is the 'first among equals'. Without equality, the superior could not be a member of the community. This is precisely what happened in the Middle Ages in Europe, when abbots and abbesses lived in their own households outside the community, enjoying a different standard of living. A community must be composed of free, adult individuals. There must be freedom in small things and real maturity. Love in a family of adults means trusting others and letting them be.

What has been said about the family as the ideal of community applies to the clan in so far as it is corporate and residential. If it is dispersed, as it usually is, then it is more likely to be a 'communion' of family communities than a real community in its own right.

As a basic community in itself, the companionship of two married persons is hardly sufficient. However, the image of a woman in a patrilineal society entering her husband's lineage group is an apt picture of an individual becoming committed to a community.

The village or settlement is the most acceptable basis for community in Africa. It is the most realistic human community. The village community is composed of both kinsmen and neighbours, and neighbourliness and good company are the predominant ideals of village life. The village works, celebrates, and takes recreation as a single unit. Neighbours share their tools, weapons, utensils and clothes. They hoe together on each other's farms; they go on hunting and fishing expeditions together. Every celebration brings the same people together, putting their hands into the same dish, drinking beer from the same pot, bowl or gourd, whether it is passed from hand to hand, or whether a number of drinking-tubes are thrust into a single vessel. Good company is an ideal based on mutuality, rather than equivalence. It comforts mutual aid and sympathy, courtesy and good manners, conversation with others. It is from the ability to converse and reciprocate that men learn wisdom. Good company is the recognition that life means living with others. An indication of this value is shown in the use of the word 'our' instead of 'my' by Africans.[8]

We have already discussed the nature of rites of passage, liminality, and liminal rituals. The threshold phase (*limen*) is the very essence of the rite of passage, and the group of initiates passing through this phase represents the ideal of a community endowed with a special role within the total human community.[9]

The liminal period is one of instability, movement and ambivalence. The liminars (threshold people) have no status. Ordinary rules and relationships are suspended where they are concerned. They are in 'the limbo of statuslessness'. There is strict equality among them, and also passiveness, humility, and poverty. This is signified by common markings, by uniform dress or lack of it (nakedness), and by a willingness to accept trials and sufferings without complaint. They are taught to act and react as a group and to sublimate selfish tendencies. Sex distinctions are minimized and sexual continence is practised. Simplicity, silence, foolishness are also characteristic of the state. It is as if liminars are in the womb or in the tomb. Theirs is what Robert Serumaga calls 'the world of shadows'.[10] But the liminal state is also strangely powerful, hedged round with prohibitions and taboos.

It is a mirror held up to society, and liminars are a *tabula rasa* on which society can inscribe its profoundest thoughts. Liminars can prophesy and criticize. Every age has its low-born soothsayers, prophets, bards, minstrels, dwarfs and jesters who claim and are given freedom to criticize the rigid norms and structures of society. Novelists and artists are also threshold people, and a strong bond of community unites them in their claim to freedom of expression and their conscious sentiment for humanity. Institutionalized forms of liminality exist in which people can experience this freedom and humanity, as in secret societies and mask societies. The liminal community experiences the 'quick of human interrelatedness' and offers mankind a reminder of the essential purpose of existence.

The Christian recognizes that his whole life is a rite of passage, and that he is ultimately a liminal person. The Church is a Pilgrim Church 'on the way', and men are strangers and exiles in this world. It is the task of the Christian to give eschatological witness, proclaiming men's ultimate freedom to be human, protesting against structures which dehumanize him, and pointing towards his ultimate fulfilment. The Christian does not claim to be better than other men; he merely claims to set human ideals in sharper relief and calls all men to a greater realization of community.

The religious community fulfils this vocation in an even more striking way. The classic example of religious liminality is, perhaps, St Francis of Assisi, who saw his friars as staying in a permanently liminal condition. Mendicancy meant instability, ambiguity, insecurity. The friars were a protest against the wealthy Church structure of the day, and St Francis employed symbolic norms which were the personification of liminal values: Lady Poverty, Brother Ass; and the constant theme of nakedness, the symbolism of the naked Christ on the Cross. The liminal communities of Africa, therefore, underline the essential witness of the Christian community and contribute to its understanding and application in Africa.

Related to the themes of community and liminality is the phenomenon of Church independency in Africa. The twentieth century has witnessed a rapid growth of Christian independency in Africa. The recent study by Dr David Barrett enumerates no fewer than six thousand religious movements.[11] Such movements attract large numbers of people both from the older mission Churches as well as from the traditional religion. The existence of independent Churches poses certain problems for Christians of the old Churches: What are these independent Churches doing and saying? How do they differ from us and from each other? What are the causes that bring these Churches into existence? What needs are they fulfilling which the older Churches have failed to cater for? What is, and should be, the relationship between independent Churches and other Churches? What is the future of independency? We shall try to answer some of these questions.

The first typology of African independent Churches was the simple one of Sundkler.[12] They were either Ethiopian or Zionist.

Ethiopian Churches are churches seceding from white mission Churches, or from other independent Churches which have seceded from white mission Churches and which have the slogan 'Africa for the Africans'. Their organization and Bible interpretation are borrowed from the Protestant Churches from which they derive, but they have a stress on rank and ritual which is reminiscent of Catholicism. Zionist Churches are syncretist Bantu movements with healing, speaking in tongues, purification rites and taboos. They have a very casual relationship with white mission Churches.

Harold Turner gives us a more complete typology, based on historical, religious, and sociological criteria.[13] He does not accept the 'Church-sect' distinction made by some writers. In fact, this distinction is odious to those who belong to these movements. They describe themselves as 'Churches' and wish to be known as such.

The first type of independent Church is called Christian, and the distinction between it and the older mission Churches cannot be described in theological or religious terms, only in historical and sociological terms. They are historical secessions, serving different sections of society; but their doctrines are similar to those of the older Churches.

The second type is called Hebraist, and is subdivided into Israelitish and Judaistic. In the Israelitish Churches God is seen as loving and helpful. He speaks through a prophet or founder. Magic and idolatry are rejected and joy is the predominating characteristic. This type of Church represents a 'radical breakthrough' from the traditional religion. The Judaistic Churches are similar to the Israelitish, but possess a new and important emphasis, that of repentance, suffering, asceticism, taboos, and laws.

The third type is called neo-pagan. These Churches are really new forms of the traditional religion, albeit influenced by Christian elements. They are revivalistic, new forms of the old religion; nativistic, desirous of purging foreign elements; or syncretist, incorporating selected elements from various religions.

When dealing with the sociology of conversion in Chapter 3, we noted that certain types of society, particularly the stratified or atomized type of society, favour the growth of independent Churches. African independent Churches certainly give a new community dimension to such societies. They are very decentralized, and they operate on the level of the local community which corresponds to the lineage, taking over some of the functions of the lineage. The independent Church, therefore, gives new support for the existing structures of society.

Anthropologists have been describing the phenomenon of millenarianism for a long time.[14] Briefly, it is a kind of belief which appears in a time of far-reaching, organizational change. People are not satisfied with the present situation. In particular the new needs they have been given are not satisfied. Moreover, new needs are continually being created. They experience a sense of frustration. The problem is transposed onto a mythical plane, and they look forward to a deliverance, or to a utopia when all their sufferings will be ended. They are waiting for a 'cargo' of all the goods which the white man enjoys and which the local people do not have; or they are waiting for a transformation when black men will become white and rule the whites who will have turned black, and so on. Such ideas are not purely materialistic, but mythological, even spiritual. The problem is solved in religious terms by a belief which incorporates elements from old and new religions. Classic examples of millenarianism are the cargo cults of Melanesia and the ghost dance religions of the North American Indians. Many of the independent Church movements have been millenarian, or have emerged from social circumstances similar to those of Melanesia and North America. In South Africa, particularly, the proliferation of independent Churches and the complex organization of these Churches is a form of compensation for the exclusion of Africans from political activity. The Churches, although small, have an enormous hierarchical ministry. There may also be many grades within Church membership, and whole complexes of councils and committees. According to Worsley, the millenary movement has the following characteristics: it is a religion of the 'lower social orders'; it integrates people, by uniting them into small units; it tends to develop into secular political institutions; there is a transition to 'passivism'—'waiting for the day'; there is the idea of the millennium, when all wrongs will be righted.[15]

Welbourn gives an even more penetrating socio-historical cause for independency in Africa. According to him, when

Christianity came to Africa it had ceased to be the 'mythological dimension of a whole culture'; it was a 'fissile myth'. In this situation the African had to affirm his Africanness. 'To be African is the most convincing way to be men in a world dominated by Europeans, where the tribe has ceased to have a meaningful existence, and the nation has not yet come into emotional being.'[16]

When a man's home is destroyed a new home has to be found. The African needed a new 'home', a new mythology radically united to the rational structures of his society at every point. The first myth brought by the Europeans was the myth of white supremacy; the second was Christianity. However, Christianity was seen to be a 'disunited decoration of Western culture' in the form in which it was brought to Africa. The African took over the elements of universal value in Christianity, but enshrined them in social institutions which were African, run by Africans, and seen to be run by Africans. In practice, however, the process is more one of 'localization' than Africanization.

So far, we have concentrated on the sociological causes of independency. Barrett puts forward the following religious theory of the rise of independency. According to him, the coming of Christianity to Africa raised widespread hopes, but the task of Church-building in the early days was so all-absorbing that the missionaries never really had an encounter in depth with the indigenous beliefs and systems of thought. The missionaries were really humanitarian co-partners of the European administrators. The early missionary respect for African social institutions soon gave way to an assault on them between the years 1885 and 1914. This shift of attitude created an unconscious state of alarm in the minds of Africans which bred disillusionment and bitterness. There was widespread religious tension and a feeling that African society was not being fulfilled by the new religion, but was being demolished by it. The family, in particular, was suffering. There was, says Barrett, a 'tribal *zeitgeist*' or atmosphere of tension.

In this state of tension it became increasingly obvious that there was a discrepancy between mission religion and biblical religion among those peoples who had the Bible translated into their vernacular. The people's grievances were articulated in biblical themes, and the main grievance was that there was insensitivity on the part of the mission Churches, an unconscious failure of love. Women suffered the most and became the spokesmen of society. Charismatic leaders appeared, and very often these were prophetesses.

There were different types of reaction. In the main, the movements were either revivalistic or separatist. Often the 'flashpoint' for the separation was a trivial dispute, but it had been prepared a long time before. In general, Protestant Churches were more likely to have congregations separating themselves from them than the Catholic Church. This, says Barrett, was because the Protestants had translated the Bible for their people and the Catholics had not.

Turner disagrees with Barrett. He thinks that the Catholic doctrine of apostolic succession made it difficult, in practice, for sects to separate themselves from the Catholic Church; whereas, among the Protestants, Church organization was much looser and decentralized, and therefore favourable to separatism. Tribalism is a major factor in separatism also.

Although this may be true in the main, it is also a fact that Catholic associations—such as the Legion of Mary with their own *mystique*, their own organization and hierarchy, and their own 'liturgy'—have encouraged the idea of separatism within the Catholic Church. Several of the independent Churches derive from, or consciously imitate, the Legion of Mary.

There are several approaches one can take when discussing the relationship of independent Churches to other Churches and religions.[17] The categorical approach sees a conflict between religions and churches competing for the loyalty of the people. The layer approach sees religions and churches as constituting 'layers' or strata, each superimposed on the other. Thus Christianity overlays African traditional religion, and independent Churches are seen as an intermediate layer. The synthetic approach, however, sees a dialectical interchange taking place between the different Churches and religions. Each religious group is a modality on a religious spectrum which they all share. This is the view of Murphree. All the denominations are syncretist up to a point, and each form of religion caters for needs not catered for by the others. The religions need each other, sociologically speaking, and the combination of complementarity and competition ensures that they cannot act as isolated units. Religion does not, in fact, divide people; the different denominations are various facets of contemporary African religion.

Independent Church movements have contributed considerably to the rise of nationalism. In the early days it was often a religious leader influenced by Christian ideas who led the first revolt against the Europeans. For example, John Chilembwe in Malawi, Simon Kimbangu of the Congo, Reuben Spartas (and the 1948–50 riots) of Uganda, Lenshina of Zambia, Elijah Masinde of Kenya, and so on. Such movements were agents of unification since they were often supra-tribal. Slowly, religious and political independency parted company and there was a transition to secular politics.

The growth of independency has been phenomenal. For example, Barrett estimates that twenty per cent of the entire Luo tribe of Kenya belongs to an independent Church. What of the future? Barrett is optimistic. He believes that the historical Jesus is central to all these religions, even though they incorporate symbols, rituals and magical elements which have nothing to do with Christianity. He believes that independent Churches are creating a new kind of community which is growing rapidly, and spreading in 'chains of independency' from tribe to tribe. It is, he thinks, 'an incipient African Reformation' of Christianity, and an expression of African religious genius. He thinks that membership of independent Churches will equal the membership of all the older Churches in Africa combined by the year 2000. Independency is 'clearly playing an increasingly vital part in the rooting of the Christian faith in the soil of Africa'.[18]

Oosthuizen, however, is pessimistic.[19] He does not see independency as 'Christian'; rather, it is 'post-Christian'. The growth of these independent Churches is due, in his eyes, to a misunderstanding of important Christian doctrines such as the meaning of the Holy Spirit and the concept of sin. The ecclesiology of these churches is ethnocentric, and they tend to become 'folk religions'. Separatism is anti-Christian. The task of Christianity is to reconcile these Churches to one another, without necessarily taking their identity away. Independency in an indication that the true challenge of missionary work is not being met. Africa can only be won for Christ by a united Church.

Turner steers a realistic, middle course. Although he detects a growth of Christian insight among the independent Churches, he finds the movements ambivalent, reactionary and dysfunctional. They seek an adaptation to African culture on the one hand, while, on the other, they set up conservative, European-type structures or cling to obsolete European liturgical usages. They provide initial psychological and spiritual satisfaction for their members, contribute to community-building, satisfy the aspirations of unsophisticated people towards aspects of the European type of life, and assist in the promotion of literacy. They also cater for persons in irregular marriage situations rejected by the mission Churches. Ultimately, however, they are not likely to last in their present form, being an unsophisticated synthesis of Christianity and traditional culture. There are indications that as people become more sophisticated, they tend to despise the independent Churches in their present form.

The final section of this book discusses service within the community, traditional and Christian ministry. We have already noted that, strictly speaking, there was no religious pluralism in traditional Africa. The idea of a Church or a religion, meaning a voluntary association of individuals in the whole field of religious beliefs and practice, was absent. Often there was no word in an African language which could be strictly translated as 'religion'. This did not, of course, mean that Africans had no religion, or that they could not talk about religious worship and religious experience. But it did mean that peoples in traditional Africa acquired their religion by being born into, and brought up by, their society—not by an act of personal adherence. Each ethnic group had its own body of religious beliefs and practices, reflecting the ecology and social structure of the group. There was no conflict between traditional religions because the relative isolation of the groups did not favour a confrontation very often, and because religious ideas and practices were often shared by a variety of ethnic groups over a wide area. Traditional religion was not systematized and was therefore capable of absorbing ideas from outside, or of reconciling its own beliefs and practices with those of other peoples.

Because of the identification of a single religion with all aspects of culture and social life, religious structures were usually synonymous with social and political structures. Religious practice was departmentalized and worship was conducted at different levels in society by rulers and office-holders on behalf of various, over-lapping communities. Apart from the ascribed associations of clan, lineage, age-set, chiefdom, etc., there were sometimes voluntary associations of individuals which had a religious aspect, although they were never exclusively religious. Such were secret societies, guilds for hunting, medicine and the various crafts.

Priesthood was not always present in African societies. Some-times the ruling aristocracy was responsible for worship at a territorial level, the paterfamilias at the lineage level, and the craft-master at the level of the professional guild or association. The most specialized priestly functions were found at the highest political and social levels. 'The temple', it is said, 'rises beside the palace.' One explanation for the emergence of priests, keepers of shrines and graves, and other cult specialists, is that when several clans or ethnic groups were brought together into one polity, their politico-religious leaders were deprived of effective power and became the specialized religious officers of their clan or other grouping.

Divine kingship is, perhaps, more typical of Africa as a whole than priesthood. At one end of the scale were the clans of 'priests' among Nilotic peoples whose task it was to make peace between feuding clans; at the other end were the kings and chiefs who constituted a permanent, centralized symbol of political unity. All kings are sacred persons to some degree, and this notion enters into the very definition of a king. However, the sacred character of the king is more strongly emphasized in some cases than in others. Frazer, the first to describe the divine king, laid down four main characteristics.[20] The divine king was a ruler with power over nature, exercised voluntarily or involuntarily; he was the dynamic centre of the universe for his subjects; the well-being of this universe depended on the king's own life and health; and the king had to be actually killed before his powers failed.

The divine king is not necessarily thought to have a divine spirit dwelling in him, though this can be the case : for example, the dwelling of Nyikang in the Reth of the Shilluk of Sudan. However, the divine king is the representative of the spirits and their instrument. In himself he is a living pledge of their favour. Often there was no real killing of the king. He was said to be buried alive, but this was not always strictly true. It was a way of implying that the king was somehow immortal—alive even in death. People pretended that the king was still alive and concealed his death. The case of Benin in Nigeria is typical in that it was strictly forbidden to speak directly of the death of the Oba or King.

There is no need to dwell at length on Christian structures in Africa. We have already seen that the Church is a voluntary association of individuals in the whole field of religious beliefs and practice. However, this does not mean that the Church should be a sub-culture, an artificial society inside the normal human society. On the contrary, Christians are expected to be a leaven in the human community. This means that they must work through the ordinary social structures of village and family. It means that the Church must be seen to have a relevance for ordinary human life; and it also means that Christians must not be 'exclusive', even in religious matters, but, in the words of *Nostra Aetate*, 'acknowledge, preserve and promote' the values found in traditional and other religions. Less emphasis must therefore be placed on administrative and juridical structures like diocese and parish and much more on real, social structures like the sub-parish and village outstation, and on the extended family.

The traditional politico-religious hierarchy of Africa has either been secularized or has disappeared. To some extent, it has been replaced in the minds of Christians by the Church's ministry. The extreme shortage of priests and the vastness of the juridical circumscriptions of the Church in Africa have encouraged this equation. This has had unfortunate results. The authoritarian character of the hierarchy and ministry is exaggerated, and the priest, being seen at the higher social levels, is considered to be a vicarious ritual officer and not a real community builder or leader at the lowest level.

The attitude to the catechist is ambivalent. Catechists were a new form of pastoral ministry which the Church resorted to in Africa because of the lack of priests. Research has revealed that people had three ideas in mind when they compared catechists to office-holders in traditional society.[21] They saw them as subordinate political officers, as religious specalists, or as social leaders. The first equation reveals the authoritarian bias. The second selects specialists who are occasionally consulted, such as diviners and mediums, rather than priests who operate at a remote level. The third stresses the value of the catechist in the local community. The pastoral ministry of the Church is unique and cannot be equated with any of these categories, but the third category comes nearest to the ideal, as long as the religious character of the pastor is safeguarded. In structural terms, the catechist is operating at the most realistic level.

On this note we come to the end of our survey of African pastoral anthropology. The future of culture and of religion in Africa lies with the people of Africa themselves. Africa is at the cross-roads. Perhaps that is a truism, since mankind is always at a cross-roads, having in its hands the power to create or to destroy. However, it is important to know at a given moment what the choices are. Only a serious study of contemporary man in Africa can help us to glimpse the ways in which Christianity may serve and develop the human values and cultural riches of Africa.

Notes

[1] Nyerere, J, *Ujamaa*, Oxford 1968, pp. 6–7.
[2] Lonergan, B, 'Existenz und Aggiornamento', digest in *Theology Digest*, 1966, 14, no 2, p. 123; and 14, no 3, p. 212.
[3] Kerr, F, 'Resolution and Community', *New Blackfriars*, June 1969, 50, no 589, pp. 471–82.
[4] Much of the section on friendship is based on Paine, R, 'In Search of Friendship', *Man*, 1969, NS. IV, 4, pp. 505–24.
[5] Evans-Pritchard, E E Y, 'Zande Blood-brotherhood', in *Essays in Social Anthropology*, London 1962, pp. 131–61.
[6] Edel, M, *The Chiga of Western Uganda*, Oxford 1957, p. 25.
[7] Kayoya, M, *Sur les traces de mon père*, Bujumbura 1968, p. 67 (author's trans.).
[8] cf. Wilson, M and Wilson, G, *Good Company*, Oxford 1952.
[9] cf. Turner, V W, *The Ritual Process*, London 1969, from whom the ideas on liminality and sense of community in liminal groups are taken.
[10] cf. Serumaga, R, *Return to the Shadows*, London 1969, AWS 54.
[11] Barrett, D B, *Schism and Renewal in Africa*, Nairobi 1968.
[12] Sunkler, B, *Bantu Prophets in South Africa*, Oxford 1961.
[13] Turner, H W, 'A Typology for African Religious Movements', *Journal of Religion in Africa*, 1967, Vol 1, Fasc 1, pp. 1–34.
[14] cf. Worsley, P, *The Trumpet Shall Sound*, London 1957.
[15] cf. Worsley, *op. cit.*
[16] Welbourn, F B and Ogot, A B, *A Place to Feel at Home*, Oxford 1966, pp. 142–3.
[17] The different approaches are described in Murphree, M W, *Christianity and the Shona*, London 1969, pp. 1–2.
[18] Barrett, D B, *op. cit.*, p. 278.
[19] Oosthuizen, G C, *Post-Christianity in Africa*, London 1968.

[20] Frazer, J G, *The Golden Bough*, London 1922 (abridgement), pp. 214–15.

[21] cf. Shorter, A and Kataza, E (eds), *Missionaries to Yourselves*, London 1972, p. 74.

Suggested further reading

Barrett, D B, *Schism and Renewal in Africa*, Nairobi 1968.

Moran, G and Harris, M, *Experiences in Community*, London 1969.

Murphree, M W, *Christianity and the Shona*, London 1969.

Nyerere, J, *Ujamaa*, Oxford 1968.

Oosthuizen, G C, *Post-Christianity in Africa*, London 1968.

Turner, V W, *The Ritual Process*, London 1969.

Welbourn, F B and Ogot, A B, *A Place to Feel at Home*, Oxford 1966.

Worsley, P, *The Trumpet Shall Sound*, London 1957.

Appendix 1

A NUMBER of recent Catholic documents and pronouncements have a bearing on African pastoral anthropology. First place among these must be given to the decree *Ad Gentes* of the Second Vatican Council on the Church's missionary activity.[1]

This decree represents a new emphasis in mission theology: away from the numerical Catholicism of a Church organized primarily for individual baptisms and towards an 'incarnational' Christian community. There is therefore a new stress on society and social institutions which are responsible for the modes of thinking and acting of individuals. To be a trained specialist in catechetics, liturgy and the apostolate is excellent, but specialists are unable to stir a finger until they know something of the social background of those among whom they work.

Ad Gentes therefore states that human beings 'are formed into large and distinct groups by permanent cultural ties, by ancient religious traditions, and by firm bonds of social necessity. The Church must be present in these groups of men through those of her children who dwell among them, or who are sent to them' (para 11). 'That they may be able to give this witness to Christ fruitfully, let them be joined to those men by esteem and love, and acknowledge themselves to be members of the group of men among whom they live. Let them share in cultural and social life by the various enterprises of human living. . . . Christ himself searched the hearts of men, and led them to divine light through truly human conversation. So also his disciples, profoundly penetrated by the Spirit of Christ, should know the people among whom they live, and should establish contact with them. Thus they themselves can learn by sincere and patient

217

dialogue what treasures God has distributed among the nations of the earth' (para 11).

The Council asks that indigenous seminarians and expatriate missionaries study local traditions and cultures. Seminarians in mission countries are invited 'to consider the points of contact between the traditions and religion of their homeland and the Christian religion', and they are exhorted to 'be versed in the culture of their people and be able to evaluate it' (para 16). Missionaries during their training must acquire 'a general knowledge of peoples, cultures and religions, a knowledge that not only looks to the past, but to the present as well. For anyone who is going to encounter another people should have a great esteem for their patrimony and their language and customs' (para 26).

On the subject of this missionary encounter, the Council says : 'From the customs and traditions of their people, Churches borrow all those things which can contribute to the glory of their Creator, the revelation of the Saviour's grace, or the proper arrangement of Christian life. If this goal is to be achieved, theological investigation must be stirred up in each major sociocultural area . . . [and] a better view will be gained of how their customs, outlook on life and social order can be reconciled with the manner of living taught by divine revelation' (para 22).

Finally, the Council singles out for special praise those 'who work in universities or in scientific institutes and whose historical and scientific religious research promotes knowledge of peoples and religions. Thus they can help the heralds of the Gospel and prepare for dialogue with non-Christians' (para 41). This is a special encouragement for those engaged in socioreligious studies.

Among the other Council documents, the Constitution on the Liturgy (*Sacrosanctum Concilium*)[2] lays down the principle of 'legitimate variations and adaptations to different groups, religions and peoples, especially in mission lands' (para 38). On the subject of the sacraments of initiation, the Council says : 'In mission lands initiation rites are found in use among individual peoples. Elements from these, when capable of being adapted to Christian ritual, may be admitted along with those already found in Christian tradition. . . .' (para 65).

The Declaration on Non-Christian Religions (*Nostra Aetate*)[3] exhorts Christians to 'preserve' and 'promote' the values that are found in non-Christian religions. The Church has this exhortation for her sons: prudently and lovingly, through dialogue and collaboration with the followers of other religions, and in witness of Christian faith and life, to acknowledge, preserve and promote the spiritual and moral goods found among these men, as well as the values in their society and culture' (para 2).

In the letter of Pope Paul VI to the hierarchy and people of Africa (*Africae Terrarum*, 1967),[4] his readers are explicitly invited to study the traditional social experiences of Africa. These are the spiritual view of life, the sense of the family, and the sense of community. The Pope has this to say about African studies:

'We have always been glad to see the flourishing state of African studies, and we see with satisfaction that the knowledge of her history and tradition is spreading. This, if done with openness and objectivity, cannot fail to lead to a more exact evaluation of Africa's past and present. Thus the more recent ethnic history of the peoples of Africa, though lacking in written documents, is seen to be very complex, yet rich in individuality and spiritual and social experiences, to which specialists are fruitfully directing their analysis and further research, Many customs and rites, once considered to be strange, are seen today in the light of ethnological science, as integral parts of various social systems, worthy of study and commanding respect' (para 7).

Finally, in his 1969 Kampala address to the bishops of Africa, Pope Paul laid down the principles of African Christianity. 'The expression, that is the language and mode of manifesting the one Faith, may be manifold; hence it may be original, suited to the tongue, the style, the character, the genius and the culture of the one who professes this one Faith. From this point of view, a certain pluralism is not only legitimate but desirable. An adaptation of the Christian life in the fields of pastoral, ritual, didactic and spiritual activities is not only possible, it is even favoured by the Church. The liturgical renewal is a living example of this. And in this sense you may, and you must, have an African Christianity.'

'The African Church is confronted with an immense and original undertaking; like a mother and teacher she must approach all the sons of this land of the sun; she must offer them a traditional and modern interpretation of life; she must educate the people in new forms of civil organization; while purifying and preserving the forms of family and community, she must give an educative impulse to your social virtues: those of honesty, of sobriety, of loyalty; she must help develop every activity that promotes the public good, especially the schools and the assistance of the poor and sick : she must help Africa towards development, towards concord, towards peace.'[5]

Notes
[1] Abbott, W M (ed), *The Documents of Vatican II*, London 1966, pp. 580–633.
[2] *Ibid.*, pp. 137–78.
[3] *Ibid.*, pp. 660–71.
[4] The full text of the Pope's letter to Africa was published in *The Tablet* of 4 November 1967, pp. 1162–5; it was reprinted in Flannery, A, *Missions and Religions*, Dublin 1968, pp. 132–49.
[5] *Gaba Pastoral Paper* no 7, pp. 50–51.

Appendix 2

A Bibliography of African Writers

NB. With the exception of the poet Okot p'Bitek, whose work is referred to in the text, the list is one of novelists only.

Abrahams, P,
Mine Boy, London 1946
Tell Freedom, London 1954
Wreath for Udomo, London 1956
Night of their Own, London 1965
This Island Now, London 1966

Abruquah, J,
The Torrent, London 1968

Achebe, C,
Things Fall Apart, London 1953
No Longer at Ease, London 1960
Arrow of God, London 1964
Man of the People, London 1966
Girls at War and Other Stories, London 1972

Agunwa, C,
More than Once, London 1967

Akpan, N U,
The Wooden Gong, London 1965

Aluko, T M,
One Man, One Matchet, London 1964
Kinsman and Foreman, London 1966
Chief, the Honourable Minister, London 1970

Amadi, E,
The Concubine, London 1966
The Great Ponds, London 1969

Asalache, K,
A Calabash of Life, London 1967

Asare, B,
Rebel, London 1969

Conton, W,	*The African*, London 1960
Dipoko, M S,	*A Few Nights and Days*, London 1966
Djoleto, Anna,	*The Strange Man*, London 1967
Egbuna, O,	*Wind versus Polygamy*, London 1964
Ekwensi, C,	*People of the City*, London 1954
	Jagua Nana, London 1960
	Burning Grass, London 1962
	Beautiful Feathers, London 1963
	Lokotown and Other Stories, London 1966
Gatheru, R M,	*Child of Two Worlds*, London 1964
Honwana, L B,	*We Killed Mangy Dog and Other Stories*, London 1967
Kachingwe, A,	*No Easy Task*, London 1965
Kayira, L,	*I Will Try*, London 1967
	Jingala, London 1969
Kimenye, Barbara,	*Kalasanda*, Nairobi 1965
Kibera, L, and Kahiga, C,	*Potent Ash*, Nairobi (no date)
Konadu, A,	*A Woman in Her Prime*, London 1967
La Guma, A,	*And a Threefold Cord*, Berlin 1964
	A Walk in the Night, London 1967
	The Stone Country, Berlin 1967
Laye, C,	*The African Child*, London 1959
	The Radiance of the King, London 1971
Mphalele, E,	*In Corner B*, Nairobi 1967
	The African Image, London 1962
	Down Second Avenue, London 1965
Munyonye, J,	*The Only Son*, London 1966
	Obi, London 1969
	Oil Man of Ohange, London 1971
Ngugi, J,	*Weep Not Child*, London 1964
	The River Between, London 1965
	A Grain of Wheat, London 1967
Niane, D T,	*Sundiata, an Epic of Old Mali*, London 1965
Nkosi, L,	*Home and Exile*, London 1965
Nwankwo, N,	*Danda*, London 1964
Nwapa, Flora,	*Efuru*, London 1966
	Idu, London 1970
Ogot, Grace,	*Land Without Thunder*, London 1968

Okara, G,	*The Voice*, London 1964
Okello Oculi,	*The Prostitute*, Nairobi 1968
Okot p'Bitek,	*Song of Lawino*, Nairobi 1966
	Song of Ocol, Nairobi 1970
	Two Songs, Nairobi 1971
Ousmane, S,	*God's Bits of Wood*, London 1970
Oyono, F,	*Houseboy*, London 1966
	The Old Man and the Medal, London 1967
Palangyo, P K,	*Dying in the Sun*, London 1969
Peters, L,	*The Second Round*, London 1965
Rubadiri, D,	*No Brideprice*, Nairobi 1967
Salih, T,	*Season of Migration to the North*, London 1969
	The Wedding of Zein, London 1969
Seruma, E,	*The Experience*, London 1970
Serumaga, R,	*Return to the Shadows*, London 1969
Samkange, S,	*On Trial for My Country*, London 1966
Sellassie, S,	*The Afersata*, London 1969
Tutuola, A,	*The Palm Wine Drinkard*, London 1952
	My Life in the Bush of Ghosts, London 1954
	Simbi and the Satyr of the Dark Jungle, London 1955
	Feather Woman of the Jungle, London 1962
Uzodinma, E C C,	*Our Dead Speak*, London 1967
Waciuma, Charity,	*Daughter of Mumbi*, London 1969

Index

Adolescence 75, 76, 81, 188–91
  peer groups of 186, 188–90
Africa
  development 2, 215
  population increase 33
  and world affairs 25
  See also Politics; Society
African Christianity 2, 219–20
  Church *q.v.*
  culture 1, 2; encounter with
    Christianity 3, 23–4, 61, 66,
    68, 69–70, 73, 119–20, 152,
    156–7, 161, 208–9, 212, 215
    (*see also* Liturgical Adaptation;
    Missionary work and Religion);
    revival of interest in 72; and
    Westernized culture 19–20,
    117–8, 143
  government: historical 4, 2, 7;
    present 18, 22, 35. *See also*
    Colonialism
  literature: modern 117–20; oral
    and traditional 58, 83–7, 97,
    99, 101, 104
  nations: building of 17, 22, 29–
    30; population of 35; economy
    of 35
  nationalism 211
  religion, native 45, 49, 52–60,
    79–80, 153, 212; after-life in
    52, 60–1, 63; belief in God 29,
    45; priesthood 213; relation to
    social and political structure
    57–8, 109, 212–5. *See also* God;
    Religion
Age-grades 27, 79, 127, 213

Ancestors 53, 59–61, 73, 109, 111–
  2, 134, 136, 149, 150, 153–4,
  170–1
Anthropological field work 218
  model: mechanical 11, 12; stat-
    istical 11
Anthropology, Physical 3
Anthropology, Social 1, 6, 8, 113
  colonial 4
  evolutionary 44, 49
  functionalist 9, 11
  pastoral ix–x, 1, 3, 4, 5, 6, 8, 74,
    217–9
  rejection of 5

Baptism 81, 176–7, 183, 217
Bible 70, 93, 94–5, 148, 209–10
  Old Testament 53, 66, 70, 175,
    182
  New Testament 53, 70, 94, 118,
    175, 182, 197
Blood-brotherhood 117, 201–2, 203
Bloodwealth 167, 170
Bride-service 81, 127–8, 166, 184,
  192
Bridewealth 7, 40, 158, 166, 167–
  72, 180, 184, 192, 193, 194

Catechesis, adaptation of 101–6,
  193
Catechists 42, 70, 214–5
  See also Liturgical Adaptation
Chiefship 28, 31, 57, 78–9, 109,
  127, 128
  mythology of 97–9
  See also Kingship, divine

Index

Childbearing and menstruation 20, 48, 126, 146, 162, 174, 191
Children *see under* Family
Christ 70, 89, 71, 74, 130, 144, 154, 211, 217
  teaching of 53, 175, 178
Christian
  community 42, 71, 177, 196, 197, 198, 206, 210, 211, 212, 217
  fatherhood 180
  marriage *see under* Marriage
  values 66, 69
Christianity
  adoption of by different culture 66–75, 78–81; in Buganda 78–9
  Catholicism 41, 58, 71, 73–4, 79, 175, 176
  historical 70
  and the Kingdom of Heaven 154
  and non-Christian religions 71–2
  practice of 41–2
  Protestantism 52, 79, 210
  Trinity, the Holy 69, 70, 95
  work of 214, 217–8
  See also African culture, encounter with Christianity; Baptism; Bible; Church; Conversion; Family, Christian view of; Prayer; Spiritual development
Church 2, 8, 70, 71, 74, 135, 153, 198, 206, 212, 214–5
  buildings 42
  clergy 179, 183, 214; location of 42; training of 42
  established 23–4
  independent 23–4, 79, 206–12
  parish organization 42
  particularism 23
  and social action 42
  in urban areas 41–3
  and witchcraft 144
Colonialism 4, 17, 22, 24, 30–1, 32
Community 25, 28, 29–30, 38, 179, 196–8, 202–5
  liminal 205–6
  See also Christian community
Conversion 2, 75–6
Covenant, breaking of a 63, 64

Death
  purification in 153, 154
  and rebirth 126, 127, 152
  witchcraft as a cause of 12, 132–3, 136, 139, 142
  See also Ancestors; Burial and mourning *under* Rites
Descent
  bi-lineal 162, 165
  matrilineal 10, 98–9, 162, 163, 164–5, 168, 173, 179, 180–1
  patrilineal 98, 162, 164, 165, 168, 172, 178, 179, 180–1, 186, 204
  legitimate 157–8, 162, 163, 168–9, 170, 171, 181
Devil 131–2, 135, 138, 144
Divination *see under* Magic

Economy 9
  currency 168, 171
Economic growth 22, 34, 164
Education
  by extended family 178–9, 186–8
  formal and school 22, 49, 81, 119, 186, 188, 189, 190
  sex 190–1
Ethnology 6

Family 156, 159–65, 168, 203–4, 209
  children: brought up by rural relatives 37; illegitimacy 156, 182; punishment of 187–8; siring c. as cause of respect 60, 61
  See also Education
  Christian view of 178, 180–1
  domestic life 20
  residence: neolocality 162, 163, 169; uxorilocality 162, 163, 164, 178; virilocality 162, 164, 165, 178
  types of: extended 38–9, 41, 163–5, 171–2, 173, 177, 178–9, 184, 186, 193, 203–4, 214; nuclear 38, 41, 163, 164, 178, 179, 181, 203
  See also Descent; Kinship; Marriage
Friendship 198–203

God
  attributes of 55–6
  concepts of 51–5, 56, 57, 62, 94, 95–6, 106; deism 57; monotheism 44; theism 56–7
  myths of withdrawal 65, 86

Index

Oaths 116–7

Parables 94
Politics 29, 208
  and class structure 27–8, 32, 33
  ideologies 17, 21–2, 24–33; capitalism 26–7, 30, 32; democracy 28; socialism 17, 24–33; totalitarianism 28
  See also Africa; Society
Prayer 54, 57–8, 61, 64, 74, 84, 101, 106–16, 144–5, 153
Prophecy 143, 205, 207, 210

Race relations 4, 24, 117, 119
Rationalism 92–3, 96
Religion 14, 21, 28–9, 44–6, 51, 53, 75–8, 210–11
  animism 58
  anthropomorphism 53, 96, 113
  Islam 23, 79
  Judaism 66, 70, 94, 148
  reincarnation 60, 165
  sacred and secular 46–9, 51–3, 62, 66, 80; sacralization 47, 149, 151; secularization 47, 48
  and science 48, 49, 50–2
  in social change 22–3
  and social grouping 66, *fig* 2
Religious particularism 21; passivism 208; pluralism 79, 80, 212, 219
  rites 112, 123, 125–6, 144–54
  worship 44, 53, 58, 61, 62, 74, 109, 147–8
  See also African Christianity; African religion; Church; Christianity; Idolatry; Prayer; Sacrifice *under* Ritual
Rites: expressive 125; instrumental 125
  burial and mourning 50, 59, 74, 122, 128
  circumcision 15, 40, 72, 73, 127, 191; female 77–8, 191
  inheritance 128
  initiation and puberty 40, 73, 81, 89, 117, 125, 127, 190–1, 196, 218
  of passage 123–4, 126–8, 134–5, 150, 190; liminal stage in 123–4, 128, 135, 150, 183, 188, 206

of purification 63, 143, 145–6, 150
twin 4, 81, 128–9
'witchcraft cooling' 138
Ritual 23, 45–6, 68–9, 74, 81, 90, 122–55
  sacrifice 64, 112, 146–52
  taboos 46, 47, 48, 62, 130, 140, 150, 205; avoidance customs 62, 177–8; food avoidance 61, 164. *See also* Incest
  See also Bridewealth; Blood brotherhood; Marriage, rites of; Religious rites
Rural areas 5, 34–5
'revolution' 22

Saints 61, 73, 154
Scripture *see* Bible
Signs 87–8, 90, 94–5
  See also Symbolism
Sin *see* Morality
Social change 5, 12, 13, 14–43, 72, 117, 143, 208; continuity and development in 24–43, 72, 77; results of: congruence 17–18, 22, 24; incorporation 18, 22, 24; particularism 21, 23, 24; tribalism 21
  culture 6, 14, 17, 18, 19; levels of 20–21
  ecology 9, 14, 17, 212
  facts 6–7, 8, 9, 10, 11, 44
  groups 15–16; parasitic 66; protest 76
  rebels 7; 'liminars' 205; nonconformists 14
  structure 9, 11, 12, 109, 123, 124, 199–200, 212
Society 6
  destruction of 63–4, 117
  male and female roles in 162–3
  physical environment of 8–9
  religion in 21, 44, 45, 77
  specialization in 17
  unitary 78–9
Societies and guilds 15, 61–2, 79–80, 124, 127, 134, 205
Sorcery *see under* Magic
Spirit-possession 23, 24, 134–5, 143–4
Spirits 49, 57–61, 62, 64, 109, 110, 126, 134, 135, 138, 144–5, 146,